# Business Shouldn't

# be this Tough

*When you get out of your own way!*

## By Steve Gaskell

## 'The Challenge Coach'

*'Be the best version of you'*

*'Be unreasonably good'*

Kim

Heres to get

into Action

The Challenge Coach.

PublishNation
www.publishnation.co.uk

# Preface

Interestingly this is my second book, although you will not have heard of me or for that matter read my first book, because it's not been published yet (although at some point you may have). This book came about through a conversation with my wife and business partner and my marketer; Sam and Michelle. As we discussed our marketing plans for the coming months we opened up the topic of my first book and how I was getting on. Well, the truth of the matter was not very well. I mentioned, however, my thoughts for another book, which I had been muddling over; Business Shouldn't be this Tough. They both loved the concept and have inspired me to get started on my second book. It's probably appropriate at this stage to make a commitment to finish my first book as soon as I complete this one and with the new-found impetus.

So, what on earth can I add to the plethora of business books which already cram the shelves in your bookstores and at the click of a button on line? What value can I add, a complete novice author, never published and who barely gained a grade in English at school? In one-word abundance. My aim is to share with you all my thoughts, learnings, habits which I utilise in my business and with my clients. I want to share with you what I have learned and experienced about success.

I'm going to share with you in the following chapters and pages what it takes to develop a mindset to succeed in life and in business. It is unlikely this book will be your golden egg, give the secret to success over night. My aim is to wake you up, and when I say 'to wake you up' I'm talking about interrupting the conversation which goes on in your head, offer you clarity in your life, give you the opportunity to become aware, truly aware. The voices in your head, which so often gets in the way of the things you really know you ought to do. The ones which create conflict in making decisions, frustrate you once you made a decision because they then start to question the rationality of it, the ones which hold you back from being the very best version of you and achieving the success you seek in your business.

As the Challenge Coach, I have spoken with thousands of business owners, leaders, executives and managers from the sole trader to multimillion pound corporations. Regardless of the size, complexity and success, there is a common denominator YOU. What I find fascinating about you is the way in which 2% of your body mass, that 3Ib mass of tissue in your head can make you do stupid shit, inspire you through unexplainable ability, be courageous, show the greatest of affection and be a total jerk, think deeply about real issues, skirt over important facts, be truly loving and brutally hateful, say the kindest things, open your mouth and speak without consideration. You get the idea.

The joy of being a coach is being privy to observing the way your brain works and the impact it has on your life. And let's be clear it is your life and they are your choices. Your mind is set to coordinates which have been determined over your life's experiences and influences. In the most part, we get on with life often oblivious to the fact we have the inner ability to truly shape the infinite opportunities of your future, through the thoughts and action you have right now.

The real purpose of a coach is to raise awareness and garner responsibility in the coachee, in the case of this book that will be YOU. As you read the passages of this book, my aim is to be your coach, to get inside your head and have you question yourself, your business and life. To raise your awareness. Now the fact you have picked this book up would probably suggest you have read many similar titles from great scholars, practitioners and other coaches on this subject and are looking for the golden nugget. Well, I hope you find your golden nugget although it's unlikely to be within these pages. My aim is to reach out to those of you who are inquisitive, are looking to get out of your own way, to make a change in coordinates, change your mindset, to realise your true potential in business and life and then actually do something about it.

One final point before you dive in. This book isn't about merely stuff, it's about unlocking your true potential. In order to unlock your potential, you need to understand the key to unlocking your drive, to take hold of it put it into the key hole and turn. Once you open that door to your potential you will be offered tools and activities to maintain your course and create velocity in the direction you want to head.

Together let's get your journey underway and towards being the very best version of you.

*'Every Adventure Requires a First Step.'*

Lewis Carol

# Foreword

It gives me great pleasure to write this foreward for 'Business Shouldn't Be This Tough'. In addition to being able to call Steve a friend he is also a significant character within our ActionCOACH community and truly embraces our 14 points of culture. Throughout this book, he emulates our commitment towards abundance. I, along with the ActionCOACH community, some 1,000 plus coaches in 87 countries globally, truly pursue and share our mission of a business coach in every business. Through this book Steve, 'the Challenge Coach', offers you as a business owner the opportunity to welcome him into your business as your coach.

Steve has encapsulated our lessons and teaching forged over the 25 years of ActionCOACH's pursuit of our mission. Business Shouldn't Be This Tough, when you get out of your own way, challenges you to take stock and truly determine where you are now, what's been getting in the way and how to achieve your dreams in life as well as in business. Steve offers you the perfect accompaniment to your business toolbox. Offering insight to mastering you, development of your business and team. Using his experience as an ActionCOACH business growth expert, and his service on the front line he'll challenge you to develop high levels of 'pig-headed self-discipline' in order to get out of your own way.

I am delighted that Steve has taken the time to share his thoughts with you through this book. As a coach, trainer and expert in performance development, you will do well to take his, sometimes blunt approach and take personal stock of where you are and aim to be. Steve has invested in his own development throughout his military career and into his passion for performance coaching of business owners and entrepreneurs. This book will not only inspire you, it will challenge you to take actions, following the time-honoured drive and commitment as an ActionCOACH towards those being coached.

Enjoy the shift.

It's time to get into ACTION.

Brad Sugars

CEO and Founder of ActionCOACH, the Global Number 1 Business Coaching Firm.

# Acknowledgments

My mindset today.

I have shaped and crafted who I am today as a result of all the people who, in my life have inspired me. Sadly, there are too many to mention, so here are the people dearest to me who I owe gratitude too in not only writing this book, also becoming 'the challenging coach' I am today.

My family, Mum, Dad and little sister, Paul, Geraldine and Marina. Let's be frank I started out here and the values, drive and commitment I have, have been forged through my upbringing. The discipline I had to have, the respect for others and the resilience to keep going whatever. Dad, I miss you and always there for you Mum and Sis.

Sam, Quinn and Phoebe the reason I exist and strive to be the very best version of me. They have inspired me in ways I can't even begin to comprehend, during my military service when in the thick of it, a moments reflection of these guys kept me true to the cause, committed and sure to come home. Today Sam is my partner in love as well as business and I feel truly blessed to have her on the journey with me. Together we gain great joy watching Quinn and Phoebe shape their lives. Love you all very deeply. I know I can be hard work.

The Regiment! It wouldn't be right not to reflect on those countless friends from my Regiment who challenged and inspired me. Sgt Brown and Cpl Thompson who reshaped a young terrified school leaver into my first version as a soldier, sadly I never really got to know them beyond their rank and surname. Sergeant Major Farrow, a true professional, hard, firm, fair and fun. Without a doubt, the first blueprint I had which shaped me 20 years later when I became Sergeant Major. Cpl Dunn, a lovable rouge who shaped me as a young Junior Non-Commissioned Officer. General Sir Paul Newton, as Commanding Officer left me with an imprint of 'seek always to be unreasonably good', it sticks with me today. Lieutenant Colonel Julian Clover; 'march, shoot and communicate'. His simple mantra turned a Battalion in to a highly operationally effective fighting unit and remains a firm reminder of simplicity. Simplicity has been a concept that has remained with me, the art of complexity is simplicity. Thanks, Colonel. Oh, and I never realised I could go so long without a shower! Finally, Major General Doug Chalmers and his lovely wife Helen. As the Battalions' Regimental Sergeant Major under his command, it was truly the culmination of a soldier's journey, my journey. His humility, loyalty, leadership, professionalism and commitment is likely never to be replicated in such a winning formula. The Battalion and Regiment loved and respected him and his kindred leadership. I should mention Helen, as she was truly the force and support behind him, as Sam is to me. So, here's to all the unsung heroes in the Princess of Wales Royal Regiment, 'Fierce Pride' lives on deep in my DNA and shapes my mindset today.

Most recently my inspiration and continued learning come from the ActionCOACH community. My fellow coaches across the globe, I should mention those who impacted on me and have helped me define who I am as a coach today; Brad the Chairman, who I first met briefly when I was exploring the thought of becoming a business coach, a charismatic, say it as it is Aussie, thank you for your continued challenge and belief. A great example of leading by example. Doug, Cynthia and Andrew who created a significant shift in my mindset when I joined ActionCOACH. I never would have thought the game of Volley Ball could have such an impact and demonstrate the lessons of life, brilliant. Oh, and must recognise Doug for sharing the lesson of 'Stop It' over a drink or two in the early morning. Chris Gibbons and Pam Featherstone as my coaches for keeping me on track through the tough lessons learnt on the journey of business.

There is also a special thank you to Traci Cornelius whose keen eye in proof reading and editing this book has been indispensable. Without her insight, I would not have had the confidence to share my thoughts with you all in my own way, authentically and from the heart.

There are so many others, too many to mention, suffice to say you all know who you are and I thank you for your friendship, council, support and challenge. That's enough for now.

Thank you all.

I am eternally grateful.

# This Book

WARNING
THIS BOOK IS BEST READ AFTER THIS INSIGHT….


As you start to devour the pages ahead (and I hope you do) there is only one rule to be aware of when reading this book, and that's there are no rules. Dig into this book, write notes on the pages, fold the corners as a reference, use 'post its' to mark pages, use highlighters to remind yourself. My aim in this book is to offer you, the reader, the business owner or prospective business owner a mirror to reflect on what's going to be important to you in your life and business. What's going to help you along the journey towards being the best version of you. Think of this as nourishment of your mind and an opportunity to make that shift you have been unable to, whatever it may be.

I'm not a veteran author, so you'll find in the pages ahead of information, suggestions, exercises and challenges which I utilise myself and with the business owners, executives, leaders and managers I have coached and am coaching. I have used these in the military with Officers and Soldiers and within various size organisations with teams and individuals, over a wide spectrum and the one thing is they work to the degrees you apply them.

Now, in this book whilst I will offer you my perspective, I will also, where necessary, offer reference, validation and education which is relevant to offer greater insight and depth of knowledge. Understanding the why of things. However, I have no intentions of getting caught up in the fine detail of academia, rather using and sharing my understanding and interpretation of it. This book is about action, I'll leave the debate for the academics. So, you'll find I aim to offer a stimulus for action through my learnings from my military career and my journey as a coach. The courses I've attended and the books I've read. The challenge for you is to act upon learnings, and I will offer you the chance to do just that throughout.

You should expect BFO's; BLINDING FLASHES of the OBVIOUS, that moment of realisation where it just seems obvious.

You just need to make sure you act upon them, write your BFO down and put a date to when you're going to act and apply it. Only when you follow through on it will you begin to make a positive change. Never merely add it to a list of stuff to do, you won't! Just to help on that note you'll find a BFO record sheet at the end of each Chapter.

In this book, I aim to take you beyond mere words and thoughts. My aim is to encourage action, to incite activity to make a commitment to yourself to influence what can be tomorrow and let go of the anchors from yesterday. There is reality regarding success, a concept that many fail to come to terms with, too embody too evoke in themselves. The journey to success and being successful is by its virtue boring. It's boring because it boils down to one thing, and that's hard work. HARD WORK!

As Jim Rohn say's you must first work harder on yourself than you do on your job. Hard work means having the self-discipline to act on your BFO's. To develop a deeper understanding and learning and the application of it. Expand your understanding in all you read in the following pages through doing and passing your learnings on. As it goes you have the discipline to do all the little things, to make the changes each and every day, which will be measured in ounces. Rather that, than at the end of your days to have the regret not to have lived the life you truly sought, because that end of life regret is measured in Tons.

Most important is your interpretation of what we will go onto discuss and the areas I will challenge you to act upon and it is there the greatest shift will take place. In order to do that I will be talking to you and aim to have you tap into your inner self, let's face it as you read this you hear my words inside your head. The greatest challenge is just how easily you will be distracted, ELEPHANT, see. Now all you can see and think about is the elephant.

'Back in the room'.

My aim is to have you challenge you, to reflect in your context to gain new insight and experience, to make the shift. It is then about commitment. Committing to make the shift you truly desire towards having the business you want and the life you want to live.

To conclude every chapter, you'll also find the BLUF, the Bottom Line Up Front. Here, you'll find the outline of what the chapter has been about, the salient points and the action points for you to act upon and your opportunity to reflect on what you aim to act upon. It's a simple way of making sure you get into action, there is no point in assimilating all this knowledge only for you to then not do something with it. The Chapter will raise awareness and BLUF will be the accountability and determine when, where and how you'll act.

Now, this may sound a little odd. Many books I have read have offered similar suggestions in regard to there utility, how to read and then apply the learnings, as have I so far. This book is no different other than one additional challenge in actually making the shift in your behaviours before you are able to conclude reading the book. You will be challenged at the conclusion of reading Chapter 3 to take the *21 Day Challenge*. I will challenge you to put the book down for 21 days in order to apply your learnings and set your conditions for success. At which point 21 days later you will be in a mind to actually finish the book, evoking the necessary motivation, productivity and commitment to achieve your success.

I should also mention that the thoughts, views, beliefs are mine and mine alone. As a coach, I have invested heavily in my understanding, education and ability towards the 'craft of coaching' and am passionate about helping people make a meaningful shift. Move towards being the version of you, you truly see in the mirror every day. My learnings, understanding, interpretation have come from some of the greatest minds in personal and business development. In another life, I would have loved to have met them; Zig Ziglar, Steven Covey, Dale Carnegie to mention a few. I have been thankful to have met and learnt from some of the greatest, Brad Sugars, Dr Marshall Goldsmith, Sir John Whitmore, Matthew Syde, Professor Steve Peters, Andy Bounds, Philip Hesketh, Allan Pease and Paul Dunn. Then there's the great minds I will be meeting in the future, Tony Robbins, Brian Tracey, Jim Collins, Michael Bungay Stanier and many many more.

The Chapters follow a structure to help make lasting long-term shift (figure 1). It will start with challenging you to determine where and what you want to achieve in not only your business, also your life. You will then need to understand where resistance will appear in you and your inner conversation and also your environment. From this position, we then need to build your resilience by applying success habits to each and every day and ultimately keeping your head above the parapet (more on that later). All the while Chapter 5 will take a look at the Business Rhythm and how it creates the foundation for your success.

Enjoy this book, the challenges and I hope the enlightening moments that will inspire you to live your life to the maximum.

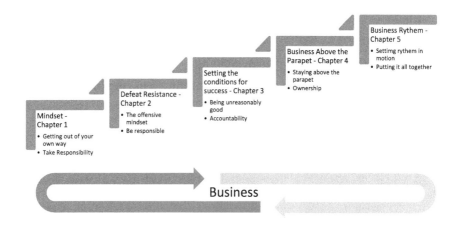

Mindset - Chapter 1
- Getting out of your own way
- Take Responsibility

Defeat Resistance - Chapter 2
- The offensive mindset
- Be responsible

Setting the conditions for success - Chapter 3
- Being unreasonably good
- Accountability

Business Above the Parapet - Chapter 4
- Staying above the parapet
- Ownership

Business Rythem - Chapter 5
- Setting rythem in motion
- Putting it all together

Business

*Outline of the Book*

# Contents

# Chapter 1

# Mindset – 'Get Out of Your Own Way'

In this book, the important factor will be the internal dialogue that you have, that conversation you have with yourself, and often the not even knowing what you are talking about or why. We, all of us have the same ability to make decisions, be a creatures of autonomy, choose our direction or define the purpose of our life. We decide what level of activity we undertake, the level of commitment to action, the motivation, the drive, you get the gist. So why is that some seem to have 'all the luck'?

The fact here is it's not about luck in the slightest. It's about momentum, it's about resilience in setting out to achieve what you decide is to be achieved. The blunt fact about this book is there is no secret, no magic pill, no success diet, it's about you getting out of your own way. Or as my Dad would often tell me as a young teenager, getting off your arse! Regardless of what you want to achieve in life, your business this book will challenge you to think differently. The book is designed to change your mental environment, the way you think, the way you respond, the internal dialogue you have with yourself, the internal conflict you may suffer, the lack of discipline, the inability to overcome your fears.

So, before you continue reading this book, make a verbal commitment to stop what's not working for you right now and to change. Commit to activity, activity which will take you out of your comfort zone, stretch you, challenge you, maybe even scare you. Act. Whether you are reading this book or listening to it what is your commitment statement? Now, this isn't meant to inspire you or suddenly switch the light on in your head it's simply a commitment to yourself that this will not just be another book to read it will be the start of your journey. So, what's your commitment?

Are you done messing around, are you over looking for the golden ticket, are you ready to take massive action? Now I'm no big name in the self-help industry, I will be, and this book is one of the first steps in my journey towards stepping over that threshold. Whilst at the moment I'm no Tony Robbins, Jim Rohn, Brian Tracey, Steve Covey I have inspired others to start out on their journey and have helped make a difference in their lives, in some way, so this book gives me the opportunity to help many.

Buying this book and reading it is a commitment in its own right, however, to allow me to help you in some small way then you absolutely, unequivocally need to take the action. Whilst there is plenty of advice in the pages to follow, you'll also find the odd nugget for you to act upon and make a difference in your life or business. Never just accept mediocrity. Where you are right now probably isn't where you truly aspire to be, go out there and make a bloody difference. Right now, say it out loud, not in your head, make a loud commitment, verbalise your shift towards success and what you want to achieve. Say it, and say it NOW! In fact, grab your pen and write down your commitment statement here:

If you didn't write anything down, what stopped you? 'I never like writing in my books', 'I read it through first', 'it's in my head so I've thought about it'. Then that's ok, this book is about you taking positive action and commitment, so it may not be for you. It's likely to look good alongside all the other personal and business development books you've read and never acted on. If you're not willing my advice, go and get your money back and accept you are who you are and you may not currently want to aspire to be anything more than you are now. Use the refund to go out and buy your lottery ticket or scratch card and good luck! Hey, that's ok.

It all starts with you.

In your life, there is one constant, one element regardless of any situation, circumstance. It's what drives the decisions you make, the responses you have, the action you take and one thing that has been with you since the day you were born. It's no secret, it's not magic, whilst complex in the depth of understanding, or realisation how little understanding of it we have, that one thing is YOU. It's your being, your very presence, your self-awareness, it's what makes us human. The mere ability to look in a mirror and firstly know, with intimacy and consciousness who is looking back at you is that factor that makes us human.

There is so much study today on what makes us tick, why our brain works the way it does, that even knowing ourselves as intimately as we do, we still have much to fully understand. Why do we act in the way and manner we do? It's very easy today to assess our behaviour as instinctual, 'wasn't me it was my brain on autopilot'. Dare I say blaming ourselves for what we do without actually being responsible for it. Let's be clear on one thing here, as a human being and making the assumption that you are in good physical and mental health it's your brain. It only responds the way it does because of the coordinates which have been set over your lifetime. Your mind is set in a certain way and that has been influenced throughout your life's experiences, your education, your social circumstances, essentially your environment.

Although it might be stating the obvious, you are who you are and we have all been defined by our upbringing and environment. We each of us have differing opinions, values and beliefs. These define each of us and shape our personalities. So, what is it that shaped those opinions, values and beliefs? From the moment, we enter the world we begin to assimilate the massive amount of information we are exposed too. Our 5-senses work overtime to make sense of it all and as we grow and as our brains develop we start to work out how we fit into this complex world.

It's interesting to understand a little of how we, and by 'we' I refer to our brains develop, so here's a little science regarding our brain development.

0 – 10 months (Pregnancy), yes that's right from conception as our brain starts to grow and the neurons start connecting we are stimulated by sounds and stimulations.

Birth – 6 years (Childhood), from developing voluntary movement through to developing reasoning, perception and emotions. We begin to shape a sense of self and begin building on life experiences and emotional wellbeing. By the time we reach age 6 your brain was at 95% of its adult weight and the peak of its energy consumption. It's interesting to understand that negative, strict and harsh treatment to this point can affect emotional consequences in the future.

7

7 - 22 years old (Adolescence), during this period the brain is constantly wiring and re-wiring as we increase our cognitive ability. With this growth, the brain begins to mature and we gain greater control of impulse and greater decision-making ability. We can see here and relate to our behaviour as a teenager and essentially what we observe in teenagers as we grow. We learn to control the reckless, irrational and petulant behaviour.

23 – 65 years old (Adulthood), at 23 our brain is assessed to be at peak performance and is likely to remain at that level for about 5 years. From that point, unless you remain mentally, physically active and eat healthily, functionality will decline. It's ironic in a way that in terms of our growth the brain takes the longest to mature and then promptly starts a road of declining ability. You'll know what I mean, 'my memory is getting worse', 'not as quick as I used to be' and so on.

Over 65 (Old Age) and the decline continues, memory and recollection continue to decline.

The relevance of this information will allow you to gain a little understanding of why you have or do behave in certain ways throughout your life. In childhood your family imprint on you and shape you. You learn from your parents and family how to socially interact, to communicate, you are developing the early version of you.

As we grow our experiences widen. We are exposed to a vast amount of information which we start to assimilate and interpret. Further shaping our beliefs, values and our identity. The people we meet, groups we associate with, clubs we join, activities we partake in, teams we play in, discussions we have, books we read etc all begin to define us. It's where our prejudices and discriminations come from, why we believe and are vehement about certain issues and topics. We are all aware of the teenage mind and the turmoil we go through trying to define ourselves, fit in, gain confidence, have a view, I'm sure you know what I'm talking about.

So what?

Well the fact of the matter here, as we have grown and continue to grow many of us just accept we are who we are and our mindset has very much been pre-set for us. Even if you think you are very much of your own mind take a moment to review your beliefs. What sports team do you support? Why? What are your hobbies? Why? What are your political views? Why? When you start to look a little deeper below the surface of who you are there will be influences imprinted on your mindset over your lifetime.

Remember what makes us human is our consciousness and own self-awareness.

'It's just who I am'. Well yes you are and that's the point, you are who you are. I'd like to pose the question 'who do you want to be?' When you look in the mirror who is looking back at you? Have you achieved what you wanted to achieve in life to date? Has it turned out the way you thought it would? How do you score yourself in terms of where you are right now and where you desire to be? We'll come to that in just a moment. Let me first ask you another ask you a question, just how important are your ego and pride?

How often does your ego and pride get in the way of the decisions you really should be making in order to achieve all you want in life? Now, this is an area I have had to overcome in my personal journey. I'll put this into a very raw context and one I have experience in my military service. During my service, I have been involved, witnessed first-hand and seen the aftermath of the very worst in terms of the human condition. In other words, the acts of senseless violence, terrorist acts and heinous atrocities on the innocent. Now in all of these, there is a personal aftermath, in the very worst cases Post Traumatic Stress Disorder. Now we hear lots of these accounts and in most instances, these are the worst cases which come to light. Sadly, there are thousands which do not. Why? Ego and pride.

They feel they are equipped to deal with what they have witnessed themselves. Their ego wouldn't allow them to seek psychological help or intervention. Their pride wouldn't allow them to reach out to family and friends for help. What about another example, which sadly kills too many people in life. Failure to go and see a doctor. Yes, that's right, knowing they have a problem and think to themselves I'll get healthier before I'll go and see the doctor. I'll diet, eat better, stop drinking, get fit and then I'll be able to see the doctor in a better place. Oops, no I died instead because my ego and pride got in the way!

These may seem like two very stark examples, they serve to emphasise the point I'm making. 'I'm not mentally ill or dying Steve!' I hear you saying, well in both cases I'm sorry to say you are, it's just a matter of how much attention and action you take when those little inner voices start talking. Let's be clear, from the moment you were born every day takes you a step closer to inevitable, death. Sorry to sound dire or melodramatic, it is just a fact. It's a fact we can't overcome, we can't cheat death, it comes to us all, what matters is what we do with the time in-between.

Live your life, stop living in the hope of a quiet existence and easy death. Let's be frank, you picked this book up for a reason. So, open up to yourself, answer those voices in a manner which will allow you to reach your true potential, to become the best version of you. Stop allowing your ego and pride to get in the way, rather use them as the catalyst for action.

The following exercise focuses on some fundamental areas of your life, it's not a definitive list so add your own criteria. The important part is to be absolutely, honest with yourself. Don't be a 'self-licking lollypop' regardless of your circumstances this exercise is simple in its context. Where are you right now and where do you want to be in the future? 12 months from now, 3 years, 5 years or the next decade of your life. What will your legacy be, what does it look like? This isn't about being 'realistic' just be completely honest with yourself, where do you want to be? Park your ego and pride and open up to yourself in the first instance to establish where you are now and where you will be.

In this exercise let's first establish where you are now. Looking at the table below score yourself between 1-11, 1 being really bad, 11 being really good for each of life's criteria. It's quite safe, there is no right or wrong because this is about your thought's beliefs and feelings. Remember one of the first steps is, to be honest with yourself, not allowing your ego and pride to take over. Afterall you're only going to be lying to yourself. Once you've marked down where you are let's take a step towards where you want to be. Let's do it in a way in which we can start to make some meaningful commitment and change. Where you can see and actively engage with your momentum, let's say on 12 months to 3 years from now where would you like to score in all of these areas. Mark your next X where you want to be. A little later in Chapter 4, we'll reflect on the gap between now and where you want to be your ideal self. I'll introduce the impact you can have short term, medium term and through your life's journey. This is exciting so let's kick off with complete honesty.

| | 1 | 2 | 3 | 4 | 5 | 6 | 7 | 8 | 9 | 10 | 11 |
|---|---|---|---|---|---|---|---|---|---|---|---|
| Relationships | | | | | | | | | | | |
| Career/Business | | | | | | | | | | | |
| Health | | | | | | | | | | | |
| Wealth | | | | | | | | | | | |

Happiness

Education/Knowledge

Sharing

Experiences

Spiritual

When you've finished this exercise, you should have two X's for each category. What we are looking at is the gap between them, what it looks like and what necessary actions will need to be in order to close the gap. Next we'll explore what has held you back next.

**Dream x Vision x Goal x Learn x Plan x Act**
What did you dream of when you were a child? In fact, what's probably more appropriate what didn't you dream of as a child? I remember as a young child dreaming of being a crime-busting police officer. This all stemmed from a school visit to my local police station, which led to a school project which led to a very clear picture of what an awesome crime buster I was going to be when I grew up.

I remember the catalogues we would have at home and spending hours looking through all the toys dreaming about how I was going to have so much fun with them. I think you'll all agree as children we didn't have any problem at all in dreaming, in fact, it probably played a major part in our everyday activity. Playing with our toys in a creative way, immersing ourselves in the deepest clarity, being on a racing circuit as we raced our cars along the kitchen floor. Playing games with our friends and role-playing, immersing ourselves in characters from the TV.

In reflection what's really interesting is how my parents encouraged me to immerse myself in these dreams. They always told me I could be whatever you wanted to be. Here's the really cool bit, 'if you just put your mind to it you can!'. Can you relate to that? So, what happened? Why are there so few really achieve the success in life they truly went after? Yet there are those who actually achieved what is interpreted as the impossible and living the life many only ever dream of. Many would state 'they must have just been lucky!' 'They had a great opportunity come their way at the right time!' Is it possible they have really mapped out their destiny? Is it possible they have really worked hard on their dream and gone after it with utter commitment?

11

In short yes. And you can as well, so let's look at how you can get underway.

Why is it important to have a dream? For me it has always been quite simply because it gives meaning. I have a purpose to fulfil during my short stay on earth. 'Wow, that sounds a bit far out there Steve', I hear you say. Well, let me ask you why it is we grow out of dreaming? Why does it get to a point where having a dream is just plain silly. The mere fact that in a book about business I'm talking about dreaming could seem to some as a little odd. So before we challenge you to take a look at your dreams and aspirations let's talk about why briefly.

When you first set out as a business owner, whether you started as an apprentice and have been offered directorship, become a partner and gained equity in the business, taken the plunge to start your own business or bought a business. The fact is you will have had a vision of where it was going to take you. From that point, it's been a slog, bloody hard work, and you've just ended up trapped in your business. Actually, nothing more than an employee, with no benefits of walking away at 5.

The key here is to have solid alignment between your business and your life. Your business should provide you with the life you aspire to. As is often the case with the business the owners I engage with, there is no alignment in their life and business. They are the busiest in the business, tired, working all the hours they can to stay afloat, stressed with the pressures and risks associated with their business. Often struggling with cash flow or a lack of it, fearful of where the next lead will come from. They face challenges with not only running the business also managing and leading the team. Sound familiar?

Without being aligned within your own business, understanding your why, the purpose, what's going to motivate and drive you, you'll struggle to reach your full potential. That's not to say you won't, just you're making life really difficult for yourself. This isn't restricted to smaller business, far from it. I have spoken with, coached and challenged multimillion businesses, their executive teams to take a moment to define their why and get aligned.

So, what's your why? Take a moment to remind yourself why you're doing what you're doing. What was it that first inspired you to start your business? Most importantly what was it that you aspired to change, what was your vision? Take your time to go right back to the beginning and reflect, establish your facts, what was the impact going to be on your life, your family, your circumstances, your future?

Try these questions if you're struggling to gain a perspective on your current alignment.

1.    What got you into the business in the first place?
2.    What were your goals then?
3.    What are your goals now?
4.    What did you aim to achieve and how have you done so far?
5.    What's the number 1 thing you would like to achieve in your business now?
6.    How has the business impacted on your life?
7.    Do you drive your business, or does it control you?

By now you'll have an idea as to just how aligned you, your life and your business are.

It's also worth mentioning at this point that your dream will expand over time, as you start to enjoy success. As you start to see the results, start to experience what you actually can achieve when you put your mind to it, you'll realise there are even greater opportunities in life. Interestingly time plays a significant role, and in the simplest terms your dreams are probably a decade away from being achieved, that's right it will take time, dedication and commitment. Stay on track and in within the next 10 years you'll see your dream start to materialise.

There isn't a quick fix here, and it's likely why most people fail to stay the course because they have little or no patience. They need stuff right now, they need to be gratified at this moment and that will only lead to disappointment. In Chapter 2 I will talk about the challenges you will face on the route to success and how utilising an offensive mindset will keep you on track and help you stay on track towards your goals.

Let's be brutally frank your business should provide you with the life you desire, not rule it, be an anchor or be holding you back, quite the opposite. You must act now, start to make a difference, let's go back to your dream and see just what you really want to achieve in this life. After all, we've already established the next pertinent point, it's your life. Be clear, the one thing which we can be certain of is we are all dying. Once again, it seems I'm again reiterating this point, let's be frank it's a key issue and wakes people up, hopefully, in this case, YOU! Let me just put it into context.

From the moment, we are born one thing is inevitable, we are on an unstoppable course, we have a one-way ticket to our ultimate destination. Death. There is but one question and that is 'what are you going to do with your time?' How are you going to make sure the time you have isn't wasted? Sorry two questions, you get the point.

We are the most interesting creatures on planet earth, and to the best of our knowledge, we are the only ones who can contemplate and think about death. In his book, 'The Subtle Art of Not giving a F'ck, Mark Manson (Manson, 2016), discusses the impact a death experience made on his life and woke him up. In his reference, it was the death of a close friend and the psychological effect which caused him to enter a very deep depression. The ultimate of all fears is death and yet there is no escaping its clutches at some point in our lives.

Mark also goes onto reference Earnest Becker's Book 'The Denial of Death'. Earnest highlights two significant issues about which are extremely relevant to and further contextualise our fears. Firstly, as humans, we have the ability to actually conceptualise and think about ourselves abstractly. Your pets never sit about worrying about where the next meals going to come from, which direction their career is going, they can't reflect on the mistakes they've made or what their future looks like. In essence, they are busy being.

Unlike us, with our ability to contemplate, visualise the future, actually, have the ability to see a world without you being a part of it. Interestingly Becker then goes on to discuss what he has coined a death terror, which is a deep anxiety that underlines everything we think or do. Why do people cry when they hit certain key dates in their lives, 30 years old, 50 years old because they are seeing themselves getting closer to death and regret the things they haven't achieved so far!

His second point and one we have touched on is how we see ourselves. Essentially there are two versions of you, your physical self. In other words, the one that eats, sleeps and works etc... The second self is your conceptual self, your identity and how we see ourselves. Inevitably your physical self will die and there is, currently, no way of escaping that. At some unconscious level, this really scares us and develops an ingrained fear. Our conceptual self-seeks to compensate for the inevitable end by seeking immortality. I've written this book, which will last far beyond my life, some seek to have buildings and monuments named after themselves and then there are the levels we go to influence followers. All in a vain attempt to create immortality and in some way overcome and compensate for death.

The point here in simple terms relates to the inability to immortalise yourself, to know you have a legacy, left your mark on the world or as Steve Jobs once said 'put a dink in the universe'. And let's be clear that's probably the case for most of us. Under these circumstances consciously and subconsciously we fear death or as Becker called it, we suffer death terror. As a result, we suffer fear on so many different levels, far too many concerns about stuff or as Mark Manson eloquently puts it: 'we're all driven by fear to give way too many 'fucks' about something, because giving a 'fuck' about something is the only thing that protects us from the reality and inevitability of our own death.

Fear will hold you back in ways you won't even contemplate and for reasons you may not be aware of. It will impact on your ability to deal with issues which haven't even happened yet and derail your ability to deal with them in a logical manner. Fear itself was designed to keep you alive, heighten your response ability, tune your sense in. Yet today it seems all too often fear is responsible for quite the opposite. Fear holds you back, so be courageous, live the life you truly seek and know it is possible.

What's your epitaph going to read?

*"Steve Gaskell, I'd rather be reading this"*

Here's an interesting exercise for you. The average life expectancy across the US, Europe, UK is between 79 – 84 years of age for the average male. There are significant differences globally and could go from 50 – 84 years. The table below has taken my life expectancy of 84 years, one square equates to one year of my life.

The lightest shade of grey years were my early childhood before I started school, followed by the years of my education, then my 28 years in the Army and the dark grey bring us to the year of publishing this book. So, at the point of writing this book, on average I have 34 years left on our glorious planet. For me that is more than enough time to reach and achieve my dreams and aspirations.

Work out your life's boxes and then work out how many you have left. When you take a look at life so abruptly and see just how long you have to go, ask yourself if you're done messing around? Are you going to waste another summer? Another month? Another Day? Another hour? Are you

| 1968 | 1978 | 1988 | 1998 | 2008 | 2018 | 2028 | 2038 | 2048 |
|------|------|------|------|------|------|------|------|------|
| 1969 | 1979 | 1989 | 1999 | 2009 | 2019 | 2029 | 2039 | 2049 |
| 1970 | 1980 | 1990 | 2000 | 2010 | 2020 | 2030 | 2040 | 2050 |
| 1971 | 1981 | 1991 | 2001 | 2011 | 2021 | 2031 | 2041 | 2051 |
| 1972 | 1982 | 1992 | 2002 | 2012 | 2022 | 2032 | 2042 |      |
| 1973 | 1983 | 1993 | 2003 | 2013 | 2023 | 2033 | 2043 |      |
| 1974 | 1984 | 1994 | 2004 | 2014 | 2024 | 2034 | 2044 |      |
| 1975 | 1985 | 1995 | 2005 | 2015 | 2025 | 2035 | 2045 |      |
| 1976 | 1986 | 1996 | 2006 | 2016 | 2026 | 2036 | 2046 |      |
| 1977 | 1987 | 1997 | 2007 | 2017 | 2027 | 2037 | 2047 |      |

going to have a focus on adding value every second of every day in order to move towards your dreams and aspirations?

In that case let's now take a look at what you really want to achieve in life, your dream.

Your Dream

Dreams are exciting, so as we discuss your dream, be an open book, be daring and courageous to define what is really possible and what you truly want. Think big. Push the boundaries. After all, we've just established you only have a finite amount of time here so why not make the impact you want in your lifetime. Unlock your deepest desires and get focus on having a mindset to get there. Having the dream is only the first step.

So, what is your dream?

With the dream have some fun, be bold, really look to what you want to achieve. Often, I have found when discussing someone's dream they immediately assume it's got to be the material stuff. It's not about a big house, expensive car and diamond-encrusted watches. OK, that's fair, your dream is your dream, it's about what's important to you. The challenge here is digging deep into your mind to establish what that is.

You're about to take a flight and you have a standard seat in economy when the air hostess approaches you and asks if you would like to take a seat in first class complimentary of the airline. Think now about your answer, do you take the seat. Yes or No? If it's yes deep inside you do crave the finer things in life. Your dream isn't about being practical, realistic or frugal it's about the myriad of possibilities in your life.

A quick search on Google reveals the 5 top regrets on the deathbed as being:

1.    I wish I had the courage to have lived my life true to myself and not as other people expected.
2.    I wish I hadn't worked so hard.
3.    I wish I had expressed my feelings.
4.    I wish I'd stayed in touch with my friends.
5.    I wish I'd been happier.

The following exercise will help you define your dream. Get a blank piece of paper, make yourself comfortable and answer these questions. You'll explore 6 areas; Be, Do, See, Have, Go and Share. This will take a couple of hours of reflection, really aim to dig deep, why not share the experience with a loved one, you'll be amazed what you'll discover when you start looking deep enough.

**BE**, here's where you really have to start to think about who it is you want to be, how you want people to remember you, and most importantly, what's important to you.

- Spiritual, meditation, church, wellbeing, mindfulness.
- Emotions, which top ten to feel daily, I just am....?
- Friendship, who, how many, what level?
- Family, what do you want to them to feel, how do you want the relationships to be?
- New Identities, who do you choose to be?
- Roles, what are your roles, daily, weekly, monthly?
- Values, and rules.

**DO**, now we can get a little more adventurous; let's look at the things you want to do, the places you want to go and the experiences you want to have in your life.

- Major achievements, business, family, investing, sports/hobbies.

- Awards, which ones, from whom, what for?
- Donations, time/money, which charities, functions, amounts?
- Kids money, how much, when, what rules?
- Hobbies, what, how often, at what level?
- Nature, where, what, how often?
- Health, diet, vitamins, your weight, vitality, mental and physical.
- Fitness, what exercise, where, how long?
- Seminars, how many a year, what subjects?
- Restaurants, where, how often, which ones?
- Fun Times, friends, how often?
- What fear do you want to conquer?
- What instrument/s do you want to play?

**SEE**, what do you want to see, experience, watch first hand?

- Sporting/special events, which ones, where and when?
- Shows, which ones, where, how often?
- What culture do you want to experience?
- See your children achieve....

**HAVE**, what do you want to have out of life, explore the physical things, toys or should I say, 'stuff' you want.

- Houses, how many, where, worth, each one no of beds/baths/other rooms, views, outside, fixtures and fittings. Answer with detail to get a real picture.
- Cars, make, model, year, colour, registration plate, interior type and colour.
- Boats, make, model, feet, colour, interior, no of berths, names, year, Jetski.
- Planes, make, model, year, interior fit-out, range, pilot's names, jet/prop, base airport, name.
- Helicopters, make, model, year, fit-out, range, name, home base.
- Bikes, push, motor, road, dirt, registration plates, colour.

- Jewellery, his/hers, watches (make, model, metal/colour stones), necklaces (metal/colour, stones, weight), rings

18

(metal/colour, stones, weight), bracelets and bangles (metal/colour, stones, weight).

- Furniture, make, model, colour, type, colour, age, antiques, modern, designer, brands.
- Electronic Stuff, Stereos, Computers, Games, telescopes, Kitchen, cameras, toys, phones, tools, motorised tools, garden tools, appliances, TV's, home cinemas and home automation.
- Art, paintings, sculptures, photographs, memorabilia, prints, waterscapes.
- Pets, dogs, cats, birds, guard dogs, fish.
- Clothes, brands, shops you are well known in.
- Library, subjects, number of books.
- Investments, self-managed super fund.
- Investment properties, residential, no of bed/bath, suburbs/areas, wealth wheels, blocks of units, monthly passive, total value per year.
- Shares, options, warrants, futures, equities, managed funds, blue chips, tech/biotech, mining, retail, transport.
- Cash, bank accounts in which countries, how much cash in each?
- Businesses, how many, turnover/profits, no of employees, no of offices/stores, industries.

**GO**, living on such a large planet there are plenty of amazing things to see, what are they for you?

- Holidays, where and how often?
- Places you want to visit?
- What nature do you want to experience?
- What extremes do you want to experience?

**SHARE**, what do you want to share with others?

- What experience do you want to share with others?
- What knowledge do you want to impart on others, your teachings?
- What wealth do you want to distribute amongst others?
- What would you like to give to society, your community or family?
- Who would you like to make happy?

So, what is the purpose of your dream, its relevance? It feels great to have gone through this process, and to have now taken some time to really establish what I'd like my life to look like, how I want to live, so what? How is this remotely relevant to my business mindset?

In the simplest terms, it's why you're in business, to facilitate the life you desire. The thing is, you've probably up until this point forgotten your purpose, just been trapped in your own business. Stopped being a business owner and reverted to being employed.

With this information, we can now take the dream to the next stage and develop the vision of how your business is going to get you there. Remember, your business exists to make your dreams come true or it should do.

Vision

*A dream doesn't become reality through magic.*

*It takes sweat, determination and hard work.*

*Colin Powell*

What part does your business play in achieving the dream, quite simply put is it the means to an end? It's probably likely your business has formed part of your dream. Clearly, we now need to establish where your business is heading, the part you play, the influence you have and the determination to succeed. Forming your vision will set out the journey ahead. The vision should be almost unattainable, really challenging. Jim Collins (Collins, 2001) in his bestselling book 'Good to Great' talks about the BHAG, the Big Hairy Audacious Goal pushing the limits of achievement.

Probably the most famous BHAG and the simplest way to offer the context was when President Kennedy shared his vision of reaching the Moon in the 1960s. He provoked a Nation's passion getting behind the vision of reaching the Moon with his declaration, "that this Nation should commit itself to achieve the goal, before this decade is out, of landing a man on the moon and returning him safely to earth." The history of the Apollo Missions speaks for itself, Kennedy created a unifying and compelling following of a goal, which the US embraced and achieved on the 20th July 1969.

Now. when we look at the BHAG we are really pushing the boundaries, which means it will take time to get there, 5 years, a decade or more. From this we can see where the dream starts to play its part, not holding back, really seeking to create a massive shift. I remember my own personal BHAG (although at the time I wouldn't have known it) of wanting to become the Regimental Sergeant Major of my Regiment. Might not sound like much, but when you're a young soldier and you're aspiring to be the number one soldier in a regiment it's a decade or two of focussed drive and commitment to get there.

It took me 22 years, at which point I became the Regimental Sergeant Major, I had made it from a cast of hundreds. When I look back on the journey and the resilience to remain on track and true to my BHAG it puts into context what needs to be undertaken to really strive to achieve. What might that look like for yourself? At this point, it's really important to understand that when I formed the vision of where I was heading and what I wanted to achieve I had no idea of how I was going to get there. When you start to create your BHAG, the vision doesn't focus on the how at all, that all comes later. In fact, focusing on the how will hold you back, remember that inner voice it will stop your creative juices flowing and you'll end up holding yourself back.

In essence, your business vision is the mountain summit the long distance view, we can then take a look at the goals which we need to achieve, the staging posts en route to the summit. We can develop the mission, setting out the guiding principle, the unifying reason of how we are going to get there. We can also define the culture, who will join us on the journey to getting to the summit, what type of team do you want with you at the summit of the mountain.

What's the purpose of a vision, no doubt you'll have often seen big business or corporation with mission statements? Some really inspiring ones would be Bill Gates and his vision to have a desktop computer in every home. Let's face it he's not far off. What about Disney, simply 'to make people happy', Oxfam has a great vision 'a world without poverty', Nike 'to be the number one athletic company in the world'. The list goes on. You get the idea.

Your vision should, in the simplest terms, set out the strategic intent of the business, the owner or the leadership. In essence, it is the businesses ultimate goal, the BHAG. It should signify the ultimate purpose of the business, be the essence of success, encourage and inspire both your team and your customers. You should take some time in setting out the vision to ensure it remains stable in terms of attaining it over time. It should motivate

21

every level of the organisation and play an intrinsic part of introducing new team members.

In my experience business owners will hold back on the vision, play safe or be 'realistic', avoid these thoughts and rationalisation. Add a couple more noughts, push the boundaries to the highest level, seek to attain what hasn't been done before, strive to be number one, aim your sights high. It will inspire, evoke excitement, encourage and give purpose and meaning to the business. If your vision feels somewhat unattainable then you're probably on the right track. Let's face it being 'realistic' isn't really going to inspire, is it?

Setting your sights high at worst could result in hitting the target a little higher than your aim. If you set your aim low, 'being realistic', then you're likely to just hit the dirt. So be bold.

Let's take a look at setting your vision, how can you develop it. The following exercise is one I use with my clients at ActionCOACH to stimulate and help shape vision. It's likely you already have an idea of what it should be, so write it down now. Otherwise, try this.

Answer the following questions in order to shape the direction of the business, have a view of what it will look like when you reach the summit, certainly on route to it.

- Where do you want to take the business or organisation in 3, 5 or 10 years?
- If you increase the revenue 2,3,4,5 fold what will the business look like?
- How big will the team need to be?
- A different place altogether?
- Maybe more than one location?
- How will you define success, what are the critical 'big numbers' not the fine details, the overall figure?
- How do you see yourself developing as a professional and leader and business owner during this time?
- What drives you to succeed and get results (this is where the dream comes in)?
- What difference do you want to make in your current role in order to start shaping your future?
- What role do you see yourself taking?

- What do you see as your purpose as a leader and business owner?
- What is your purpose in your current role?
- What is the ultimate mission or contribution you are making, to yourself and to others?
- What are your values that define how you work?
- With what kinds of people do you like to work?
- What are the values that you reject or that violate who you are?
- With what kinds of people do you not like to work?
- What are your top talents?
- How are you able to express these talents as skills and knowledge on the job?
- What talents, skills, or knowledge would help you in your job, and that you do not have?
- What talents do you have that you are not using in your current role, and wish you were?
- What about your work makes you passionate?
- What gets you excited to get up in the morning and come to work?
- What about your work would you like to stop?
- What are your passions in life?

*The Organisational Chart outline the structure of the organisation*

Having answered these questions the next exercise will help you to determine additional detail regarding what the business will look like. Take a blank piece of paper and a pen and draw your organisational chart 3, 5 or 10 years from now, ideally draw it as it would look when your business is finished. Make sure you highlight the size, the various departments, appointments within and size. Diagrammatically this will help to determine where the priorities are for the vision, you'll be able to see just what you are currently responsible for and delivering and where you want to grow the business.

Look back over the answers to the questions and the organisational chart and when you review them what is it about the business that will inspire you, what makes you tick, how hard was it to look to the future and define where you want to go and what you want to achieve? How much of the business is your responsibility, are you conducting or the head of? Focusing on your vision will also help you define the future path you will take with some detail. You'll identify your development needs, the skills, knowledge and learnings you'll need to gain. It will give you an insight as to your fit within your business right now. Are you an employee, a business owner, enjoying what you do or stuck? It will give you the outline of the team you're going to need to help you get there. Most importantly it will give you a sense of your ambition, drive, positivity to achieve your vision.

Having the vision is one thing, how it really impacts on you, the team and overall the business is the real test. Having formed the vision you really want to make it a vivid proposition. In the vivid context is there a picture or pictures you can associate with it, maybe an infographic, animated picture of the future, a picture modified to give a view of your business in the future. I'm sure you get the idea. You could create a poster, brochure or flyer with the vision depicted. Better still you could go to the next level and create your Vivid Vision.

The Vivid Vision

In his book Double Double (Herold, 2011), Cameron introduces the concept and methodology of the Vivid Vision. Complementary to the BHAG Cameron suggested we focus on a tangible time frame, 3 years. Just enough time to remain very real in terms of the distance whilst sufficient time to ensure a massive impact in terms of achieving the vision.

Regardless of completing your vision, BHAG or indeed the Vivid Vision Cameron's advice on stepping out on the right path and have the right focus to develop your vision will help with your mindset. In short:

> • Get out of the office. If you attempt to write your vivid vision in the office, even if you hide in the broom cupboard you'll soon find yourself drawn back into the routine. Get away from the office, away from the distractions of your routine and not accessible to your team.

- Turn off your computer. Go back to good old pen and paper. Go on try it, you'll soon find you haven't forgotten how to write. There is an energy with putting pen to paper. Oh, and when we talk about turning your PC off we also refer to that little handheld one we call a smartphone.
- Never ask 'How' think 'What'. This is tough, I guarantee you'll try to focus on how you're going to get there, suddenly you'll rationalise, be realistic and start to listen to the 'know it all' voice in your head as it starts to convince you that it's not achievable. Be realistic! Being realistic won't stretch you, your team or excite anyone. Your vision must get you out of the comfort zone. How comes later.
- Think outside the box. Another matter is that of engaging the creative right side of your brain, get thinking about stuff you are going to achieve. Getting away will also allow you to really think outlandishly without being told that's silly. Rule of thumb, if it seems too outlandish, far out, then make sure you include it.

To help with the Vivid Vision here's Cameron's checklist. To get you underway, first imagine you have travelled in a time machine into the future. The date is today 3 years from now. You are walking around your company's headquarters with a clipboard and pen (or tablet and stylus)....

- What do you see?
- What do you hear?
- What are your clients saying?
- What does the media write about you?
- What kind of comments are your employees making at the water cooler?
- What is the buzz about you in the community?
- What is your market like?
- Are you marketing goods/services globally now?
- Are you launching new ads on TV?
- How is the company running day to day? Is it organised and running like a clock?
- What kind of stuff do you do every day? Are you focused on strategy, team building, customer relationships etc?
- What do the company financials reveal?
- How are you funded now?
- How are your core values being realised among your employees?

Look under every stone leave none unturned, look at every aspect of your company, see the organisational chart you drew in reality, the departments, the heads of department and their teams. With this level of information, you can now produce a written document, approximately 3 pages in length, articulating the summary of what the business will look like 3 years from now. It doesn't consider the details of how to get there it rather highlights what will be achieved. The document will inspire your team, inspire those who are yet to join your team, it will impress your clients and wow prospects, it will give you drive and the commitment to stay on track.

Whether you author your Vision, BHAG or Vivid Vision it's important it comes from you, it's not a detailed plan of action, that comes later. It's not a work of word magic with every buzzword you'd expect in a corporate, difficult to read and frankly shallow. It helps you and the team understand the business they are a part of and what that means. It's the guiding rail, the point of reference for daily decisions. It paints the picture which you can actually see of where the business is heading. Your vision needs to be about being 'great', not just about beating your competition. It's inspiring and not just about the numbers. Most importantly it inspires everyone in the business, touches the heart and spirit and helps them to see the role they play and how they can contribute to its achievement.

### Goals
So, you disappeared to a secluded Caribbean island for a 3-day retreat to write your business vision uninterrupted or the back room at home if you're like me. You've clearly understood the why behind having clarity in your vision, now what? How do we get there? We have a structured approach to being able to measure our progress and develop the actions required. Just setting out a plan would be far too complex, we need to set stages along the way to achieve, follow progress and measure our results.

Goal setting isn't just a case of listing stuff to do. So many of the business owners I talk to create a list of things which need to happen, to be frank, you can do that without the assistance of a coach. Probably you'll still have the same challenges of not achieving them, never reducing the list of stuff to do or plain and simply the wrong focus. The focus here is that of now turning the clarity of the vision into actionable activities with a focused outcome and generating momentum. This is where we begin to work just how we are going to make our dream a reality.

Let's be clear, having a dream is the easy part, once you are open to the idea that you influence what happens in your life and you have the ability to determine your future. Gaining a sharp clarity of what the future will look like helps to set the agenda. Setting goals are committing to action, setting the agenda for your success. Having multiple opportunities tomorrow really needs to be focused to which you will pursue with vigour and commitment, goals help to achieve that.

Your brain and that internal dialogue play a significant part here, the voice which pushes you that bit further, keeps you true and challenges the negativity and easy option. Our brains work best with goals set and pursued. Just think about the activities you undertake on a daily basis, before any activity, you determine the outcome, define what it is you will do. Go shopping, cook a meal, visit friends, you will determine what you aim to do more often than not and on a subconscious level. In this fashion, we will merely bring the subconscious to a conscious level.

The greater clarity you can determine in your mind on the desired outcome the easier you will find it to achieve. Your brain is probably your greatest untapped resource, give it purpose and focus and watch what happens. Give yourself purpose and the activity will follow, set the goals and you will have the focus to work towards achieving them. Conversely, those who do not set goals get what they planned to achieve; nothing. As we used to say in the military failing to prepare is preparing to fail.

Being SMART about your goals.

I have no doubt many of you will have heard of and be familiar with the principle of setting goals. There are many schools of thought regarding what framework to use.  The point here is following a framework or a checklist of criteria as you set your goals will give you the greatest chance to actually achieve them. Remember the New Year's Resolutions, so many are forgotten, given up on, not even started because there was no structure to follow.

Setting your goals should take contemplation, let's remember this is about the impact on your future, shaping the results for tomorrow. Whilst the idea may be impulsive, there needs to be a thought process to follow, a checklist. Coming from a military background I like and look for structure. Setting SMART goals will give you the handrail you need to remain on target for your goal.

So, what is a SMART goal? Whilst there are a number of different meanings to the SMART acronym I tend to focus on the following when setting my goals and coaching.

- **SPECIFIC** The goals should always be clearly and positively defined in terms that are behavioural. They need to be defined and not vague. In this way, they should relate to outcomes and actions that are specific rather than ones that are general. Rather than simply saying that we are going to be a better manager or that we are going to get fitter, or we are going to empower our team; we should be looking to describe in exactly what way we are going to be a better manager and in exactly what way we are going to get fitter and just what we are going to do to empower the team.

- **MEASURABLE** The goals should also be objectively measurable such that we have a benchmark against which to monitor our progress and achievements. In order to do so, we should be asking ourselves how we will know when we are a better manager and how will we know when we are fitter, indeed how will we know when the team has been empowered. If we look at the goal-setting process as a path that we intend to follow, we need to know where the path starts and where the path ends. We also need to have established milestones along the way in order to ensure that we are not deviating from the path that we have chosen.

- **ACHIEVABLE OR ATTAINABLE** Many people set goals that are completely out of reach for them or knowingly impossible to achieve. Although this practice is clearly self-defeating, many people do this in order to have a built-in excuse for not achieving their goals. We must always have a realistic chance of reaching our goals, combined with a belief that we can reach them, in order to stay committed to them. This is the essence of "realistic" goal setting, although we must be careful how we use this term – extraordinary things are not achieved by realistic people! The use of "fantastic" OR '10X' goals – those that relate more to the original dreams and aspirations that motivated us towards making our goals in the first place – can be extremely useful too. Incorporated within our visualisation they can be extremely motivational and help support our realistic goals – so long as we employ them appropriately. We'll cover this in the book shortly.

- **REPEATABLE** Fundamentally, performance and achievement are a process of "constant and never-ending improvement". As such, our goals should reflect this by having a long-term outcome and growth opportunity. Short-term and

28

intermediate goals (sub-goals), meanwhile, provide useful "stepping stones" that can help us to maintain our focus. In order to do this, however, our goals not only have a measurable aspect, they also need to be repeatable too. In this manner, a goal can be increased at the next juncture through the learning attained during its first iteration. Then through replication, we can effectively leverage the outcome through experience, with a focus on further improvements along the way.

• **TIME PHASED** In order for our goals to be measured in any real way they need to be time-phased. All to often people have goals that they are going to commit to "someday", it's an open-ended agreement, the finish date slips continually to the right. Goals such as these are very rarely achieved and certainly not within the timeframe originally intended. Having developed the goal we should immediately place a "start" and "achievement" date and use this time scale to monitor our progress and maintain and inspire constant action and activity.

Now for those of you who are familiar with the SMART formula you will have noticed that I haven't included REALISTIC. For those of you who are not, this will be an added education on setting your goal without boundaries. I'm not a fan of realistic, because it is often used as knowingly or unknowingly as an excuse. In fact, let's be quite clear I find the word repugnant as a coach, it's just a big barrier.

*Realistic: 'Having or showing a practical idea of what can be achieved or expected'.*

Let's take realistic just for a moment and determine in your life what it is. Take a moment to reflect on your current circumstances, your current environment, the circles you move in and ask yourself how much has been truly influenced by you? In his book, 'Think and Grow Rich', (Hill, 1937) Napoleon Hill says "You are the master of your destiny. You can influence, direct and control your own environment. You can make your life what you want it to be." Is that currently true for you?

Being realistic simply means you will limit what you can achieve on the assumptions and beliefs of others and what they think. Let's face it, they probably haven't truly achieved their ambitions and desires, and that's fine, not everyone is focused enough to take action. You are though! Right? So never base your goals on what others think is possible, never base it on what other successful people have done. Rather base it what you aim to achieve because you have the ability to achieve what you want in life.

When you look at the numbers we are among many who have and will continue to live their lives averagely, are influenced heavily by others, which probably links into the way you were brought up. If you want a little evidence of just how influenced you have been answering these few questions:

- Are you religious, if so why?
- What language do you speak, why?
- Do you speak any other languages, if not why not?
- What are your politics, why?
- What are your values, why those?
- What are your prejudices, why?
- What do you discriminate against, why?

I think you'll get the idea. Being realistic will hold you back from truly getting out there and getting into action. Grant Cardone (Cardone, 2011), in his fantastic book The 10X Rule, if you haven't read it needs to be the next book on your list to read, makes a really important differentiation when he talks of setting your goals. In the simplest terms, your success is *your duty, obligation and responsibility*. Your future is yours to define, not anyone else's; anything is possible, your potential is vast so be bold, thankfully success doesn't suffer from recessions or shortage. Now take a look at your goals and re-think them and be prepared to get into massive action.

What gets in the way?

You will get in your own way when it comes to setting goals. How many of you follow the yearly ritual of setting your New Year's Resolution? How's that been working for you, are you now the prime specimen of yourself, in your dream position at work, have the best job in the world, started out on your own having set up your business, had the quality time you yearn for with your friends and family, you get the idea.

You may have read a personal development book devoured all the positive talk and insight, it may have even inspired you. Although, in reflection, there is little evidence of change. You now need to read this stuff because it's 'brilliant', it will change your life … for or a moment you believe it. Months later you find the book, dusty and discarded on your bedside table. 'I'll start it tomorrow!'

Remember this book has one primary aim to focus you on action, taking your business to the next level, and facilitating the life you want. Sadly, for the vast majority, this book will reside amongst the other great titles on your bookshelf, it will look impressive in your office, even demonstrate your education being able to suggest it as a title for someone else. To be honest, right now I hope you're feeling a little pissed at me for maybe being so blunt and generalist about you, the reader, even though we have never met. Good.

Let me be clear it's not about you, it's about the vast majority who will not, repeat will not commit to their goals and make the difference they need. There needs to be a shift in mindset regarding achieving your goals, committing to the action required. There's a reason I've started this book with the challenge of your dream in life and conversely the vision of what you need to achieve in order to get there.

Here's an interesting thought. This book whilst it has a positive undertone IT'S ABOUT ACTION, not positive thought! You may have a garden full of weeds, looking at it and thinking positively will not rid you of the weeds. You need to get into positive ACTION, get on your hands and knees and pull out the weeds. Sure enough, you'll then be able to enjoy a weed free garden.

Now, if you've really taken a view of the real dream, where you truly want to get to, I'd imagine there is a significant challenge ahead; great news. You'll have developed a big enough dream and gain the clarity with your vision to see there is a need for action. Here's the thing, it's going to need to be massive action. If that's not the case go back and review your dream, set the vision with no holds barred, be daring and dream big.

As a result, your goals will need to evoke massive action as well. Let's be clear, your goals need to be in direct relation to where you are heading. It's worth noting at this point that we have been focused on the future. We have defined where you are heading and what you and your life looks like in the future. Remember this is all about opportunity, letting go of the anchors which inevitably have or could hold you back. Weigh anchor, let's get some forward momentum because that's where you can truly influence the outcome. You can't change the past so let it go. You can, however, influence the infinite opportunities in the future with massive action.

So, how are you likely to get in the way of yourself? What anchors will you need to let go of? The following are some of the common reasons why achieving goals can be such a challenge for some and actually gets in the way of commitment.

- **Unfamiliarity** You may never have heard of the concept of goal setting, uncomfortable with the process of accountability. A lack of knowledge will be an excuse as to why it wouldn't work for you, it makes you feel uncomfortable, amused or even embarrassed. Well, read on, just to help I'll define what goals are and how to structure them.

- **Lack of understanding** You may have heard of goal setting, you just might not understand the benefits of goal setting. Even when understanding the benefits, there is still uncertainty as to how to set goals and the process involved. Being unsure as to the benefits of goal setting, you need only consider peak performers, professional and semi-professional sports people, their levels of performance and what they achieve and do, that makes them peak performers – goal setting will play an intrinsic part. Hopefully, by now you'll be stoked, having looked at your dream life and the vision, so there should be clarity on what the benefits will be.

- **The Fear of Failure** Is a big one and leads to a total lack of commitment. Invariably some people believe that it is "better not to have tried at all, then to have tried and failed". Unfortunately, this can sometimes create a problem with low self-esteem, which creates a perpetual cycle of underachieving and not hitting the goal. As a result, there may be a reluctance to declare what we want and set as goals in case failure to achieve them leads to demotivation and a further lowering of self-esteem.

- **The fear of rejection** this is where there is an understanding towards the importance of goal setting having the fear that other people might laugh at their goals or make "fun" of them for wanting to improve their performance and achieve more. By declaring our goals to other people we always risk ridicule or rejection by other people and more often than not those who we think we are closest too. This is especially true of people who are afraid that we might "out-achieve" them, or people that have low self-esteem themselves and feel threatened by our goals. Although we often need other people to support our goals, it is often a good idea to be selective as to whom we share them with, although we can always use a person's comments of rejection as a form of personal motivation.

- **The fear of success** Strange as it may sound, some people find that continued failure provides a certain sense of security, dare I say excuses and reasons. Such people invariably like to blame their failure on external factors or other people because it absolves them of personal responsibility. For others, repeated failure might make other people feel sorry for them and provide them with a certain sense of belonging or importance. They fear success, therefore, because by achieving it, their attention is inextricably drawn to the potential that resides within them. This forces them to take personal responsibility for their actions and results and can make them feel uncomfortable. Or they might fear to lose the sympathy of others as an "acknowledged failure" for whom nothing has gone right in the past. It is only by taking personal responsibility, however, we can start to realise our goals and our true potential in the future.

- **A lack of purpose** Not really connecting the dots, knowing your why. If you are vague or have a lack of understanding where you want to go and what to achieve, you'll have little chance of setting the parameters towards which you need to set your goals. In this manner, you gain clarity and purpose in relation to where you are heading and how it all fits together.

There are numerous other excuses and reasons which will get in the way and challenge you in not only setting your goals, also sticking to them. You might be a serial procrastinator, devoid of responsibility for your own life, listen to the doubters, have a negative outlook on life or be surrounded by the wrong people and in the wrong environment. We'll pick up on these matters in detail a little later.

Setting Your RAS

The Reticular Activating System, your RAS located in your brain stem plays a significant role in your existence. I'm going to offer some insight into the role and the importance your RAS has in the pursuit of your success and in achieving your goals. It's all about raising awareness. Understanding a little of what the RAS's function is means you'll start to think differently, in essence, my aim here is to strengthen your ability to think success. As we will discover your RAS is your ECU (Electronic Control Unit, which controls all the functions in a car) in many respects, the control centre your compass and critical in the background functionality we just take for granted, your subconscious.

33

Now I'm by no way qualified or experienced in the workings of the RAS, my understanding allows me to 'set my RAS' for success. My aim here is to give you some background understanding of what it is and does in order to allow you to 'set your RAS' for success. My research has come from the communications expert Allen Pease, (Pease A. , 1998) who I have had the pleasure of meeting and attending his lectures. His explanation, which I will try to recount, is by far the simplest I have encountered.

The RAS is located in the brain stem and is a group of neutral fibres referred to as the Reticular Formation. Your RAS plays a significant role in the beating of your heart, sleeping, breathing, walking and in behavioural motivation. In addition, the RAS also plays a part in your appetite, arousal, eating, going to the toilet and controlling your consciousness through raising awareness, bringing certain things to your attention. So, you can see it plays a significant role in your control day to day.

The RAS is essentially the initial point of contact in your brain where your thoughts, feelings and external influences meet. Essentially everything you see, hear, taste or feel goes through your RAS and results in the areas of responsibility in your brain being switched on. Sending the signals to the relevant parts of the brain to motivate responses. As your control centre, one of the major functions is to sort out the millions of bits of information your brain is processing every second. However, the conscious part of your brain can only deal with a very small percentage of that incoming information, 0.01%. 99.99% of the information received goes unnoticed. Your RAS or the control centre filters the information received and responds between the subconscious and conscious brain to ensure the appropriate responses. Your RAS responds to your name, anything which threatens you or anything which you need to be aware of and think about. Think for a moment why is it in a crowded place having a conversation when in amongst the cluttered noise you suddenly hear your name. Your RAS has picked up on that piece of information and alerted your conscious brain.

There is a wealth of research and information regarding the RAS and what it does, I want to focus on how you can now, this minute, start to programme your RAS for success. To set the direction you want to go and make sure you are tuned in to every opportunity which avails itself to you. It's often interesting to listen to people discuss the rich and famous and to qualify their success to luck. Luck plays a part I have no doubt, here's the thing, what is luck to some people is an opportunity for others who have programmed themselves to be tuned into the opportunity. They have their subconscious constantly seeking out the smallest glimmer of an opportunity.

It's not about luck, it's about belief, about knowing what you aim to achieve and looking for it constantly, it's about having clarity in the vision of where you are heading. So how do you go about setting your RAS? Let's put your RAS into action today. Think of something you would like to have right now; a great example would be a car. So, picture your next car, what colour is it, what model, how does it perform, what's the make, get some real clarity on what it looks like. Get a picture of it on the desktop, a screen saver, on your smartphone. Now in all likelihood over the coming days, you will start to see the car in your day to day activity. Because you have spent some time programming, thinking about what you want, you begin to see more of it.

In setting your RAS you can get a greater focus on your vision, where you are heading and what you want to achieve, be programmed so your conscious brain is alerted to opportunities via your RAS from the unconscious brain. The greater clarity you are able to achieve the higher the probability of picking up on these opportunities you'd normally miss. If everything goes through the control centre you need to make sure you have locked in deep into your subconsciousness just what you're going to achieve.

As we have already mentioned the greater the image and clarity you can define for the future you want to achieve the more likely you are to be aware of opportunities going forward. Write your goals in detail, be descriptive, articulate in detail, define the numbers and support think of your success, in achieving your goals in the past tense. Later in the book, I offer success habits which will enhance your journey towards success.

Your RAS is the compass, the control centre and filter to ensure you are tuned into the opportunities you are seeking. When you set your goals on the journey to success then make sure your conscious mind sends the RAS the clearest message to ensure you are tuned into the opportunity when it avails itself; what others call luck we call success.

**As Henry Ford said;**

**'Whether you think you can or can't you are probably right.'**

I often use this analogy to assist with your conscious ability to decide what you want to think about. Setting the RAS is one thing, let's not forget your RAS is probably already set in some degree in line with your current environment, it will probably be alerting you and raising your awareness to less than helpful thoughts feelings and situations, unknowingly. It is these thoughts that 'derail' you, let me explain my view on this.

I suspect you will all have heard of 'train of thought', well here's my take on it. If you start out on a less than helpful train of thought, what happens? As we've just discussed you build a level of dissatisfaction and that starts to take over all your thoughts. In essence, the train starts to gain momentum, it gets faster and faster as the thoughts, feelings and emotions start to take control. What happens when you get on an ever-speeding train is you can't get off and if it keeps going, what's going to happen? It's going to derail and that means, in essence, it's going to quite literally derail you.

I would suspect you know what it feels like when your thoughts, feelings and emotions have derailed you. The funny thing about our thoughts and feelings is we can't necessarily define what, at any particular moment, we will think about. In all likelihood when thoughts seem to randomly pop into your mind it's probably your RAS and subconscious at work. Here's the point, at the moment any particular thought enters your mind, which you know will lead to derailing you, creating dissatisfaction, then get off the train, shift your train of thought.

The second those feelings, emotions and thoughts step onto the platform don't even allow them onto the train. Get away from that train of thought and actively think of the train of thought you need to be on right now. The important thing here is to recognise the derailing thoughts early, remember you can't get off a moving train and ultimately it will derail and that means a train crash. In Chapter 3 I'll offer a series of habits which will assist in the process of shifting your thoughts, feelings and emotions and ultimately setting your RAS and deciding which train you want to be on and when.

The Law of Attraction

Have you ever used words like:

| Out-of-the-blue | Fell into place | Serendipity Synchronicity | Coincidence |
|---|---|---|---|
| Luck | Fate | Meant to be | Karma |
| Calling | Destiny | Fluke | Fortuitous |

No doubt you have, and maybe chalked it up to a random set of circumstances. What about a call from someone, where you greet them with, 'Wow how bizarre I was just thinking about you'. Maybe you had a song in your mind and then you heard it on the radio. How about that friend who seems to have all the luck or maybe the unluckiest? The book 'The

Law of Attraction' Michael (Loiser, 2003) offers additional insight that, in my view, supports the idea and concept of programming or setting your RAS. The Law of attraction is defined as:

'I attract in my life whatever I give

Attention, energy and focus to

Whether positive or negative.'

The Law of Attraction focuses on the energy we give off in the form of vibrations. Have you ever had that sense of a good or bad vibe? There's no surprise here we use the phrase positive and negative vibe. There is a reason for this and science which supports the law of attraction and hence why it is a law. This is the same context as the law of gravity, physics, conservation of energy, conservation of mass even thermodynamics. Now I've already stated that I'm not a biologist and in the same context here I'm not a psychologist or physicist. I'm merely passing on my interpretation and understanding of the science which supports the 'Law of Attraction' so here goes.

We are all made up of matter and all matter has energy, there are many forms of energy; atomic, electromotive, kinetic, thermal and potential. Energy cannot be destroyed. You might also recall that all matter is made up of atoms and each has a nucleus, containing protons and neutrons around which orbit electrons. These electrons orbit the nucleus in prescribed orbitals or energy levels that assure the stability of the atom. With the addition of energy, these orbits may get higher or emit more energy when they assume lower orbits.

Where atoms are aligned they create motive force or vibrations, all pulling together in the same direction. We can see this with magnetised metals as the molecules align in the same direction. Essentially the creation of the positive and negative poles. Positive and negative poles are a fact of nature and science, these are physical laws which cannot be disputed currently. Now I say currently because there are still physical laws which cannot be observed and qualified in various fields. From this we can determine the Law of Attraction isn't magic, it's set against a solid and rigorous foundation within the laws of nature, every atom which makes up your being is in constant response to the positive and negative vibrations.

I would be surprised right now if you're less than sold by the idea let alone the science. If you are, take a moment to reflect the facts that we as a living being create energy and that's measured, electric activity measured in brain waves. The positive and negative poles. You can't see microwaves, yet they heat our food, you can't see radio waves yet we can hear the radio and so it is with the Law of Attraction, you can't see it yet you pick up the vibe.

In your life, day to day, moment to moment you have thoughts which create your feelings and they are either positive or negative, which in turn create a positive or negative vibration. Just go back to the words we have already highlighted, the fact you are able to pick up on the intangible is the fact with far greater awareness you can really begin to apply the law of attraction in your life. Having a bad feeling about this, it doesn't feel right here, they give off such a good or bad vibe. You already have the ability to pick up on these vibrations, you've been doing it for a while now.

So, what do you emit?

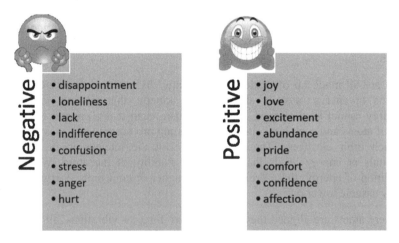

**Negative**
- disappointment
- loneliness
- lack
- indifference
- confusion
- stress
- anger
- hurt

**Positive**
- joy
- love
- excitement
- abundance
- pride
- comfort
- confidence
- affection

If you emit a positive or negative vibe the Law of Attraction's response to that is positive or negative. The universal energy around you obeys the science of physics and responds to the vibrations you are sending out, it matches your vibration by returning a vibration of the same wavelength, positive or negative.

How many times have you been in a situation where the negativity or positivity seems to have been compounded. It's resulted in multiple events and responses. Think of those days when you use phrases like 'things couldn't get any worse', 'why does it always happen to me', 'what have I done to deserve this?' or 'what else could possibly go wrong today'. Or conversely 'I have just had the best day ever'!

As with much of what I have written in this book, once you become aware, take responsibility and understand the power you have, you can start to evoke the response in life you want. There is a direct correlation here with actually being able to achieve your goals. Having the focus of what you want, what you want to attract in your life. When you set your RAS you are tuning your subconscious and visualising what you want. With the Law of Attraction, it's about tuning yourself to the positive vibe to attract it.

Now if at this stage you remain a non-believer, that's ok. It's a choice you make. You chose to allow your circumstances to determine your state of mind, the way you feel and the actions you then find yourself taking. Now you choose your response to the ideas written in this book, you choose how to interpret them, the thoughts, feelings ideas and BFOs are yours and yours alone. The difference comes with the actions you commit to and take. So, my advice here is to give it a go, what have you got to lose? Choose to be positive, decide to have a positive outlook and watch what happens.

Understanding that we all emit a vibe, be it positive or negative is the first step to being able to set your vibe and shift your state of mind in order to focus on positivity and attracting positive results. Whether you believe this or not, the practice of being positive leads to living a fulfilled and successful life in my opinion. The key here, as it is with so many aspects of what we have and will go onto discuss are words. The words we use will determine and be the preset for attracting what we truly seek in life. In this case, there are four words I will challenge you to stop using, **don't, not, won't** and **no**.

Stop! Think for a moment, and you will see and use words in your mind's eye. It could be said that words make us. You will have read words, hear them spoken, you see written words everywhere, when you sleep words will form your dreams. Our very existence, consciousness and subconsciousness resolve around words. Unsurprisingly words impact directly and indirectly on our levels of positivity and negativity. With a simple shift in the use of certain words, you will promote far greater positivity. The use of **don't, not, won't** and **no** will inadvertently create negativity. They set your vibe to be a negative one because you are then focused on what you don't want.

Every time you express something you don't want you're giving attention to it and in terms of the law of attraction you're sending out a negative vibe. You need to stop expressing what you don't want and align yourself with what you want. I don't want to….. Then conversely express what you want.

Sounds simple, doesn't it? The challenge will be tuning into all the times you use **don't, not, won't** and **no**. And let me be clear here, this isn't about what you verbalise, rather what's going on in your head. The focus going forward is to shift your thoughts from what you don't want to what you do want.

Types of Goals and Goal Setting

A goal, is a goal or is it? When we look to establish our goals, we should be aware there are 3 types of goal which offer differing levels of control towards the desired results. They will also have relevance to your situation, circumstances and the type of person you are. Additionally, the following goals also offer a hierarchy of purpose and will, when viewed sequentially offer an overall development of the goal.

The 3 goals are;

*The 3 types of Goals*

- **Process goals**. These goals relate to what needs to be done in order to make the goal a reality. They are described prescriptively in terms of behaviour and are concerned with how the goal is to be achieved. Large process goals are normally broken down into interim or sub-goals. Process goals are important for monitoring what works and what doesn't work, focusing on technique and strategy. They will enable the greater improvement in regards to the improvement of execution of ability and skills

- **Performance goals** relate to predetermined standards against which achievement is measured. They are described objectively in terms of cognition and are concerned with what the goal actually is. Performance goals are very important for focus, control, and recognition of goal attainment. There is a high focus on variables to be measured and can be viewed as key performance indicators, the KPIs. There are tangible results here to actually measure the achievement of the goals in real time.

- **Outcome goals** usually relate to desired results and can be linked directly to the dream and vision. In other words, they are aspiration goals, which can be expressed as a mission statement or vision. They are usually described subjectively in terms of emotion and are concerned with why the goal is important. Outcome goals are often compared to other standards and achievements, benchmarks from others who may have already achieved the goal. They are important for motivation and commitment.

The Hierarchy when setting goals relates to the amount of control you are able to exert in their pursuit. In the pursuit of your goals, it is likely you'll develop the outcome first, what you aim to achieve. The destination or dream. From here you'll aim to focus on developing process, what needs to take place in order to reach the goals, the technique, and strategies you aim to apply. As this process evolves you'll naturally start to develop the performance criteria you can then measure, actually see the goal start to materialise.

As an example, you set the following goal.

*As an outcome* to increase the business revenue by 30% over the next 6 months, from £100,000 to £130,000.

This goal then develops into the following *processes,* in order to gain greater focus; the business will develop a referral system, send out a mail campaign and look at increasing prices in order to increase revenue by 30%.

With the collection of data, the performance can be a targeted focus, with the referral campaign currently accounting for a 25% increase in revenue we will target an additional 5%, in order to reach the target of 30% increase in revenue.

What are the Motives

At this point, it's interesting to take a look at what motivates you. The reason you bought this book in the first place, the effort you placed on your dream not to mention the clarity you have created through your vision. If you haven't done it yet, then go back and do it now. I'll still be here at this point ready to pick up on what motivates you.

*Motivation: 'A reason or reasons for acting and behaving in a particular way'*

What are the reasons you bought this book? The why? Assuming you are committed to taking your life and business to the next level, right now, what has motivated you to take action? The chances are you'll be motivated by either an away from mindset or towards.

Away from.

Take a moment to reflect on where you are right now and where you are heading. What is it right now you are seeking to change in your life? Your circumstance because of a lack of satisfaction. Are you trying to get away from something right now that you dislike? There is no doubt that irritation, dislike, anger, urgency or maybe even fear are prime motivators. Are they the right motivations intrinsic to our human rationale?

Away from motivation is linked in many respects to primal instinct, as Prof Steve Peters (Peters P. S., 2012) in his book The Chimp Paradox, calls it the chimp! Our primal instinct doesn't have a full-time job today so it's often associated with our instinctive decision making. In the case of away from motivation, you can link it to the freeze, fight or flight response. Essentially when we don't like something our instinct is to distance ourselves from it. This is good news, after all, we don't want to get eaten by tigers!

So, if you are currently not happy with your circumstances and you are seeking to distance yourself from your own circumstances, you will. You will be able to tap into a level of motivation to make a change. Here's the thing, it's highly likely that as a result, it will be a short-term change, you won't create sustainable and consistent change. There will be no significant direction or plan of action it will just be to get away from it! Whilst that's ok it's not the solution.

Let's put the concept into a simple contextual scenario. If like many people, you have a phobia, spiders are the obvious one, what happens when you suddenly become aware that one is on the wall behind you? You move. You move at speed in any direction. You're not even worried at this stage what you're moving towards or in what direction. Your motivation is to move away from the spider. Away from motivation works in the same manner although the timescale may be somewhat longer.

You act and you make decisions, the challenge here relates to the long-term sustainable change you'll make. How consistent is the motivation? Essentially, you'll be focused on action until you have moved away from the circumstances. What then, all stop!

Towards

Now when we look at what motivates us, and the focus is towards something, this is in tune with Dreams x Vision x Goal x Learn x Plan x Action. When you go on a trip you start with a goal in mind, where you are going, from there you're then able to determine the goals you need to achieve to get there. The need to work out which way you'll go, fuel the car, pack your bag etc. Now think for a moment the amount of preparation you completed for your last holiday, weeks in advance you were likely preparing and completing a list of goals associated with getting to your sunny destination.

I'm sure you'll agree that whilst you may have found some of the tasks tedious, you nonetheless completed the goal. The similarity here comes from the sense of achievement once you step onto the plan, all the activity which got you to that point was a form of 'towards' motivation. Having real clarity in where you want to go and what you want to achieve will give you the real motivation to commit to action.

Your mindset plays a significant role here too. "It's all well and good Steve, but with this focus I don't manage to achieve my goals." "I never manage to achieve my yearly New Year's Resolution!" A towards goal is you shaping your future, just take a moment to write down the previous goals you made and ask 'what was motivating me'? I would be surprised to hear that in the vast amount of cases there was an away from motivation or a strong connection to it. Go back and make sure now you have clarity in your dream, you have the detail in your vision of what your future looks like. Then tell me what it feels like.

You'll have a feeling of wellbeing, happiness and excitement, you get the picture. These are the real feelings which motivate, these are the real feelings which inspire action, keep you on track. As I write this book, I become frustrated with my ability to get the words down on the paper quick enough (well on the screen). I am so excited about becoming a bestselling author. I can see the book on the shelves in the bookstore, on sale with Amazon, signing books at my local store. I have real motivation in being a published author.

I can feel the motivation in the pit of my stomach, I get excited when I am able to sit down and spend time writing because I am so driven to publish my thoughts, advice, and guidance. For me, this has caused a real focus, drive and commitment to writing. Interestingly even though, at this point when I was yet to finish I was also thinking about my second book (well first if you read my introduction).

A towards goal will inspire you if you have the clarity, belief to accompany it. It's not about clichés or inspirational quotes, it's about what you believe you can achieve and the purpose, the why, that will give you the motivation you're looking for. You are the only reason you fail or achieve your goals, no one else. We spoke of that inner voice, what's it saying right now? If at this stage it's telling you that this is all bull shit, then you're probably right, grab your receipt and go and get a refund for this book, because it won't make any difference in your life until you decide it will.

A towards motivation will create a far greater sense of motivation to remain on course, a consistent approach to achieving your success. To overcome the fear, the inner dialogue, the Nay Sayers. So, if you are still focused at this stage on an away from goal it may be worth establishing what you are moving away from and more importantly define what exactly you are aiming towards, where you are heading.

GROW

By way of summary and to assist in defining the goals you aim to achieve I like to sum up using Sir John Whitmore's GROW Model. In his widely-acclaimed book Coaching for Performance (Whitmore, 1992) he developed the GROW model which today is used to develop and commit to achieving goals. The GROW model asks essentially 4 questions:

> **Goal Setting** – This is a question which focuses on and pays attention of the outcome or performance goal ultimately desired. It's important that we employ all the tools and guidelines applicable to goals and the goal-setting process as we have discussed, such as being SMART. The outcome of this stage should be a goal that is both clearly and precisely defined – accepting, of course, that it is focused on changing your future, creating a shift and stretching you. The type of questions we might ask ourselves at this stage could include "what do I want to achieve", "how might I make this goal more specific", "how can I make this goal measurable" and "do I really think that my goal is achievable by me through my own efforts"? In addition, we would also consider any sub-goals that might need to be included as milestones along the way and determine the time scale in some detail to further aid accountability.

**Reality** – What is the reality for you now? This stage involves us considering your current situation and circumstance. Where you are right now and reflecting on where you are now in relation to your goal. The most important principle for doing this is objectivity, in order to stress what you aim to achieve. Don't be surprised if you or your environment distort the reality now with the opinions, judgements, expectations and the doubters. It is this reason it is important to maintain a degree of detachment and be descriptive in focus rather than evaluate too deeply. Having been through this process you'll be able to define the validity of the goal; a coach is the most impartial and effective way to help determine and review the reality. Many people find that they need to amend it in light of what they have learned about themselves during the reality stage. Essentially take a moment to review what you have discovered in this stage. Ask yourselves, "what is my current situation now with respect to my goal"," how close to my goal am I", "what are the reasons for this" and "how do I think achieving my goal will make me think, feel and act in the future"?

**Options** – Having looked at the reality of the current situation, this stage involves considering the options available in terms of making the goal a reality. It is important to recognise, however, that the purpose of this stage is not so much to find the right answer, as it is to create and list as many alternatives as possible, seek out the 'art of the possible'. Looking at the options openly will also encourage blue sky thinking, thinking outside of the box, whilst reflecting objectively on the relative strengths and weakness of each option, the various courses of action. Here we will also determine what already supports each of the options, and any additional resources, the support we may require.

Throughout this stage, we have to beware of negative assumptions, the emergence of the barriers, such as "that option wouldn't work" or "I wouldn't be allowed to do that". By asking effective questions, or better still ask your coach, we can over-ride this negative and self-limiting tendency, limiting beliefs and challenge the reality of the situation by asking ourselves "what are the reasons for me thinking this way". Similarly, the "what if" "and what else" approach often produces yet more options. In this way, we might ask ourselves, "what if I had more time" or "what if this wasn't the case". Here the external dialogue will often uncover the options and opportunities which alone we might be unable to see.

Here, we might ask others, "are there any options that I haven't yet considered?"

Having asked the question, we must be prepared to consider the answer. Examples of other questions that we might ask during this stage might include "how might I achieve this goal", "how have other people achieved similar goals" and "what other options might I have open to me"?

**Will** – Whilst the Options stage is about what we "could" do, the Will stage is about what we "will" do. This is arguably the most important stage because it is the one in which decisions are made and from which action is derived and commitment made. It is during this stage that we ask ourselves "what option or options are available to choose from?" Having run down our list of options and summarised them, which will be the preferred option and in what order priority will they be executed. Alternatively prioritising several options on the basis of "if that doesn't work then I'll do this" having contingency will also increase the will to achieving the goal. With a decision made, it is often a good idea to check that our chosen course of action will help us achieve our goal. It's then essential to commit to our time scale by asking ourselves, "when will I start working towards my goal?"

If we have employed the GROW Model properly, committing to our action plan in this way is the natural conclusion to the goal-setting process. It naturally leads to the development of the plan. Interesting and an area where there is often limited focus is learning. What will your learning agenda need to be?

## Learn
Learning is an area so often overlooked. Whether it's ignorance, arrogance, just plain uncertainty or misplaced pride, one thing is clear you need to invest in yourself. You need to embrace learning, if you're going to reach your true potential, if you're going to be the best version of you, if you're going to live your life to your full potential, if you're going to achieve your dream and make your vision a reality. One thing is clear with those who have achieved real success in their lives they have the knowledge and they didn't start out with it.

In the business context, it's a simple mantra you need to embrace; 'if you want to earn more you need to learn more'. So right now, what are you doing to better yourself, to increase your knowledge, improve your own ability and maybe excel your own beliefs?

How much time do you spend learning, actively engaging your brain? Your brain is an amazing thing and has the ability to consume vast amounts of information and learn new things you just need to have the belief that you can. In their book Sort Your Brain Out, (Lewis & Adrian Webster, 2014) highlight the fact that you can teach a dog new tricks. Your brain has the resources to create new neural pathways to learn new things.

Another characteristic of learning new things is having the resilience to remain focused even when it seems you are making little progress. You need to have the confidence that you will break through and learn. Let's face it, as a child you learnt how to talk a language, to walk and what's interesting is you did all this through an inner resilience to keep at it. Where would you be now if you had given up learning to walk because you fell over one too many times?

All too often the challenge comes from our childhood, we found ourselves influenced by significant grownups in our lives; our parents, relatives, teachers who often reinforced beliefs of not being very good at something. Therefore, resulted in us believing we were bad at something. It creates a self-fulfilling prophecy if we are continually told we are bad at something. Then we will reinforce that belief and guess what, you'll be bad at it. You wouldn't have the resilience, persistence or enthusiasm to learn, rather you'll just accept you're not good and continue to reinforce that. You wouldn't have the determination to learn and therefore wouldn't stretch yourself. There it is, a self-fulfilling prophecy continually played out in your life. Does that sound familiar?

Interestingly this happens to be a significant focus as a coach, helping others to stretch themselves. So, in your life, if you have a person of influence whose opinion, views and guidance you trust, the opposite can be derived. If they reinforce your ability to learn a new skill, to develop new learning you will have a greater focus on stretching yourselves and in return, you get motivated to do more, be better, get to the next level.

Now you may be thinking, as children, we soak up learning because we have young minds resulting in soaking up new things. Well, let's take a look at that for a moment. As children, we live in a learning environment, preschool everything we do is new, playing is new in stretching our imagination, our interaction with grownups is a learning experience. We then head off to school where we spend all day learning. Learning is a habit, it requires a level of dedication and personal discipline to learn new things. The excuse of 'I'm too old to learn' simply is rubbish. The simple fact here is you need to develop the habit of learning once again.

Knowing we all have the ability to continue the learning cycle, in the biological sense, in other words, your brain only stops assimilating knowledge because you get lazy in nourishing it, seeking out new things, learning new things etc. Here's a simple focus I have on the impact, requirement, and importance of learning, and it's easy to remember; L.E.A.R.N

> L – Learning Gives Leverage. Leverage is all about more with less. How many times have you attempted to do something which you have no background knowledge of? It's fair to say it would have taken you considerably longer than had you had the knowledge. Learning saves you time, creates greater efficiency, which is great leverage for you.

> E – Educate Others. One of the easiest ways to cement new learning is to educate others and let's be clear it's a real win-win, you gain a far greater understanding and you're able to share your learning.

> A – Assessments of your Learning. Gain assessment of your learning. Have others, professional bodies, teachers, coaches assess your learning. Seek every opportunity to qualify your learning. Where you can get qualified, get external recognition to be open to being assessed and tested. It will give you greater confidence, challenge and stretch you to go that bit further.

> R – Research what you don't know. Don't just accept what you know to be what you know, seek always to challenge and gain a deeper understanding. Whilst you may have specific beliefs, ideas, values seek always to understand the widest context. In this manner, you will become an expert and maybe the first to uncover the next concept, idea or thought.

> N – Never Stop Learning. Probably the most important element is to never stop your learning. Always seek out new things to learn, can you play an instrument, can you talk another language, is there another skill, sport or interest you could go out and learn. Always seek to constantly nourish your brain and by virtue, you'll live a fuller life.

Upgrade

It's time to upgrade your operating system. If you're going to live your life to its fullest, become the best version of you, you will need an upgrade in belief. You must believe you're able to be that person you aim to be. You will need to spend time learning to learn once again, to assimilate new knowledge and maybe reboot old learnings which have laid dormant since leaving school. You will also need to ensure the learning environment, and reinvigorate a thirst for knowledge, once again become a sponge for new learning. You'll need to challenge your brain to start learning once again you will be amazed at what you uncover.

So, what is your learning environment right now? The sad reality is once many of us finish education there is very little undertaken to continue to actively pursue education. Let's take reading. There are a variety of different polls available when you ask Google, however, the overall statistics seem to offer a similar message, certainly in 2018 when I wrote this book. Over a fifth of adults will never read a book, it's suggested on average we only read 6 books a year. Wow, that's 1 book in two months. Learning has never been so available than it is today, yet there is a significant limitation when it comes to our continued learning.

Interestingly 45% of us in the UK would prefer to sit in front of the TV for hours consuming mind-numbing drudgery, fiction and fantasy. Just think about that for a moment. How long do you spend in front of a TV? If you're not watching TV you're probably playing a game, does it really add value to your life. Oh, and what about our smart technology, we are glued to it. From the moment, it wakes you in the morning to being the last thing you look at before you go to bed, you are consumed by it.

Today when you walk down a street you have to dodge those on autopilot, mindless walking down the pavement head down consumed by their smartphones. Now I'm not against TV or gaming, the fact you are reading this book would suggest you have a drive to better yourself. So, it's really about asking the question; how much time do you spend learning?

Upgrading your operating system is, in fact, easy today especially when we can utilise our technology to an educational purpose. With the ability to watch what we want when we want to, are there educational documentaries you can watch? You'll find just about all the leading business personalities have their own YouTube channel. Check out some of the great names; Brian Tracey, Anthony Robbins, Zig Ziglar, Brad Sugars, Richard Branson, Peter Jones, Grant Cardone and many many more, all of whom can be streamed directly into your living room for your education. Oh, and that includes my YouTube channel as well.

Books have never been easier to read and consume, to the point you can read a book on one device and then pick up the audio where you left off in your car. Let's take the car for a moment, with the nature of in-car entertainment you can turn your car into a virtual classroom. Just think for a moment how long you spend in your car in a working week. If you are merely travelling 15 minutes to and from work every day, that's 30 minutes a day, 2.5 hours a week, 130 hours a year, that's about 16 full days of study. Ramp that up to an hour in the car per day and you end up with a full 30 days study per year; what could you teach yourself?

As for reading, could you start to have a book on the go constantly? On average I read 2-3 books a month, I have a pile of books I read on my bedside, I have a book in the office and I listen to audiobooks when in the car. Subscribe to those who inspire you, subscribe to TED (Technology, Entertainment, and Design) Talks are a major source of insight and inspiration. If you want to get a sense of what's available, then check out the top 25 most watched TED Talks.

Upgrading your operating system is a simple choice and if you truly want to be the best version of you, if you truly want success in your business and to live the life you want to lead then you have to educate yourself. The next time you sit in front of the TV, aimlessly watching fantasy then ask yourself if the balance is right. Better still lock your TV away and try a couple of weeks without it. You won't miss it as much as you think. Likewise, with your smartphone, stop defaulting to it, stop seeking a hit of social media at every moment of the day.

The more books you read the more knowledge you have the more you will gain positive momentum in the direction in life you want to head. Start your upgrade today. Make a commitment to your education, to your learning, to your future. Stop making excuses.

Competence versus Incompetence

With the focus having so far been about defining what you aim to achieve in your life you will start to uncover and discover where you lack knowledge, essentially what you are going to need to learn to get to your destination, to realise your dreams and achieve your goals. You will, in fact, start to realise just what it is you need to understand and learn. In the 1970s an employee named Noel Burch of Gordon Training International first defined the 'conscious competence' model.

So how do we define competence?

'The ability to do something successfully or efficiently.'

Essentially the required state once you have learned. Learning gives you the competence to be successful and efficient. Essentially why learning is so important. Right now, you probably have no idea or understanding in reference to knowing what you don't know and what you are going to need to know in order to achieve your goal. This is the first stage of your learning agenda and is termed as unconscious incompetence. The aim of the learning is to ascend to the other end of learning to become unconsciously competent. So, let's take a look at the four stages to give you context.

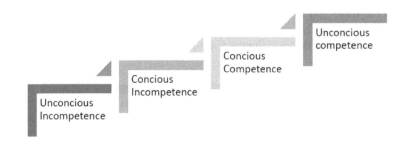

*Conscious Competence Model*

*Unconscious Incompetence.*
At this stage, you will have no idea or awareness of what you don't know. You won't know just what it will take, what you will need to learn and develop in order to make your dreams come true to make them a reality.

*Conscious Incompetence.*
This will be the moment at which you realise what you are lacking, what you may need to learn, to develop to understand. This will often be the point you have a BFO (Blinding Flash of the Obvious), suddenly realising you need to gain competence in a new area. From here you can define just what the learning agenda will need to be, what you need to learn, to gain the competence in.

*Conscious Competence*
At this stage, your new learning is being utilised, you are aware of what you have learned and consciously apply it. You will require to actively engage with your learning as it will require significant concentration to be applied, you will have to think about what you are doing. This is the process where you develop the learning or learned habit.

*Unconscious Competence*
In short at the stage it becomes second nature, require little or no thought to complete. In fact, the power of your subconscious is engaged and in many respects takes over. A system upgrade.

You will have experienced this progression in learning a number of times, think if you hold a driving license what it took to first sit in a car not knowing how to drive, change gear, be aware of your surroundings, then think today about your drive to work and how everything just happened. Or, if like me you can type with two fingers, you have the ability to type at speed. Have you ever tried to get a blank piece of paper and write out the order of the keyboard? In all likelihood, you would struggle to remember, yet when you type your fingers simply identify the location of every letter automatically.

The process of moving from incompetence to competence is a major part of your development and you have been doing this all your life. Now to live the life you truly want you'll start to identify those new areas of incompetence in order to gain competence.

Wisdom

The ultimate acclaim in the pursuit of your learning is to attain wisdom. Wisdom can only be achieved through experience and experience takes time, commitment and relentless pursuit. What does that look like in your life, in your business in the dreams you have? What level of wisdom do you aspire too? When you take a close look at your destination, in all likelihood you will ultimately have to master something.

Your pursuit will start with collating data, which you are immensely well equipped to do. Each and every day you assimilate millions of bits of data, everything you see, hear, smell, taste, touch and see feeds you data, which you then turn into information. The skill in developing your ability to learn is to know what data you actually want to be tuned into and in turn collate. Knowing what data is important and what's 'white noise'.

As you gain the information you will start to develop your knowledge, creating ideas, formulating concepts which you have pieced together. This is the critical element of your learning as you define your learnings. With the development of your learning, you will then develop the skills to act upon. Actively putting your learning into action. From here, the more you act, the more you achieve and with every iteration, you gain more and more experience and ultimately wisdom. You become an expert in your field of endeavour and expert at what you do.

In order to gain wisdom, mastery and true expertise of your field it is thought to take 10,000 hours. Matthew Syed in his book Bounce (Syed, 2010) has determined that in order to truly succeed, to master your chosen profession or endeavour will take 10,000 hours. Interestingly his extensive research has highlighted there is no shortcut. Now, if every waking hour was engaged that alone would take 1.14 years. Even if you were able to engage 12 hours a day you're then over 2 years, so you can start to see that attaining wisdom is a lifelong process and why if you are going to achieve your dreams you need to truly engage learning.

**Plan**

Having set your goals and started out on your learning agenda there is now the question of achievement. Developing and determining your plan will ensure you have the necessary focus on the level of effort and actions required, set within the available resources you have; time, finances, levels of autonomy and the constraints. Interestingly we had a saying in the military, 'no plan survives contact with the enemy'. The same can often be said within the business environment, although you can probably change 'contact' for 'exposure' and 'enemy' for a 'client, customer or member'.

Interestingly the plan remains a vital focus, in order to understand the business environment, to have an outline proposal of how you aim to get from A to B, to achieve your goals. And the goals should remain the focus and you should have an adaptive, flexible and proactive to shifts in the delivery of the plan. Your plan is the outline of how you are going to achieve your goal, to keep you focused on your desired outcome to measure your progress and monitor success. There is no doubt in my mind that in planning you need to be adaptive.

This may seem a little counter-intuitive, why plan if it's highly likely to change? It's about setting out with a focused approach. In the planning process, I will share with you shortly you will also establish or at the very least have contemplated the contingency. What happens if? What do I do when? What are the 'actions on'? Planning, when it's conducted diligently will have allowed you to take a detailed look at a variety of outcomes. To determine the appropriate outcome, you seek in relation and on track for your vision. However, if you fail to plan and you are of course planning to fail!

What will be the process, the actions, activities needed to get there, to deliver the desired outcome? Think of that elusive health New Year's resolution, the loss of weight and the toning of your body. You're clear on the goal, the target weight, the measurement, the question then is how to reach them? How to get there? It won't just happen. You'll need to determine when and what exercise you'll undertake, how often will you train? How hard, how it will escalate in tune with your steadily increasing ability? What about your diet? What will you eat? What will you need to change about your food shopping? Each of these elements forms the plan, the detail required to achieve the proposed goal or goals.

With the focus, we have defined to this point we are aiming to facilitate your dreams through the success of your business. The context of my focus will work equally in a variety of different situations, sports and improving overall performance, in education and in life in general. So, to recap by now you'll have taken a deep look at what it's all about, what you want out of life in general, you'll have refined to achieve the clarity of where and what you need to achieve in order to get there, the vision. And we have now taken a look at the stages or goals you need to achieve to get there. Well, that sounds ok but how do I now make a plan for the rest of my life?

Starting within the end in mind is the key here and we have looked with some detail as to what it should look like. Steven Covey in his acclaimed book 'The 7 Habits of Highly Effective People' (Covey S. , 1989) stresses the importance of having clarity of what your end looks like. Essentially, he adds credence to what we have discussed so far. So, in developing the plan to achieve the goals we have to work back from the long-term goal, to the medium-term goal to where you need to be in 12 months to know you are on track.

Mission

Before we delve into the plan of action, just how we'll make our dream a reality through action. I want first to offer my thoughts on the need for a mission statement and the importance of having one. A good mission statements should be presented to evoke full engagement, inner drive, encouragement, motivation and ultimately unify effort within the team, organisation or business. In a similar manner to the vision, a mission statement should be a focus on what's to be achieved currently, in terms of its customers, the team and the business owner. Ultimately it defines the reason for the existence of the business and pursuit of its vision for you and your dream.

You have your dream, a focused vision and have set your goal or goals, the mission statement should now be a concise, clear and direct statement. Whilst a clearly written statement it would not be unusual to have implied meaning between the lines, this, in turn, gives the mission statement far more depth, meaning, and utility. It should offer a unified focus for the business and team as a whole. Offer a unifying purpose, act as a focal point and give a higher level of purpose and it also evokes a greater level of engagement and alignment. We'll explore this in more detail in Chapter 5. Essentially if all else fails and the employee has only the mission statement to refer to then they should be able to make an informed decision with the aim to achieve the right outcome.

G-OST

There is much debate and many schools of thought regarding delivering the results derived from setting the Goal. My aim is always to keep it simple and following the context of how goals fit into defining your direction. I'd like to share my take on a seamless fit for the plan. Having offered extensive insight to defining and articulating your goal down to the detailed structure of a goal, how do we then set about achieving the goal. G-OST or Goals – Objectives, Strategy & Tactics, whilst these sound similar they actually offer a structured approach to achieving your goals and ensuring they play an intrinsic part of your plans, as we will go onto see. There is no need to regurgitate our discussion on Goals so let's look at the additional 3 elements in turn.

## Objectives

An objective is specific and measurable and in all likelihood, there maybe numerous objectives to complete in order to achieve the goal. You can look at objectives as the step requirements towards the desired goal, in essence, the milestones along the way. When you remind yourself of the SMART principles we can immediately see where objectives fit in Specific and Measurable. Knowing what the key objectives will need to be will also assist in the formulation of the big picture, what the strategy will need to be in order to then actively accomplish it.

## Strategy

Strategy is often a hot topic, bandied around profusely within business with very little understanding as to its true impact. Strategy is the responsibility of the business owner and the leadership. It doesn't need to be confusing, rather part of the process in terms of delivery of the goals set for the business. It's quite simply, and remember I'm a fan of simple, the 'BIG PICTURE'. Your strategy will focus ultimately on the delivery of the goal. It will define the guiding principles in order to truly align the organisation. It will also assist your subordinates, management and the team in making decisions, remaining on track. It will reinforce what needs to happen, the milestones which need to be achieved and what should be avoided and define the 'rules of the game'. It articulates 'the how' and not 'the what'.

## Tactics

Now we get to the grassroots, as tactics are about doing, delivering on strategy. More often than not this is where confusion resides. Business owners spending more time doing stuff with no real strategic focus. Not looking at the end game or heading in the direction of the objective and ultimately the business goal, rather a belief of heading in the right direction because of being busy. This is a route to disaster. Working IN the business with no real purpose.

Another area of confusion and concern is at the other end of the scale when we spend too much time strategising and not enough or no time at the tactical delivery, grassroots. A simple rule of thumb here is the focus on how much time you allot to strategising and the delivery of the tactical outputs. The rule is one third two thirds. Essentially never allow yourself more than two-thirds of the time available for strategising and preparing the strategic plan. Now whilst this may not equate directly to business overall, stargazing for 4 months of the year and delivery over 8 months. It does as a rule of thumb reinforce the principle of less time at the strategic level and more time at delivery. All too often business owners and leaders seek to have the ultimate strategic plan before getting underway with the tactics.

At the tactical level, you will need to ensure the team have clarity on the actions required, have the tools and resources to fulfil them and be really clear on what needs to be completed and by when. At the tactical level delivery should be viewed with levels of flexibility allowing adaptation in application and decisions made to create best practice and focus on the systematisation of the business. Thus, creating the techniques, ploys or responses which give the business the edge, leverage and higher profitability.

G-OST

| Goals | Objective | Strategy | Tactics |
|---|---|---|---|
| **What's the end game** | What's the game plan | How the plan is to be played out | What are the plays, moves techniques to be applied |
| **A general outline of what is to be achieved.** | A defined step to step account of reaching the end game. | A general outline of how it is to be achieved. The methodology. | Definitive actions and activities which need to be completed. The implementation |
| **Aligns and Motivates** | Gives Direction | Guidelines | Outputs |
| **Set by the Business Owner** | Divided within the team | Team Coordination | Team and individual contributions. |

*G-OST definitions*

Regarding the business plan, there are essentially two levels, the strategic plan, and the tactical plan. Your strategic plan is the 'big picture' of where the business is destined and what is to be achieved in the long run. It is more often the case that when businesses have this level of plan you'll find them in file 13 and is at best only ever used as a reference to what has been achieved. Dust it off and then take a look at 'how we have done'!

The second and probably most important relates to the delivery at grassroots, the tactical plan of action. This is where you monitor, measure and maintain the necessary levels of action and activity in the pursuit of the strategic plan.

The Strategic Business Plan

If you are producing your long-term business plan then there is a great deal of information which you'll need to establish towards getting there. This is not a document which is then filed and dusted off once a year, rather it forms the overarching definition of the route to success for you and the business. The plan will determine, in detail, the outcomes across the business. It will ultimately be the definition of success. It will also be an organic document which along the way when reviewed may need to be amended, to take into account over or underachievement.

Traditionally this would be an annual affair, bringing the team together and review the plan and see how we've done. As a Business Coach, this should at the minimum be a quarterly activity in order to ensure your current situation can be reflected in terms of the overall direction and desired outcomes of the business. You can influence the tactical delivery in a swift manner and stimulate responses fast to impact on the growth of the business.

Within ActionCOACH we have a dynamic strategic planning system which can be monitored and updated at the touch of a button and the input of fresh data. It will remain current and always be able to take into account what's happening in your business environment right now.

As a guide the following headings can be followed to create your business plan:

- The Business
  - Vision
  - Mission
  - Purpose
  - Your offering and objectives
- Your destination

- The 5-year long term goal
    - The 3-year medium term goal
    - Your 12-month goal
- The Roles, responsibilities and culture.
    - Your roles
    - Your Key performance indicators
    - Your people
    - Your ethos, values and culture
- Business analysis
    - A SWOT or PESTLE analysis.
- Sales and Marketing
    - Your target markets
    - The ideal customer
    - Where are your customers
    - What your customers want
    - What your customers need
    - Why choose you
    - Your lead generation strategy
    - Test and measureing
    - Your competition
    - Your customer lifetime value
- Client fulfilment
    - Your products and or services
    - Customer service and support
    - Delivery and distribution
- Business operations
    - The pricing policy
    - The payment and account terms and conditions
    - The reporting and compliance requirements
    - Supply contingency
    - The systems and technology
    - Business insurances, licenses, accreditation and certification
- The finances
    - Financial history of growth
    - Financial forecast
    - Financial backup plans

Defining the detail in regards to these headings will determine your strategic outcome for the business. It will give you the annual targets, which you can then go onto preparing the tactical plan of action.

Whatever your long-term goal is you will be able to determine where you need to be at the halfway point to know you are on target, ahead or have an additional activity to catch up on. You can then apply the same approach to where you will need to be in 12 months, this is the essential goal as 12 months is a very tangible time span, you can see with clarity what will need to be done. It will give you a real understanding of what you'll need to do, the activity, the targets to know you are on track to reach the 12-month goals.

Knowing the end state, we can then start to develop the tactical plan of action to get there. Creating the plan or determining the actions required to get there can be a very complex or indeed a simple process. From my military service, the creation of any plan required the need to first conduct the estimate process. Whether you were forming a mental picture of an immediate problem or the required plan of action for a complex military operation, the estimate process stimulates thought and gives structure towards the development of the plan. From my experience, I have taken the estimate process and offer you the Business Planning Estimate, 7 questions which you can answer to develop your 'tactical plan of action' based on your environment, now and where you seek to go at the strategic level.

The Business Estimate – Tactical Planning

So, what do you require for a plan? Information, facts and your assumptions. In order to establish a plan, there is some analysis required, some preparation in order to piece everything together. You'll need to make some deductions from the available information and assumptions you make. Now often the case will be that the plan sets itself out in front of you quite clearly, in order to get from A to B I do x, y and z. How many of those plans have worked for you? How often have you abandoned the plan owing to the changes encountered? The obvious answer is known as 'the most likely course of action'.

In this planning process, you'll determine the number of courses of actions or COA's. You will determine the least likely COA and a number between that and the most likely COA. This will allow you to prepare for other eventualities, have the agility that if or once the plan changes you can adapt swiftly knowing what you need to do.

You might be thinking right now 'that's ok in the military context, business isn't like that'! Let me ask you now if you have a cash flow forecast? From my experience, very few small and medium-sized business will develop a cash flow forecast. Essentially determine the most like COA in terms of their income and outgoings within the business. Even allow you to manipulate the figures if x,y and z don't happen. Let's be clear in business you're going to want to avoid the avoidable. As I've already mentioned, here we can shape our future and the infinite opportunities tomorrow offers, we can now make some assumptions to what happens when they become history.

In developing the business estimate there are two elements we will now take a look at and offer some focus on applying them. The first is situational awareness, taking a good look at the environment in which your business operates. The impact of competition, the habits of your prospects and the impact of external influences; political, economic, social, technical, legal and environmental (PESTLE). The second is the development of the plan, the first step to piecing the plan together in a cohesive and logical manner.

So, let's take a look at the business plan estimate. In the first 3 questions we look at your situational awareness, how much do you know about your business environment, your competition and marketplace?

**Question 1 – What's happening in the marketplace/industry and why?** In order to make some assumptions towards creating your plan you'll need to take a look at the following:

What are the current market/industry trends which affect the business environment? What assumptions can we make about the habits of the potential customers, why are they buying, where are they buying, how much are they buying and what stops them from buying from us? From this what are likely to be the COA's; most likely, probable and least likely?

What are the competitions capability in these highlighted areas and what do I need to do in the business to counter them?

What are the intentions of my competition in direct response to or in reaction to my actions?

What will be the likely financial consequences of these?

**Question 2 – What is the purpose of my business and why?** From your vision what is your purpose, why are you doing what it is you're doing? What are the driving factors here, what is it that will set you outside your competition? What are the drivers of the business? Why do we exist? What drives the business, the team and indeed our customers?

What are the constraints we have to take into account in regards to our purpose in relation to time, team, finances, marketing, sales, logistics or any other relevant impact on the business and opportunities? Which of those do we impose on ourselves? Which are imposed on us and outside our control?

What are the specific outcomes and deductions I aim to achieve from in relation to my business purpose? What is absolutely essential? What are the critical numbers required; the break even, the gross profit, the net profit, lead generation, conversion rate, production requirements, service levels, the prospect habits, locations, and needs?

What are the implied outcomes and deductions required from my business purpose? The standards and values; service/product quality, quality assurance, customer relationship management, skillsets and training required etc?

It's important to ensure you evaluate and re-evaluate throughout this process to ensure the circumstances and the market situation remains the same in context to what you aim to achieve. That the concept of the plan doesn't escalate and become over complicated.

**Question 3 – What impact do I want to have on the marketplace and what must be achieved in order to achieve that; the key performance indicators?** In answering this question you'll start to gain an idea in direct relation to what you want and need to achieve within the marketplace. This will help to determine the level, consistency, and quality of action and the potential resources which will be required. You will further develop specific targets and goals which will need to be achieved in order to have the desired impact.

You will further establish what the major focus is, what is the desired outcome, in terms of revenue, new business, clients, leads generated and from this where the focus needs to be. What will all the actions be focused on achieving? You can also develop and determine what the main effort will be. In all activities what will be the one major outcome, the impact which will be desired. In this manner, you will remain focused on achieving the overall impact.

Areas to consider in the market: market segmentation, targeted marketing, who you are targeting, where will you find them, what they seek, what they need, your USP. In terms of measurable you might want to consider: lead generation, conversion, average transaction, average spend, hourly rates, break even, gross profit.

The next 4 questions will allow you to start to develop your plan, what actions and activities need to be defined in order to achieve your goals.

**Question 4 – What are the business objectives and how can I best achieve them?** Having a clear understanding of your business environment, you can now begin to take a look at developing a plan of action.

What will the objectives and outcomes be for marketing, sales, logistics, operational, financial, HR etc? Who will be responsible for the delivery of the outcomes, what team collaboration will be required and what managerial support will be needed to support the activity?

You can determine what the mission for the plan should be, which will give the business the outline guideline of what must be achieved. As a reference, it will keep the team on track to accomplish the plan.

**Question 5 – What will be the resource's need to accomplish the objectives?** Here you can determine what you will need to assign to each of the desired outcomes in order to ensure they are delivered. How much time will need to be allotted? What are the financial implications and how much will be required to invest? Who will be given the task and what levels of managerial support will be required?

In addition to this what levels of constraints will be required, what are the decision points, what activity and action when accomplished or when it happens will trigger additional actions, outcomes or choices of direction to go? What are the levels of autonomy in regard to making decisions?

Probably most importantly here is what direction and support do you need to ensure is in place to facilitate the delivery of these tasks and outcomes required. How much detail will be required for the team to undertake the activities?

**Question 6 – When and where will the activities take place in relation to the overall desired outcome?** What will be the timeline in order to synchronise and deliver the outcomes of the plan? When will activities take place and what will be the priorities of the activities? What will need to happen in order to trigger the following activities? You'll also be able to define where decision points will be, at which point a multitude of alternate actions can be defined only by the specific outcome of the previous action. In these cases, it may be a financial target that will trigger a certain level of marketing or different marketing activity.

This is referred to as the Gantt chart in the project managing world. As a visual aid, it can be extremely beneficial in monitoring the progress of the plan, individual activity, market trends, sales activities and your operational outputs.

**Question 7 – What control measures and limitations do you need to ensure are in place?** In order to create momentum and facilitate the delivery of the plan without you becoming the default solution to every problem or issue you will need to have clearly defined limitations for the team. At which point do they need to seek clarity. What happens if the situation changes and when do they need to refer to you for guidance.

**Act**
Colin Powell was quoted to have said 'a dream doesn't become a reality through magic, it takes sweat, determination, and hard work'. The toughest element of gaining the forward momentum and maintaining it is getting underway. Everything pales into insignificance if you don't act. Getting into action really takes hold when you've got real clarity in where you want to go, what the dream really is and what it means to you. If it's hot air and guff it will never evoke activity, it's just not strong enough.

If at this point you're not feeling it, it's not evoking the excitement it should then you haven't got it right, it's not big enough and you need to go back and get it right. Let's be frank there is no point in getting underway half-heartedly. It may be you're still unable to really focus on the dream and are holding yourself back, with that dreaded word 'reality'. Your reality will be what you desire it to be. It's not about conforming to the belief of others, sociality or limiting what you can achieve.

The other limiting factor once you have the dream is gaining clarity in the focus of the vision, really bringing it into high definition vision, not allowing it to blur. Let me put this into context with a simple equation:

**D x V + FS > R**

What does that actually mean? Dissatisfaction x Vision + First Steps being greater than Resistance. Now mathematicians will be up in arms at this point highlighting that's not an equation, no you're right it's an analogy and one which works, stay with me here.

Think back to the last time you felt dissatisfaction, now that may be a feeling of anxiety, worry, pissed off or anger you get the idea. At that point just how motivated did you feel? In all likelihood, you probably felt anything but motivated. It's quite the opposite impact. Probably made you feel inactive, unmotivated and probably didn't inspire any action. So, as a result of a high level of dissatisfaction, you failed to act. There was no motivation. No get up and go.

In simple terms, there was probably a sense of defeat, a resistance to doing anything. What's the point attitude. Hey, you may even be feeling sorry for yourself. Whatever the level of dissatisfaction it almost certainly has contributed and resulted in a significant loss in activity. Now whatever the circumstances, in life or business I'm sure you have either experienced it first-hand or observed others in suffering from it. Now with all we discussed so far, it's a great opportunity to make choice to focus on the vision and where you're heading and by virtue maintain tempo and a higher level of motivation.

Now this book is called 'Business Shouldn't Be this Tough, when you get out of your own way' and at this point, it is extremely prudent. If this is you if you suffer from an inability to act that's down to you, no one else before we can continue you have to agree to get out of your own way. It's all too easy to allow these thoughts and feelings to derail your dream, to blur your vision and to cause inactivity. STOP IT. Yes, it's that simple and if right now you're having a bit of a hissy fit because there are psychological factors at play here, then that's your belief. It's not mine and after all, this book is sharing my beliefs and thoughts and I don't believe in it. I believe that if you want something and have a dream and clarity in your vision you go after it with gusto.

So, stop pissing around, get out of your own way and start to have some self-belief in what you want. Bring your vision into clear focus, gain some clarity about it, don't allow it to fade, to diminish, reinforce it daily. Don't worry if it's an area of challenge In Chapter 2 I'll introduce to what's likely getting in the way right now. I'll also be sharing with you later in the book some habits which will assist in cementing it and creating a higher level of resilience in you.

In terms of dissatisfaction and our equation higher levels of dissatisfaction and poor or no clarity in the vision result in a high resistance to first steps of taking action, in fact, greater resistance to anything. I'm sure you'll all have your own examples of where you've experienced this. Think back to our earlier example of the New Year's resolution to get healthy. Did you have clarity, was it written down and did you manage to achieve it, for those of you who didn't I'm sure you will relate to the dissatisfaction created when you fail to reach your goals and the impact it then has on continuing to pursue it.

Having highlighted the impact of dissatisfaction, clearly, we need to create a stronger vision. What happens when you have clarity in the destination, where you are heading, the vision? The opposite, in essence, you start to gain momentum, it's motivating, exciting a driving force. Interestingly the impact of this mindset, the state of physiology impacts directly on the level and quality of your activity and action. It drives you. Getting the idea, the clearer the vision, the more clarity you have the less likely the resistance to act on it, the less likely the resistance period.

It's a very simple mind over matter focus. There's no voodoo, magic or higher intervention, it's simply about how much you want it. Telling your brain i.e. you, that its non-negotiable, it's going to happen, it's going to be achieved, it's going to take place and then doing it. Remember setting your RAS. This is the point where you have to 'get out of your own way'. Stop creating your own barriers and limiting beliefs and start to break them down. Your vision will reduce if not remove any thoughts of inactivity, of resistance to moving in the direction you desire, towards your vision. It means you'll get into action.

The difference between your success and failure boils down to the level of activity, moving in the direction you want. Sit there feeling sorry for yourself, lackluster, what's the point, it's just not worth it, can't be arsed, it's too hard, too difficult, too far away, I don't have the discipline, I'm not determined, I don't have it in me, I can't and you're probably right, you won't. My advice is simple at the point you're prepared and I mean truly committed to living the life you want then pick this book up and start acting like a winner. One thing is sure if you don't have your life's dream, the vision and start to focus on how you're going to get there you won't.

Let's be clear your inability to act is the reason you're never going to achieve what you are truly capable of. If that's the case those who do make it, don't and haven't relied on luck, they have merely been driven towards the success and life they desire.

*The Process*

**BLUF – Bottom Line Up Front**

Let's take a brief look over what you have established in this the first and arguably the most important chapter. This chapter has been all about you getting out of your way. Opening up to the belief you can live your life to the full, you can achieve what you want to in life you just have to go after it. If at this stage you're not feeling it, can't see it, not hearing the inner voice telling you that it's possible then go back and read it again. Make notes, gain clarity, carry out the exercise and establish your DREAM.

By way of a summary:

- It absolutely starts with you.
- Dream x Vision x Goals x Plan x Learn x Act = the steps towards creating the best version of you, starting out with a commitment to become the best version of you and live this ONE life you have to the fullest. Don't make excuses, just get out there and do it and do it NOW.
- Be SMART, set out your goals in a specific manner, have clarity and detail about what exactly you want to achieve. Measure progress to establish growth and forward movement. Attainable and achievable, you know what that means to you? It doesn't mean an excuse to underachieve! Make sure you stretch yourself. Repeatable, once you have completed a goal, it by virtue will be repeatable, you'll have the skills, knowledge and attitude to do it

67

again and at the next level. Most importantly make sure you have a time in which to achieve it. Hold yourself accountable, don't let it be an open-ended goal as you'll never achieve it and it will just be stuff to do.

• Set your RAS. Make sure you set your Reticular Activating System to success. Be clear on what you want to achieve and solidify it in your subconscious.

• With your goal or goals set out what does the big picture look like what strategy will you apply to set out your plan of action?

• Set a clear and concise mission statement.

• Always L.E.A.R.N

If you haven't gained a greater level of clarity at this point, go back and read the chapter again. Make sure you commit to take action and list your actions from Chapter 1, the impact and commit to a date to have them implemented.

**My Action**  **The Impact**  **Achieved by**

# Chapter 2 –

# Defeat Resistance, the Offensive Mindset

As you begin Chapter 2 I truly hope you have taken the time to determine where and what you want to achieve in your life, the Dream. If you've followed the dream x vision x goal x plan x learn x act you have a new level of clarity towards starting your journey. Now that's all well and good and if only it were that simple, sadly there is more you will need to deal with and prepare for if you are going to maintain a real focus on being successful and living your life in full and not to someone else's agenda. With an offensive mindset, and that's not related to being rude or disrespectful, it's about tuning into where the potential threats are and having the ability to deal with them, being prepared to counter their impact indeed being actively prepared with an offensive spirit.

Your offensive spirit will have to deal with both the internal and external influence in your life, which will constantly attempt to derail your mindset, get you onto the wrong train of thought. What's more, these are more often than not, the elements which are directly outside your control. For me it's often white noise which I choose not to tune into, the background muffled sound of other people's lack of success or fear of failure, maybe even your untuned RAS. In this chapter, we need to deal with the plethora of distractions which will cross your path, attempt to block your way or bar entry to a world where you achieve success, where you are able to live your dreams, where you are the best version of you in life and in business.

Right now, you have an imprint which you will likely be unaware of at this moment. It will have been shaped by the environment you have grown up in and it will have shaped your conscious and subconscious behaviours. Your beliefs, values even prejudices will have all been shaped by your surroundings. Throughout your life, you will have been exposed to the opinions and beliefs of those around you. Your parents will have had a significant influence on you, as will any siblings. Your friends, teachers, employees, the social circles you have moved in. So, as you can see you are likely carrying a large amount of baggage which might need to be challenged, reshaped or merely dismissed in terms of where you are you now and aim to head.

Then there are the external influences from society, what is deemed to be achievable, right, appropriate or realistic! Some will be vocal, some will see your pursuit of success as self-indulgent. They will actively or covertly attempt to derail your pursuits, knock you off track, hold you back for various reasons all of which have meaning to them and not you. Think of the stereotyping, putting people in boxes, making assumptions on what their expectations should be. In all likelihood of benefit to them and not you.

It will be difficult to deal with this level of resistance along your journey to success. Let's be quite clear this is a battle of your will against your subconscious, those who don't share your dream, can't see your vision and fail to embrace the challenge of living the life you desire. You will need an offensive mindset to deal with, tackle and defeat the barriers to reaching your success. So, let's take a look at the route to success, the obstacles, potholes and barriers you will have to encounter and need to defeat on your journey towards success and what you will need to do about it.

At no point have I suggested that the journey you are embarking on towards success, which your business will facilitate, will be easy or quick, quite the contrary. It will take guts, determination, willpower and investment in time. Interestingly your willpower will be tested most when you encounter others who don't share your belief and resolve to succeed. In fact, those closest to you are likely to struggle with your ambition; your friends will give you the advice to play safe and there will be those who merely seek for you to fail.

In this chapter, I'm going to highlight the challenges you're going to face if you aren't already on the journey to success. Before I begin to highlight some of these areas I'd first like to challenge you to read on with a wealth orientated mindset. In order to counter these barriers, internal and external influencing factors you will need to be equipped with a mindset from which to counter them. In his book 'Secrets of the Millionaire Mind, Think Rich to Get Rich' (Eker, 2005) T.Harv Eker talks extensively about the impact on our thinking and relationship with money as the rich and the poor mindset. Essentially what it is to have a millionaire mindset.

Understanding the difference between a rich, wealthy and abundant orientated mindset and a poor, poverty and deficient mindset is the first step. This is about moving towards the version of you, you see in your mirror, who it is you aim to be, the best version of you. In all likelihood, we have to focus on why you are the way you are and then upgrading your personal hard drive to the latest version you want to be, in pursuing your dream. Eker states that "it's not enough to be in the right place at the right time. You have to be the right person in the right place at the right time." Supports the focus on setting your RAS and that it's not about luck, rather being tuned into the opportunities for your growth.

Before I go onto define the difference between the rich and poor mindset, I'd like you to think about your response to this scenario. You're about to go on holiday and you have bought economy class tickets for your flight. You board the plane and quickly move down the aisle to find your seats. As you are making yourself comfortable the air hostess approached and quietly and discreetly tells you that you have been upgraded to first class. What's your response? Do you accept or decline? For most people when I pose this scenario to them, although many will seek more information to define why what's the catch etc, they say yes.

Now you're in a safe environment, you're not at one of my seminars or workshops where I ask this question openly, so you can answer absolutely honestly. And why wouldn't you? I would imagine the majority of you answered yes. Now the point here is you would very much like to travel first-class, right now the question is would you pay for it? You clearly see the value in it, if you answered yes! The poor mindset wouldn't, the rich mindset would, the mere fact you have potentially answered yes would suggest that the only factor denying you first-class right now is wealth. The fact is you want to travel first-class means we need to focus on increasing your wealth in order to allow you to travel first-class, we need to focus on your rich and wealthy mindset.

The relationship you have with wealth now will also directly impact the knowledge you have with money. What level of understanding do you have with finances, in your life, in your business or outside investment? Do you feel qualified and knowledgeable enough to make solid financial decisions in direct terms to having money work for you? Let's take a moment to start to take a look at your relationship with money. When you think of money what are the first 5 things you think of, what do you associate with money? What emotions, thoughts and memories come to mind when you think about money?

We have already discussed in brief the environment we live in and the impact it has on us, Eker refers to this as your blueprint. Essentially your blueprint will be the reason you associate certain beliefs with money, you will have been imprinted and as a result, will impact on the financial beliefs you have. In terms of wanting to succeed in life and through your business you will need to have a mindset to support that. A millionaire's mindset, or as I will describe it as a wealth mindset.

So where are you now? When you were growing up what was the relationship with money you experienced? Money doesn't grow on trees, money doesn't buy you happiness, money doesn't make you happy, do you think I'm made of money, watch every penny we spend, don't spend it all at once, I hate money, if I have money I'll lose it anyway and on and on it goes. If that's anything similar to your childhood, then you'll likely have poor a mindset and the relationship with money will be a hindrance to your growth.

A poor mindset will hold you back and even if you were to suddenly strike it rich you'd probably end up losing it. Your blueprint will have resulted in the level of knowledge you have with money. Think of it in the context of a mechanic, having all the tools you could imagine to fix engines with no idea how to use them. It would be pointless having all the tools. It's the same in regards to you and the accumulation of money. Unless you are equipped with a wealth mindset and have the knowledge, the chances are you wouldn't know how to have it work for you in order to increase your wealth.

Tony Robbins (Robbins, 2014) in his book 'Money Master the Game' makes a great point in terms of his relationship with money. It's a tool, and you'll need it to fulfil your life's dream. So, what do you need to do with your blueprint? If you have a poor or impoverished mindset in relation to money and needing more of it, then you'll need to start to shift that mindset. You'll need to accept that it's ok to want more of it, it's not about greed, self-indulgence or anything which would make you feel remotely guilty in the pursuit of it. Rather it's a tool, and you'll need more of it to live the life you want to live.

So, what will your blueprint need to look like, what shifts in money beliefs do you need to make? Is debt ok when we look at using other people's money to help the growth of your business, through wise investment in the business such as marketing? Not fearing debt because we have always lived outside our means. What about the focus of being an employee in your business right now versus being the business owner? What shifts do you need to take in placing a value on your time and working towards always achieving that? In other words, not undertaking the roles and tasks which don't truly add the value you have to offer as the business owner.

It maybe you are seeking instant gratification always looking for the next best opportunity to earn more. You're extremely bad at saving, never able to live the life you want right now because you're always outside your means. Let's be clear today it's a tough challenge because access to more money is incredibly easy. The sad fact is we have a culture where it's ok to run up thousands in debt merely to have shiny things now, to live outside our means. The reality with the wealth mindset is you put that money to work now to earn you more money, which in time allows you stability in the life you want. Long-term thinking and investment.

One way to look at this will be through conducting a need versus wants analysis. What is the difference between the two?

| Want | Need |
|------|------|
| •Why power | •Will Power |
| •Towards | •Away from |
| •Drive | •Driven |
| •Stretch | •Restrictive |
| •Rich mindset | •Poor mindset |

*Need v Want*

### Intelligent Preparation for Business Success (IPBS), the Offensive Mindset

If you have taken the time during Chapter 1 you'll probably have shaped or been shaping your mindset, started to reset your RAS and have connected with your inner wealth mastery. The first step towards the offensive mindset is to determine if you have a poor or wealthy mindset. Once you understand you'll then be able to tap into your inner resource in the pursuit of your dream. You'll also be better equipped to deal with the elements which will seek to defeat your offensive mindset. You'll be able to adopt intelligent preparation for business success.

In order to help and assist you in developing the offensive mindset for wealth, it is first necessary to have some expectation of what to expect along the way. What are you likely to encounter both from yourself and your subconscious, at least until your RAS has been 'reset' and the external influences filter through it. On the journey to success you'll encounter; self-sabotage; limiting beliefs; overwhelm; short-term thinking; fear; out of your depth; making bad decisions; loving doubters; haters; shiny thing syndrome; scarcity thinking; the superhero complex, to name but a few.

From my military experience when planning for offensive operations we would always spend time focusing on the enemy. Referred to as Intelligent Preparation of the Battlefield or IPB, where 4 factors would be looked in depth to ensure that we could be as thoroughly prepared as possible. The battlefield (Business) environment - your marketplace and industry; battlefield (business) effects – what ability we have within the marketplace and industry; the threat analysis – the risk or accepted risk; courses of action or COAs – what are the most and least likely responses our competition will have to our activities?

In preparing ourselves for the obstacles we are likely to encounter we should first understand what they are, the circumstances in which they will arise and appear, the effects on us and our mindsets, the levels at which we could expect there presence and the courses of action we need to have prepared with our offensive mindset. Essentially, we could look at this as the Intelligent Preparation for Business Success, IPBS. So, let's take a look at what you are almost certainly going to encounter on your journey to business success and how shaping our offensive mindset will combat these challenges ahead.

## Self-Sabotage

The tell-tale sign for self-saboteurs is a simple one, what do you rate your ability to succeed right now? Score one to ten, ten being ultimate belief. If you're anything less than a ten then you have doubt and doubt is the combat indicator that you will be your own downfall. Remember this book is called Business Shouldn't be this Tough, when you get out of your own way, for a reason. Simply before anyone else can impact on whether you will succeed or fail you will have to decide. Now, this isn't about pumping yourself up, saying 'I can do it', it's about real belief about real commitment about a tangible gut feeling which makes the shift in your belief and as result will lead to committed action.

Do you often focus on what's not working? What's not going right for you? The negative aspects of what's going on in the business and in your life? The challenge is? The problem is? It's not working! If that's the case you need to shift towards a focus on what's working and determine how to do more of it, to have the concept of success bleed into the other activities. When something is not functioning as it should how do you deal with it?

Here's a very real example of self-sabotage in action. You read a couple of similar adverts for a position in an organisation you would love to have. Although described in a very similar context, one position commands £50,000 per year and the other £250,000 per year. There's a good chance you are qualified for both positions, which do you go for? The saboteur in you will be answering the add and submitting your CV for the £50,000 per year role. Does that sound like something you would do?

There is also an interesting debate, which relates to our ability to self-sabotage, though likely in a less conscious manner and is driven by your subconsciousness. It's the case of effort versus talent. There have been plenty of studies conducted on the effort and hard work school of thought versus the talented. Essentially over time effort can outperform talent and actually is seen to encourage and motivate action. However, there is a school of thought where talent is seen as a limiting factor. Have you ever heard of talented students at the point where they should be preparing for their exams go out and get drunk! It allows them a get out clause that if they return a poor result they have an excuse, I was hungover.

It's not unheard of, for talented people to have a fear of losing their talent, not performing to expected standards and as a paradoxical result, their performance dips. They in effect, through trying to protect their talent through not failing then fail to progress. They hold themselves back. Conversely, hard work and effort reward itself through continued commitment. Sadly, the environment we grew up in also impacts on this.

Picture this; a young child brings home from school a picture. The child comes in excited they have created such a work of art for mummy and daddy. The parent immediately lavishes praise for what they have achieved before they have even picked up the picture. When they pick up the picture they further praise the child for being so good, having such a great talent.

A second child from the same class comes home to their mummy and daddy with their picture equally excited. In this case, the parent asks to see the picture and praises the child for the effort they put into the picture. Telling them they have done really well and it's a great deal of effort.

Child number 1s environment will focus on the child as having talent, without actually having to work hard at the picture. Now whilst this may sound ok, child 1 soon learns that they don't have to work particularly hard as they know whatever happens they will be praised for the talent they have. In the case of child 2, they start to associate effort with the need to perform better. The will seek to work harder to continuously be rewarded with praise directly associated to the effort they put in. Now whilst these two examples may be very simplistic, which camp did you grow up in, rewarded for just being you or the reward associated with the effort you put in?

In whichever camp you grew up in, how much impact it may have had on you the fact remains that self-sabotage is a focus you need to have in pushing your performance, seeing that with effort you can achieve what you want to achieve. As we mentioned earlier, it's not about luck, nor is it about talent. Yes, there are talented individuals, in all likelihood when you ask them about how well they've done they will certainly highlight the commitment and effort to getting to that level.

Do you feel you have value to add, or do you feel worthless, always seeing others as better than you, feeling put down? Do you compare yourself to others, wishing you were like them? Which often results in a feeling of inadequacy and low self-esteem and confidence. Another symptom maybe you never seem to reach your goals and as a result, don't bother with them. When you look back what did you achieve when you set goals, was there some movement forward, did you have some focus on what you aimed to achieve? When you take a detailed look, it is highly likely that there was some shift and it's not so much never working rather never committing!

Right now, have you sabotaged your own commitment to actually putting some of the advice and guidance in this book to action or is your inner voice quietly saying to yourself that whilst it may be interesting, it's all bull shit! I'll never be able to succeed! I haven't got the commitment! It wouldn't work for me! Well before you close the book and place it on the shelf, let me remind you that the voice you hear is yours, no one's else, it's yours. You decide whether you have got the courage to step up to the challenge, to make your dreams come true, to live the life you want. Stop messing around, stop sabotaging your life, take control and focus on what you can achieve. Your performance can be vastly improved with time and effort.

## The Offensive Mindset

You'll need to start to really focus on what works, what you're good at, what success you have enjoyed and how it made you feel. Here are some habits which you can use to start to combat the self-saboteur in you:

1.      Always make sure you focus on what's working for you, no matter how small. Fix it in your mind and you'll grow your self-belief in your ability and commitment to succeed.

2.      Keeping a journal makes you focus on what you have taken from the day, being able to actively record your momentum forward and your growth.

3.      Stop worrying about others, you can't influence them, and they can't make your life right. Focus on what makes you good and maybe even better than others. A great exercise is to write down a list of your 6 best ever wins, what they were, why they happened, how they made you feel then and how they make you feel now. Write them down in as much detail as possible, the more the better as it will help to reinforce your self-belief.

Self-Sabotage will absolutely derail the pursuit of your dreams, it will cloud your vision and it will have a negative impact not only on you also those around you. Self-Sabotage will lead to self-pity, feeling sorry for yourself and no one wants to be around a whiner. It will also lead to and cement your limiting beliefs.

## Limiting Beliefs

As a coach, I often have to deal with the limiting beliefs of my clients. Limiting beliefs are a sure way in which we set our RAS to failure. Self-Sabotage leads through reinforcing our thoughts to real limiting beliefs. There is a significant shift here as we start to internalise and believe we just don't have the ability, discipline or commitment to do something we want to do. I can't….. I'll never….. I couldn't…. I don't have the…. If only I could…. All of which is a coward's way out. Yes, I said it, a coward's way out. Let's be clear in life it will take courage to go after the life you want. It's not going to be presented to you, rather on your death bed you can reflect 'if only'.

To get over the limiting beliefs you will need to focus on your inner dialogue, that voice again. One thing which I'd almost guarantee is we all have limiting beliefs. If you don't believe me go and take a good look in the mirror and tell me if you like what you see. Tell me right now you're the best version of you. No? Isn't that interesting. When you see your reflection looking back, is it as educated as you would have liked, healthy, able, disciplined, driven, nice, wealthy, engaging, courageous, connected, respected, loved, kind, giving, strong, and the list goes on. There's only one reason for that and that is your belief in attaining those characteristics you desired.

I'll help you make the shift with one word. BUT.

The first shift you need to make is to remove this word from your inner dialogue. More often than not when we use BUT it is in a limiting manner. You have a great idea, something you want to do and your inner self-agrees....... BUT. Now it's likely you are not tuned into your inner 'BUT' right now, so listen out for it. When you next make a commitment to yourself and then fail to commit ask yourself what got in the way, why didn't you commit? BUT will always seek to talk you out of what you actually want to achieve. How many times have you really wanted to do, or complete something and never managed to see it through to fruition?

Clearly, the other area is when you verbalise it to others, talk them through what you aim to achieve, your next great idea and then add the BUT CAVEAT, that's right you qualify in advance the reason you are likely not to achieve it. It's ridiculous and another prime example of the need to get out of your own way. Get tuned into your inner BUT and combat it, destroy all remnants of it, take it out of your vocabulary and if you need to replace it use AND. AND will challenge even further, keep your mind open to opportunity, make you think in addition too not taking away from.

**The Offensive Mindset**
To empower your offensive mindset, you will need to start to write down what you aim to achieve, funny enough we covered this in Chapter 1. Write down your dreams, the vision and your goals, it will assist in really cementing the end state, where you are heading and what you will achieve. Here's the really interesting part here, you won't write BUT. BUT won't feature in your written dream, vision or goals. Indeed, quite the contrary you'll actually define the detail to succeeding and how you're going to get there. Getting the detail on paper will also help to reset your RAS, gain the clarity within your subconscious and start the process of eliminating your limiting beliefs.
This also links, interestingly, very closely to defining your poor versus your wealth mindset. I'd be quite certain when I asked to review your blueprint earlier in this chapter you may have found a few BUTs sneaking in. Don't let them hold yourself to account, dismiss them instantly and seek an

alternate response, BUT adds no value to your inner growth and your ability to commit and stay committed.

### Overwhelm

What causes the feeling of overwhelm? Why is it that life can seem like there are too many things to do all in one moment? How does overwhelm seem to suddenly appear? From my experience overwhelm is caused in the simplest terms through a lack of or no planning. Added to this being consumed IN your business. This relates back to being employed by yourself. Think for a moment in your business just how busy are you? In all likelihood, you will be the busiest in your business and as a result, you'll have little time to spare in relation to making the achievements you desire.

Now there will be a number of you saying that I have a plan, I have to do the work in the business as I'm the only one who can, or I'm the only one. Yes, you're right. Here's the thing, how detailed is your plan, is it written down, does it take into account you have to balance working IN the business with the focus ON the business and its growth. I probably wouldn't be far off the mark if I made a few assumptions here; the plan is in your head, the business solely relies on you and would fall on its arse if you weren't there, you're the only one you trust to do the job right, if you have a team they all default to you for solutions, your customers all have your personal phone number and default directly to you for business, you're probably also doing the bookkeeping, marketing, sales, problem-solving and cleaning!

Is it any wonder business owners suffer from overwhelm?

The classic analogy here is being in a forest and not being able to see the woods for the trees. In life let alone business we are confronted with so much it's not surprising we suffer from overwhelm, whether you are starting a new business venture; growing your business; have a critical project underway.

A major challenge from overwhelm is our inability to make decisions and good ones at that. It may be we just don't know where to start. You might find you make the easy, less complex decisions, focusing on the easy outcomes and not focusing on what really needs to happen. The consequences of the decision we make can also play a part, seeking to focus on those decisions with limited consequences and thus may miss the bolder more important decisions which need to be made.

Being overwhelmed will incapacitate you, create negative thoughts and result in focusing on the wrong things. Incapacitation will only serve to shift you away from being able to deal with and respond to situations to a state of almost panic and in some cases simple panic. Your cognitive ability to respond rationally to situations in the business will escape you. Rather you will lose the ability to focus on what needs to be done. For some, it will result in a state of paralysis and actually not being able to respond, give direction or work out what needs to be done.

What about the impact of the negativity? This links back directly to the train of thought and impacts it will have if you allow these thoughts feelings and emotions to take hold. It's back to that challenge of being what you believe you are. If you think it, it will reflect in the world you are in. In relative terms, you will exacerbate the situation, make it worse, it would likely snowball and that's just going to lead you down the wrong path and derail your journey.

**The Offensive Mindset**
In this instant, your offensive mindset will need to kick in swiftly to negate the feeling and impact of overwhelm, here's how. In the first instant, you have to take control of your mindset, they are your thoughts and feelings, so control them. Get off the train of thought and get back onto a meaningful focus. Knowing when these symptoms show themselves, the trick is to shift yourself away from overwhelm and refocus. Breaking the thought process will give you the opportunity to look at and reassess the bigger picture.

Take a view and focus on what's happening currently and then logically establish what needs to happen, break it down, focus on the simplicity of solving the current situation or problem. If there are multiple issues remember you can only deal with one at a time so to prioritise. You may have deadlines for some activities, some activities may need to be completed first in order to facilitate others. Act with purpose not with panic, evoking your positive mindset here will encourage a swifter resolution. Be in no doubt the overwhelm and negativity won't give up easily, they will be lurking in the background wanting to derail you at a moment's notice. You have to consciously work hard at this, it's not as easy as it sounds.

This next focus takes us back to Chapter 1 and is a sure way of avoiding overwhelm in the first place. Having a plan in place and sticking to it. Furthermore, having a planning mindset. The plan is one element the delivery of it is the next and requires a focus at each level. Now not all of you out there are high in detail and so the mere thought of planning is going to be a challenge. So, let me be clear here, plans are critical in moving

81

towards your success, and one thing I say with some experience from my military service is the necessity of planning.

Often, it's not about the actual plan. As the saying goes 'no plan survives contact with the enemy'. The same is try in business, often the best-laid plans are not directly followed or achieved. What's critical is that you have taken the time to determine the plan. It is the act of planning which is so often missed, the fact you have taken the time for deep contemplation and thought in regards to your business.

Whilst some of you may not like planning or the detailed focus, one thing you will all have or be lacking in various degrees is your level of self-discipline. Planning is a discipline and one which you will need to master. From having the plan of the strategic objectives, the bigger picture, that which will take you towards the success, achieving your vision and dreams. To the discipline of planning the actions and outcomes for tomorrow and having the focus to make sure you complete today's tasks. I'll touch on self-discipline in the next Chapter.

Having your plan written down will force you to cement the detail for progression, what needs to be done when, what are the key decision points, what activities complement each other, what we will have to measure success and so on. It takes the guesswork out and gives you a guiding rail to stay on track. It will also assist in the ability to further establish and plan the smaller activities, what's the focus for tomorrow, what needs to be achieved, what are the priorities. As we have discussed in Chapter 1, have the long-term vision and then bring it right back to the activities I need to focus on tomorrow to know I am on target. This is crucial.

Remember I introduced you to the idea and concept of the Business Estimate and as a result, you would have to think about the most likely and least likely courses of action. As we will be aware plans often change or deviate, having as part of the process of formulating the plan you have contemplated other potential outcomes is it conceivable that you may have looked at solutions already. So, if you have a positive mindset which is prepared for the unexpected it is far less likely to derail your progress. Don't allow overwhelm to slow you down, derail or halt your focus, in the simplest terms you can be prepared for it.

**Short-Term Thinking**
As a business coach, I come across this pattern of thinking all too often. However, I have first-hand experience of this in my life and I think you'll have encountered the same. What is short-term thinking? Do you own, or

have you ever owned a store card, maybe credit cards or even an overdraft limit in the bank? These will all entice and encourage short-term thinking. It gives us the ability to live outside our means to have stuff right now we can't afford to have and so we use credit to buy them. This is short-term thinking, this is need and want over patience and aspiration. I'm sure you can relate to having had the desire for something that right now you really couldn't afford.

In context with the wealthy and poor mindset, this is firmly fixed in a poor mindset. Not having the commitment or patience to wait and build the disposable income to such a point it becomes affordable and merely creating a bad debt is a poor mindset. Interestingly and as was the case with me, it's almost addictive once you have seen how easy it is to use other people's money for stuff. I walked into a shop and decided I was going to have the very latest camera, and not only that, all the additional add-ons to go. In less than an hour and having racked up £500, limited to that only because of the cards overall balance. With a couple of signatures, I walked out of the store.

I then walked next door into a very famous high street clothing shop and did the same once again. By the end of the day I had accumulated over £1000 of debt and I felt great. I had worked out just how I was going to be able to pay it back whilst having only to forgo a few elements of my life. Now had I at the very minimum been able to keep to my plan of repayments it might have been ok. Unfortunately, I didn't and the next few years were a real lesson in patience and a focus on how I should have made a better, wealthy decision. Sadly, it didn't end there and the story goes on to add a holiday to Florida, mid-way through an operational tour in Belize.

What was the main cause? In the simplest terms the need for self-gratification over patience. I see this all too often today in my coaching. There is limited focus on the long game, where the outcome results in sustainability and consistency and ultimately the level of incomes where you can enjoy many more of the things you dream of. The reason so many fail to achieve their dreams, feel unlucky and have a view it will never happen to them is down to their need to be gratified right now. A quick shot of gratification and everything will be ok again. Let's face it, today it's never been so easy for people to do exactly that and sadly keep doing it.

In business, it's the same. I often come across business owners who are spending their money on stuff which adds no value to the business, offers no return on investment and by virtue merely eats away at the profits. There are those who have their heads stuck in the sand and take drawings, dividends and cash from their business without the slightest idea of its effect, merely because they had a good day. It's all short-term thinking and if unresolved will ultimately result in the demise of a business and quite the opposite of a feeling of gratification.

The other aspect in addition to the hit of gratification is being in a hurry to get there. Let's be clear when we spoke of the dream and your long-term vision we were talking at a minimum a decade. Of course, there will be those of you who will accelerate the results and arguably your goals will get bigger and you'll aspire to greater things, so there is a commensurate focus to achieving your goals. As you achieve success your goals will get bigger.

Being in a hurry will have an impact on the outcomes of what you want to achieve, you can't hurry success. My military career spanned 28 years and went from Private Soldier to Regimental Sergeant Major and then Captain. There was no point I could have made the journey any quicker. I needed to grow, learn and develop into each rank, appointment and role throughout my career. The net result was a well-rounded, experienced, operation hardened Captain who had all the attributes and qualities associated with and for the position I would hold. As a soldier having progressed through the ranks to being commissioned, what's referred to as a Late Entry Officer or LE, there was no shortcutting that. And whilst some of you maybe thinking it's a little self-indulgent of me to highlight my journey, I would encourage you to go and talk to anyone military or otherwise who has experienced success on their path and they will say the same. Take a look in the mirror, what has been your journey to this point? What success have you enjoyed?

The same can be said in Business. As you will all be clear there are some sad statistics regarding the success and failure of business. Sad as it is 20% make it to through the first 12 months, of those 50% make it to 5 and years and only 40% remain at the 10 years anniversary. The fact here and something we can draw from is the successful businesses don't and haven't suffered from short-term thinking. Just reflect on Chapter one, the point here is to have a clear focus on your future, 10 or 20 years from now.

In business, short-term thinking will cloud your judgement. You will be less likely to invest your income and the retained profits back into the long-term growth, rather you are likely to spend it on stuff! You will be less likely to focus on what the lifelong value with your prospects will bring. Rather you will miss opportunities because you are looking for the short-term gratification of offering your business, products or services NOW. There are and will be occasions where you are likely to lose on your first sale, which is ok as long as you have looked at the long-term value you could make from a long relationship.

## The Offensive Mindset

As we can see there are dangers associated with short-term thinking and you need to have a clear focus on the long-term outcomes. The vision always maintains the clarity of where you are heading fixing it firmly in your mind. The challenge here is training your brain to dismiss the need for short-term gratification. Brilliant get the swanky car, the shiny stuff right now, it's not going to offer you the satisfaction you seek long term. In all likelihood without a long-term game plan, you soon find it becomes unsustainable. Sadly, you significantly increase the risk of your business not making it.

Whilst having detail in the plan the real key here too long-term thinking is its execution and the consistency in your actions. Too much focus *in* the business and none *on* the business and you'll lose sight of where your heading, failing to see the 'wood for the trees'. So, in addition to the plan have the goals set out, get a level of accountability in the business, fellow directors, a coach or your accountant. Essentially if you are someone who has a poor personal discipline record then appoint someone to hold you accountable. Remember this is about getting you and your business above the parapet, more on that later.

## F.E.A.R

Of all the emotions, we experience through our journey in business and life FEAR is probably the most prevalent, so it worth understanding a little about why we experience and what we can start to do to control it. In his book, Emotional Intelligence Daniel Goleman (Goleman, 1995) offers insight into our ability to first understand our emotions and through understanding better control and use them. The concept of EQ, emotional intelligence and having an understanding falls into two prominent aspects:

- Firstly, having an understanding of yourself, your goals, intentions, responses and behaviours and all other associated emotional feelings.
- Secondly, having an understanding of others and their feelings.

From this Daniel goes on to discuss in depth 5 domains of EQ:

1. Knowing your emotions.
2. Managing your own emotions.

3.    Motivating yourself.
4.    Recognising and understanding other people's emotions.
5.    Managing relationships.

Whilst we are focused on fear I have introduced the concept of EQ because of the myriad of emotions we experience, in my personal experience if you are unable to understand why and how fear impacts on you at whatever level, it will debilitate you and derail you from your path ahead. Your mindset has played a significant part throughout the book to this point and it is that mindset which will stimulate the emotion. With all emotions they are prompted and promoted by irrational thought, they don't focus on the logic, often when we experience fear it will form the making of the excuse and a way out. Essentially without an understanding of fear, it will compromise your focus for the future and what you want to achieve.

Here's the thing, how do you begin to understand fear if we do all we can to avoid it. Surely to understand it we have to become comfortable with it, we have to experience it in order to really determine how to to deal with it. We have to become familiar and to an extent comfortable with it, used to its presence. I'll pick up on this shortly as I share with you my experiences.

Let's put this into context for you right now in your business, what are you fearful of? Fear of failure; fear of success; fear of not knowing where to start; fear of getting finished; fear of being seen as a smart arse; fear of not being an expert; fear of losing everything; fear of change; fear of regret; fear of public speaking; fear of making decisions; fear of not knowing; fear of cold calling; fear of not reaching your targets; fear of committing; fear of being uncommitted; fear of not attracting customers; fear of criticism; fear of letting others down, fear of debt; fear of investment; fear of running out of money; fear of trusting others; fear of being on your own; fear of the unknown.

The list is not comprehensive, and you will probably have others we haven't mentioned here. When you go back through the list. What's interesting in direct relation to the irrational aspect of fear is the paradox with many of the fears, the opposite often exists in the same context. Fear of success may lead to the fear of failure! You see you really need to take control of these emotions and take a logical reflection as to what triggers it. In the same context, you'll be able to identify fear and then utilise it as a strength to motivate yourself.

All too often fear will lock you away in your comfort zone in a bid to protect you. You will not seek to expand yourself, challenge yourself because it's nice in your comfort zone, it's safe in your comfort zone no one can touch you in your comfort zone. In all likelihood, you won't be reading this book because it's out of your comfort zone. Rather you may be looking to challenge yourself. You need to confront fear and to do that you will need to expand your comfort zone and that will require you to step out of it.

You will need to nourish yourself in order to reduce the fear, stop being irrational and start to think rationally. You will need to develop, learn, gain greater experience, shift your perspective and be doing it continually. It is only then that you will start to determine what can actually be achieved, what you can become. Don't allow yourself to succumb to the fear.

False Expectations Appearing Real

False Expectations Appearing Real is probably the most widely used acronym in relation to discussions about fear. Which on the face of it is a relatively good way, to sum up the source of fear. Being fearful of an outcome which may happen or may not happen in the future. As an irrational emotion fear will, if left to its own devices, derail your progress, stop you from achieving what is truly possible. I'd like to take a moment to reflect on fear in its rawest terms, the confrontation of your mortality. Now I'm no expert, from my own experience, learnings and insight fear is also an indication and signal that you need to proceed with care and attention. Not an excuse to halt or freeze or switch off, quite the opposite. As one lady shouted out in a workshop when asked what is fear, the response came f__k everything and run! Funny as it sounded at the time, when you reflect on that, it's probably the response most people have. Irrational with a need to create rational responses and commitment.

Throughout my military career, I have had to confront fear on many levels, most notably in combat. So, just how did I and all the soldiers and officers I served with manage to overcome the fear of 'not coming back'. Conditioning, training and having an understanding of what to expect, becoming familiar with just how fear feels. I often remember the quiet reflection just prior to deploying on operations, it was probably the only moment were fear would suddenly come into the forefront of your mind. The reality then was focusing on the job in hand and having confidence in your abilities and being a part of the team. It didn't result in inactivity but rather a quiet confidence and inner reflection from becoming comfortable with the presence of fear. The key to being able to function effectively despite the presence of a fear of losing your life, being injured or one of your mates being killed or injured required a significant level of mental robustness. Learning, training and being comfortable with it.

In the first instant, the training is extremely comprehensive and pressured to enable you to operate at such levels for prolonged periods. With such high levels of training your reactions to situations almost becomes instinctive. You are able to programme your mind to immediately act. Often the reality once onto operations you had to take control of your emotions in order to make sure you were able to operate effectively. You can see from the insight to EQ, this was a significant ability required to deal with the rigours of operational life. It allowed the rational thought process to take charge and decipher the threat and response to it in a comprehensive and measured way.

Now I am only really touching the surface here, in order to offer context to the fears we encounter in business. One of the additional key aspects in understanding the impact of fear is understanding what physical and physiological signs you would need to be tuned into. Let me take a moment to give you some insight into the levels and impact of fear and what the likely signs and symptoms are. Often referred to as the 'combat mindset' the mental state of a soldier in combat conditions heightens the physical and mental stress.

In a high threat life or death situation the body will have an alarm reaction and the freeze, fight or flight reflex will kick in. This creates a host of responses when the soldier finds themselves in a combat situation some of which might be:

- Increased heart and respiratory rate.
- Nausea.
- Chemical cocktail of adrenaline + endorphins results in shaking, clumsiness, slowness.
- Pupils dilate and both eyes open wide.
- Tunnel vision.
- Tachypsychia, which is slow motion time/space distortion.
- Auditory exclusion, a temporary loss of hearing.
- Precognition, foreseeing what's going to happen.
- Conflicting memories

This cocktail of biological reaction results in various degrees of physical reactions, which some will, over greater exposure, adjust to and manage and others may not. Interestingly when I talk to business owners who are in a constant state of stress or fear it's not unusual to talk of these symptoms. Why because our bodies are hard-wired to respond accordingly to threat.

The challenge here is that fear is debilitating, when we do not take control of it and understand it. It negates your ability to function cognitively because your brain is only tapping into the simplest of brain functions. You'll have all heard of your lizard brain or the chimp brain, well that's the part of the brain we have managed to keep from our ape decedents. It's like a PC going into safe mode. It stops all other processing activity other than what's going to protect and preserve itself. Hence the freeze, flight or fight mode.

Tame Your Inner Chimp.

Professor Steve Peters in his book The Chimp Paradox (Peters P. S., 2011) for me provides one of the easiest, understandable models of how and why our brains function the way they do. The three key elements to the brain are the frontal (Human), limbic (Chimp) and the parietal (Computer). In context, the Chimp is the emotional part of your brain, and essentially thinks for itself, its independent, neither good or bad, it is quite irrational. Remember we already mentioned the irrational behaviour and responses triggered by our emotions.

The human part of your brain is where 'you' reside and your rational thoughts. Your day to function is managed from here, your logic, ability to think problems through and so on. The final piece to the jigsaw is your computer or your hard drive, where you store and reference information. Interestingly the computer store both information assimilated by you the human and your chimp. This essentially is your psychological universe.

Now I understand I am not necessarily giving this the full introduction it requires, in which case I strongly recommend you check out the Chimp Paradox for further reference, stay with me, it will make sense. The reason you may currently have little control over your emotions and in this case, we remain focused on fear is owing to the relationship with your chimp. Right now, your chimp is there in the background monitoring all that information being passed through your RAS. Now the moment there is a perceived threat your primal instincts kick in, the chimp, now a chimp is far stronger and quicker than the human. Hence emotions just seem to happen. Ever experienced a moment's fear, when something has happened. One minute you're ok the very next you're in full freeze, flight or fight mode. That's the chimp reacting on instinct.

The fact of the matter here is you, the human is unable to reach anywhere close to the same speed as your chimp. However, with EQ and training and learning we can programme our computer (goes back to setting the RAS) which does respond faster than the chimp, so we can effectively allow the human a moment's notice to respond before the chimp is alerted and makes a rational decision.

Now take a moment to reflect here in terms to the fears you may be experiencing. Are they irrational, in the context of what we have discussed? And what of the impact they are having on your ability to think rationally, to make the right decisions? Is it holding you back? Are you in freeze mode unable to respond rationally? Are you in flight mode, maybe a little denial turning your back on it in the hope it will just go away? Or maybe you are in fight mode and it is soaking up all your attention and distracting from the actual activity required to negate it? It's your chimp taking control.

Whatever the impact likely it will be a major distraction from what it is your aiming to achieve. Now here's the paradox, fear is a good thing. What are you on about Steve? I hear you saying. Well let's go back to that chimp brain, it links back to your computer and RAS, the only difference here is it's part of your programming, it's the way you are wired and it is designed to keep you safe. Now because the vast majority of business owners are no longer being hunted by sabre tooth tigers there are very few risks which will be focused on eating you, your chimp needs to be stimulated with other threats. So, with less life-threatening risk today, our chimp brain and our response to risk are now defined by experiencing fear. The result is your subconscious triggers a response when there is a risk. Essentially it keeps us sharp, helps to constantly monitor what's going on overall. It's working in the background to keep us safe from the risks we face today.

Feeding Fear

We've discussed the appearance of fear and why it's there, what purpose it serves and how in the business context to manage it through your chimp and programming of the computer to support your rational human thought process. Nonetheless, there is one factor we are yet to discuss which will feed your fear unless you absolutely take control; time.

Grant Cardone (Cardone, 2011)in the 10X rule probably describes this in the clearest context. Time feeds fear. Think about that for just a moment. Let's think about the following example and this is one that most of the business owners I've spoken to have. You need to generate new leads and fast, probably one of the fastest methods still as an option today is to call them. You have your list of prospects, you absolutely know the value you offer them and that right now you really need to feed your pipeline, to add more prospects to your sales process. So, we decide we are going to spend an afternoon calling them, that's right picking up the phone and having a conversation! Can you feel the anxiety in the pit of your stomach already? Likely for many of you just reading this will start to feed your fear. The time approaches and you are almost ready to start making the calls, what happens?

For many of you out there reading this it will be a case of thinking about picking up the phone and the fear breeding the irrational thoughts of the rude responses, rejection, stuck at the gatekeepers, being asked tricky questions, being shouted at etc etc. You don't pick the phone up you are too scared and have just spent far too long feeding your fear with time; time to contemplate and define all the reasons why it will be safer not to call. All of which your irrational mind will have supported, with little or no thought to the fact that your business will fail without new customers!

Time feeds fear, whatever the situation you fear in your business, whatever it is currently which is holding you back if you feed it you will not achieve it, fear will win over, your chimp will be victorious. Don't over-think it, decide when and then just get on with it. Stop derailing yourself, it's irrational and you are the only one to blame. Time + Fear = Failure. Don't feed fear with time, act.

**The Offensive Mindset**
So, fear is good, in terms of making sure we have overall awareness and tuned into potential threats. When it debilitates us, it becomes a problem and also when it's not present at all. Without fear it would suggest we are not really stretching our abilities or making irrational foolish decisions, pushing for growth or making the real business decision which will help us to really achieve our long-term dreams. Challenging ourselves is the most effective way of pushing the boundaries, in your business if you're not pushing the boundaries, doing what others won't in the marketplace then you're just in the mire along with all your competitors. Push yourself, challenge yourself, feel the fear and use it to your benefit in reaching the next level.

Avoid the interFEARence. The fact that fear will create psychological and physiological responses in you requires you to truly understand the impact. There is often an irrational reaction and that's the start of the descent into the mire of interFEARence and will simply stop you from truly achieving.

You need to manage your chimp and the best way to do that is through the programming of your computer and RAS. Reinforce your beliefs, shift your mindset to that of a wealth orientation focus and make sure you are challenging and stretching yourself. Probably one of the biggest fears is fear itself, don't embrace it when it arrives, be in control, understand why it has shown itself and remember don't feed fear with your time, use it to drive activity forward.

**Out of Your Depth**
Before I go on to offer insight into feeling out of your depth let me first say it's a good thing to recognise. That's right it's good. Why, because it's a sign you are either expanding or need to. This is about expanding your comfort zone, the only reason you feel out of your depth is usually because you are stepping or being forced out of your comfort zone. That's a great sign, it means you are growing, its business growing pains.

In a similar context to a feeling of being overwhelmed being out of your depth or at the very least the feeling will impact on your productivity, quality of focus, activity and focusing on the real priorities. What causes you to feel out of your depth? In all likelihood, in business, there will be one of 3 levels where you will experience being out of your depth, which relate directly to the experience gained as you develop your business.

The 3 levels are the first three rungs of the entrepreneurial ladder. It's important to understand the context of the first three rungs and just how they can have a negative impact on your ability to function as a business owner and prove a challenge in the pursuit of your dreams, vision and business goals. The entrepreneurial ladder actually starts with your feet firmly planted on the floor where you are deemed a student, we then step onto the ladder as an employee; then self-employed; then manager; then business owner; then investor and finally the entrepreneur. We are going to focus on the transition between being self-employed and ascending to manager then to business owner.

The major cause of being out of your depth relates directly to growth and the transition from one state to the next. Do you remember how you felt as a child when you went from the safety of being in primary school to over the period of a summer holiday finding yourself thrust into the medley of secondary school? Where you, some of your friends and a bunch of kids you didn't know all congregated in the playground equally stunned, shocked and feeling way out of their depth. What about when you finally left education and suddenly realised you had a responsibility to your own destiny, earning money, paying rent, paying your way, being absolutely accountable for your own actions and decisions, just having a sense of being free? In each of these situations, it's likely the memories you have are quite vivid and you remember the feeling of being out of your depth.

In the first level of being out of your comfort zone will have been when you went from being employed to being self-employed. Now some of you will be thinking I circumnavigated that because I went straight to being a business owner from being employed. You probably didn't, let me explain.

When we are employed essentially, we have a sense of security, we have a job description and in exchange for our ability and time, we get paid. Essentially this is the majority agreement that most people will remain comfortable with for the life in employment. Happy with their lot, contented in employment and the security and safety which comes with being employed.

*The 3 Levels of being Out of My Depth*

The first experience of a sense of being out of your depth comes from the moment you decided to start your own business and venture. Now unless you invested in buying another business or started the business with employees, the chances are you transitioned from being an employee to being self-employed. Now that's not to be a slap in the face or a flippant comment, rather a state of fact. Taking your technical ability and then rather than having someone else benefit and making a profit from it, you decide to set up a business for yourself. Whether a sole trader or registered business you will suddenly have a number of additional responsibilities. You will have to generate leads, make sales, pay yourself, submit your own financial returns. The chances are these will create a feeling of being out of your depth. What have I let myself in for?

Being self-employed means, you will have to develop new skills associated with being responsible for yourself. Now for the large part, you'll have the skills and knowledge associated with your technical ability, whilst lacking in the wider context of owning and administering and managing the business needs and requirement.

The next level of being out of your depth comes in direct proportions to growing your business and that at the point you take on employees. At this stage you start to build a team, you will start to leverage other people's time, you will become an employer and exchange their time for their skills and expertise. With this comes the direct responsibility to ensure you cater for their needs as an employee. Just think back to the point you were employed (if you have been). What was it in addition to your salary that gave you a sense of security? Having a job description, positional agreement, a staff handbook, HR support, knowing you worked in an environment where you were safe, having health and safety in place and what about the tools of the trade, being equipped to function in the specific role.

Suddenly you are a manager, you have the responsibility to others, your employees. You need to constantly assess their performance to ensure you cover your cost and are profitable, you need to manage and have a constant eye on the team and the business. Let's not forget you'll have all the previous responsibilities as well. It's not just about you and new business it's now a responsibility to a growing business. They are hungry beasts which need to be constantly fed, nurtured, tended too and cared for. You might have great leverage with a growing team and with that comes even greater challenges, holidays, illness, poor performance, managing multiple relationships.

In this instant, the feeling of being out of your depth is, in all odds, complemented with the challenge of feeling overwhelmed. There are so many moving parts, how did it get so complicated? Not being able to see the wood for the trees is not unusual at this stage, a feeling of losing control will also be prevalent. Following on from this we enter into the transition to becoming a business owner.

Now being a business owner will actually reduce the feeling of being out of your depth. It is this transition which will suddenly open Pandora's box to the many areas which need to be focused on. Essentially going from being a manager to a business owner your business will need to function in your absence. Your business will need to be thoroughly systemised on all the fundamental business functions. Go back to the planning to establish what is yet to be focused on in your business. This is often where I come in as a business and executive coach and suddenly here I am raising awareness to the many areas needed to be focused on within the business. It's not unusual for me to then have initiated the feeling of being out of my depth.

The thread which runs through the 3 levels is a simple one, knowledge, education and accountability. We only ever feel out of our depth when we are taken out of our comfort zone. I open this section with the explanation of expanding your comfort zone, so how do I do that?

**The Offensive Mindset**

In the simplest terms when we need to step out of our comfort zone we need to get comfortable in the expanding zone. If your instinct is to jump back into your existing comfort zone then you need to be clear that you will never reach your true potential, achieve your dreams and be the best version of you in this life. Now that's only my humble view, reflect for a moment and I'm sure you'll see it makes sense.

In order to expand your comfort zone, you will need to gain a wider understanding, you will need to become a well-rounded business owner. In one of the best books out there in reference to the fundamentals of creating a great business Michael Gerber in the E Myth (Gerber, 1995) sets out a very simple picture of what it takes to grow a successful business. Now I mention it here because there is a direct correlation to the feeling of being out of your depth. Michael talks of Entrepreneurial Seizure. Michael defines the three mindsets required by any business owner as the Technician, the Manager and the Entrepreneur. Let's just take a look at these:

- **The Technician** – This goes back to my opening comments in regard to being out of your depth and relates to your technical abilities and why you started the business in the first place. Your ability is the intrinsic focus for you in your business. I'm a coach so my technical ability focuses on being a coach. Whatever your technical ability there is a very high chance that it is the focus on which the business offering revolves around. What you do well and what it is you sell. As a technician, you will be very much focused on the present.
- **The Manager** – In every business as a result of the delivery of the service, product or process there will be a requirement to deal with information which will need to be

recorded, logged, processed and complied. Essential as a result the business will have an auditable trail of information to maintain, its history. The manager has an eye on the history of the business or the past.

- **The Entrepreneur** – Now in all likelihood it will have been the entrepreneurial self which will have first challenged you to make the transition from employed to self-employed. You will have had an idea of what you wanted to achieve, where being in business for yourself was going to take you. What your future looked like. The entrepreneur focuses on the future.

When we start to feel out of depth, it's our technician which is being stretched. It is at this point we start to have the feelings of being out of depth, overwhelm and as Michael terms it has a sense of entrepreneurial seizure. You will feel the busiest in the business, working very hard without seeming to get anywhere. This is where you need to develop as a business owner. In the simplest terms when we start to experience a sense of being out of your depth you have a choice; sink or swim! Allow it to get the better of you and sink, and we all know what that will lead to or swim. So, when you feel out of your depth what are you being told to learn? In all likelihood, it will relate to the business acumen you need to learn. In Chapter 4 I'll introduce the levels required to grow as a business owner above the parapet.

### Making Bad Decisions

What leads to making a bad decision? When was the last time you made a bad decision and for you when you reflect what was the cause? What's more, do you actually go out and aim to make bad decisions? NO. Yet we still do, and what's more, I would be extremely surprised if you haven't got your own examples and if you're like me, you'll have plenty to reflect on. The major fact here is the person and circumstance or your environment.

When you look back over what we have discussed or rather raised your level of awareness of, it is possible as you have worked your way through the book, as you have leafed through the pages you will have reflected and been able to see your habits. Connect with what has been discussed both good and bad. Making bad decisions is the result of who you are; whether you have a rich or wealthy blueprint; whether you have programmed your RAS for success or not; if you have an employee or owner mindset; being tuned in to what will open up the opportunities for your success, or as some like to refer to it as luck; might be you have limited control over your chimp and a plethora of other psychological challenges.

Now here's a real smack in the face for all of us who have made bad decisions and it relates directly to the cost. In a wonderfully written book, A Road Less Stupid, Keith Cunningham (Cunningham, 2018) hits you square between the eyes when introduces you to 'Dumb Tax'. In the simplest terms, Dumb Tax is the cost of all those bad decisions. Hey and I know you've made them, I for one have made my fair share. So, every time you made a bad decision what did it cost you, I'm sure if you take a moment to reflect you'll see just how much you have spent on Dumb Tax. I want you to really think about the impact of making bad decisions and what it could potentially cost you in Dumb Tax from this point. I think you may start to sit up and take notice.

As with all we have discussed you need to shift your mindset towards the success you want to achieve. The challenge of bad decisions will only ever reside with you and you need to be in the right mindset to make the right ones. Yes, this will challenge you and there will be those decisions which will take you out of your depth, scare you and focus on your long-term aspirations, not short-term gratification.

With the impact of bad decisions, what are the circumstances which you will find they will have an impact? The following are example areas where you will experience bad decisions. Just before we go through some of the situations and circumstances let's be absolutely clear bad decisions will derail your progress and end up shifting your mindset to a less favourable place. I never do anything right; I always get it wrong; can't do anything right; I never know what to do; I just can't make decisions.

Now, this isn't a definitive list, rather my experience as a coach in both the military and in the business community, whatever your take these examples serve to emphasise the fact you firstly need to get comfortable in making decisions, understand the need for making them and ultimately make decisions and be decisive. Here are my top 12 reasons why bad decisions are made.

1. **Focusing on and Expecting the Worst.** This links directly to your ability when planning to contemplate the worst and most likely course of action. It's true there will be a range of outcomes for every decision we make good and bad. If you always focus on the worst-case outcome you will not be able to make real growth orientated decisions. You'll have or nurture a negative view on the outcomes and every outcome for the decisions you

make. You'll become your own worst enemy, unable to move forward creating and empowering your limiting beliefs.

**2.      Poor Discipline, Being Lazy.** Putting decisions off because you feel someone else will make the decision, not committing to what needs to be done to make a decision. If you are of poor discipline, you will find it very difficult to make any commitment going forward, you will struggle to actually get to a point where decisions need to be made. Ultimately you won't be in business very long and you certainly won't aspire to achieve the level of becoming a true business owner in the true meaning of the title. You'll only ever be self-employed at best. You couldn't make a decision to bring someone else into the business because it can always be put off until tomorrow.

**3.      Ground Rush.** This is a very dangerous limitation to making the decisions which need to be made and whether it is as a result of ill-discipline, laziness or fear leaving a decision to be made until the last moment can be costly. Let's take those financial decisions which you need to make either as a result of compliance with the tax office or offers which have a date associated with them or other parties, whatever it can be extremely costly. What's interesting here is the levels of denial after missing an opportunity, not unusual here to hear, 'oh well some people have all the luck'. The other impact which is often associated with ground rush is the fact you merely feed the fear and all the negative aspect of the decision will be at the forefront and will simply reinforce your poor mindset. You won't get better at making decisions, just worse.

**4.      Fear of Failure.** Picking up on feeding the fear, failure is often the other side of the decision being made. What happens if it all goes wrong? Failure is a risk, it's a certainty if you feed the fear because you'll never move forward, you'll never grow, you'll never achieve your dream. And yes, shit happens and sometimes it may go wrong and fail. The fact you had the courage to make the decision will allow you to learn, develop and make better and better decisions as you maintain your momentum going forward and grow. Let's also be clear you're not reading this book in isolated passages, rather developing a fuller picture and so knowledge also plays a significant role in your approach to confronting fear.

**5.      The 'I Knows'.** Now we will pick up on this in Chapter 4, it's relevant here in your ability to make decisions. If you are an

'I Know' person, the decisions you make will be based on what you know and perceive to know. Not knowledge and understanding, so it's possible you will simply be ill-equipped to make truly informed decisions. The other side of being an 'I Know' is you would never seek outside influence and guidance, rather think you know best. This can be twofold, in making bad decisions and not making them at all. In business 'I Know' is probably the most expensive two words there are. Just think about that for a moment and contemplate the situations where you may have used it or it has been used on you. It's not conducive to gaining knowledge because you are blind to any further opportunity and without knowledge just how good are the decisions you're making?

**6.      Reactive not Proactive.** A lack of forward thinking will render you and your business reactive to the marketplace, your customers and the financial environment. If you are always making decisions because you are reacting to changes in the environment, your situations or your position in the marketplace you will always be behind, never able to focus on the, as yet undiscovered opportunities which are the future. You are probably a dinosaur, not open to embracing new technology, see it as a fad and won't last. Not agile enough to look at your business and seek out diversification. Your growth will be at best stagnant.

**7.      Gratification over Gains.** Making the wrong decisions is as bad as making no decision and one which we have covered in short-term thinking and one I see all too much of is quick fix decisions. When we seek instant gratification and the quick solution we miss the point of long-term gains. There is absolutely a requirement for a decision which needs to resolve issues in the here and now. Often the challenge comes when we then fail to seek long-term solutions or requirement. More often than not these decisions are made on the grounds of feeling good right now. In the business context making a decision which is the easy or a less risky option. Short term solution over the consistency of a long-term gain. The quick fix will only ever be that and will lead to other challenges, overwhelm, fear and short-term thinking all of which will derail your momentum, erode your long-term thinking.

**8.      Uncontrolled Chimps.** Your chimp will try and have its say in many different circumstances and will show itself in your decision making. Interestingly who do you think it is that needs the short-term gratification, the human and rational thought process or the irrational chimp in your head? An additional area to seek to manage here are the occasions where swift decisions need to be made. Let's be clear, regardless of the circumstance, unless it is an actual life-threatening situation, where your chimp should make the decision you need to be the one to make the decision. Having understood and deliberated over the evidence and circumstances you will then be better equipped to make the decision on the facts as they are presented. Making a rash, hasty or impulsive decision will often be the wrong one. And let's not confuse this with a decision is better than no decision, it is when you are making it. Now you're probably saying there are circumstances where there is limited available information, in which case my simple question is are you making an emotive decision or informed?

9.        **History influences the now.** Here's one of the most significant barriers to making decisions let alone make the right ones. How often do you reflect on what has been, what you've done previously, what you are convinced doesn't work? There is an intrinsic problem with basing your decisions on the past and it's significant. Too many business owners are committed wholeheartedly to their past. That doesn't work in our business, in our circumstances, never worked before what's different now? Here's the problem, there is no way you can influence the past, so being stuck in it will not move you any closer to the decisions that will make the positive shift in your business. Now don't confuse this with not learning from our past, the history. You absolutely should be taking the lessons as you go. Determining what has worked and what hasn't. Here's the thing when we learn from our past it allows us to actually make better decisions going forward and is not based on old assumptions. It may be that a small change in an idea is all that is required to make the difference. Not on the basis of tried it and doesn't work. Rather try forward thinking as to how, what and where we could have done better, may offer far better results. In Chapter 4 I'll introduce you to the concept of feedforward and how to use our learnings and experience to move forward not use them as an anchor to the past.

10.        **Lack of Knowledge.** Now we have already touched on the absolute necessity to learn and invest in your learning as a business owner. Being the technician in your business, being the centre of your business universe and the all-knowing oracle should be the default setting for making all the decisions. Now I understand there would be limitations, constraints on some areas of

business decisions, certainly on the journey to becoming the 'Business Owner'. Then there are also decisions you won't be equipped to make. That is unless you take the time to learn or invest in others having the knowledge for you. What are the areas of your business that you don't understand fully? Financial, HR, systemisation, team, operations, administration etc. Would hiring a financial manager give you the knowledge in the business, would hiring an HR specialist to give you the information you need, would investing in a lean consultant give you the knowledge, in short, yes. Henry Ford was challenged by journalists and he told them to come to my office and I will answer any questions you have regarding the business. They duly did and asked a question at which point Mr Ford pressed one of many buttons on his desk. When asked what he was doing and to just answer the question, he replied, yes of course, at which point a department head came in, Mr Ford asked him the question and he promptly answered. As Henry Ford said, there is no need to fill your head with every detail of the business you are growing when you can gain the knowledge from others.

11.      **Indecisiveness.** Should I, shouldn't I, have I been given all the facts, is there more information I require before I make the decision. If there is one thing which is certain, there are no certainties. Often an indicator of indecisiveness is over analysis, let's make sure we have all the facts and more before we commit and make a decision. Let's just think about it a little more. How many times have you been personally caught out by your inability to make a decision? How many missed opportunities, meetings, investments, prospects or any number of other various chances have been missed because you were unable to assess the information in front of you and make a timely decision. This one often shows up hand in hand with fear.

12.      **Isolation.** Business and being a business owner is a lonely place. Being solely responsible for every decision can be and is tough. Nonetheless, you need first to be comfortable with making decisions and then build your support network, of strategic partners, trusted confidants, consultants, coaches and so on. Surrounding yourself with like-minded individuals will encourage you to reach out when you feel you need assistance in making decisions. As with knowledge in a business you can also then start to leverage others within who are right for making certain decisions, as we discussed in number 10 and a lack of knowledge.

101

**The Offensive Mindset**

There is no doubt that business is tough and as the business owner, it's often down to you to make decisions. And you will need to make decisions, having awareness indirect reference to the 12 reasons why you will make bad decisions is a step closer to making good ones. Whilst there are those of the school of thought that the worst thing when making a decision is to make no decision, I don't necessarily conform to that. Outside of a life and death situation understanding your decision-making profile and the process will help you, in the course of time to make better ones. As you start to piece together the elements of this book, which will form your above the parapet business mindset, you will naturally become comfortable with making decisions. What's more, as your business grows you will become comfortable with the team making the decisions.

**Doubters**

Sad as it is there will be those who will be just waiting for you to fall on your arse. Sorry to say it, but there you have it. Now I'm pretty sure you will have your own examples of those who watch only from the sidelines in order to see you fall. There are two levels of doubters, those who doubt from a position of love and affection and those who do not, these are the loathing doubters.

The Loving Doubters

These are the tough ones, especially those who are really close to you, the wife, mother, father, sister, brother and so on. Now, these don't generally doubt from a position of hate. Far from it. It is their love and affection which gets in the way. Let's be clear you have chosen to pursue your life's dream, to have a vision and aspiration in this one life you have. You have chosen to no longer be a party to the mass indoctrination of being employed, rather break out and be an employer.

One of the biggest challenges here for your loved ones is they may have followed the route of employment, giving their time in exchange for money and likely have a poor blueprint. If when we spoke of the poor and wealthy mindset and you established, you have a poor blueprint not be surprised by the cautionary tales in relation to what you are doing. They will not have the capacity to understand the wealthy mindset and what it is you are undertaking.

Ironically it is often their fears and lack of courage to step out and do what you are doing. Now that sounds quite cutting, it's not supposed to be. It's merely a fact, there are those who will push themselves and absolutely want to be the best version of themselves in life and there are those who are happy with their lot. Because you have challenged their norms they feel it is their duty to warn you of your woes, the peril that lies ahead, the risk you take and the impact it could have not on you on them! The question which comes to mind here is one regarding the fact that their free-flowing advice comes from a place where they haven't had your courage to give it a go. Or they have and failed.

Interestingly anyone who comes from a background of a family member who has achieved success, stepped out and given it a go themselves is less likely, much less likely, in fact, I'd be surprised to hear a successful individual warn you that it's too risky, do you really know what you are doing, be careful. Rather they'd turn to you and encourage you to give it a go.

What's tough here, is what's said and not said will have an impact on your mindset because these are your closest loved ones. There is almost certainly a feeling of owing who you are right now as being down to their love and affection. You owe them the courtesy of acknowledging their concerns! Bullshit! They should focus their love and affection to support your journey, to give encouragement along the way. Or they need to quietly harbour their concerns to themselves. Now this is my opinion and it might not be a favourable one, what I can assure you is the lack of support from your loved ones will be far more debilitating if you allow it into your mindset.

The best response is to simply and politely acknowledge their concerns and then tell them that whilst you understand they have their own fears and concerns they are not yours. If that is to be their contribution to your journey, then politely ask them to keep it to themselves. Or make a positive contribution and join the journey with you. As quoted from a movie; 'you've got nothing to say, and you're saying it too loud'.

The Loathing Doubters

Now, these are a completely different ball game. These folks merely want to see you fall, they are not interested in supporting your success, they want to see you fall on your arse. They are not friends, although they masquerade as such, they are not business colleagues, they are quite the opposite. Often, they will be or will see themselves as in competition with you. They will be the smiling assassins.

They have no interest in you, your business other than to watch you fail. Often these will be watching your progress intently waiting for it to all go wrong. They will quietly or not so quietly offer commentary regarding your progress, question your ability, undermine you to others in the marketplace and socially. You may even find those who today feel that it is ok to openly comment and offer their perspective on your social media.

Interestingly you need to relish the moment you find yourself in this sphere. Grant Cardone (Cardone, 2011) makes a great observation here and at the point, you start to receive criticism it's likely you have shaken your competition or at least those who feel you are in competition with them. In essence, you are resonating in the marketplace to such a level that they feel threatened, they see you as a contender, they are worried about their position, not yours.

Now at this point, Grant raises a great focus and that is of domination. That's right resonating at a much higher level, aim to dominate your marketplace. And why wouldn't you, after all your business vision is likely to talk about being the best in your space. So, maximise any opportunity to do so. Don't retreat, apologise or lessen your activity, rather get stuck in, do more, much much more.

Your loathers should be a source of inspiration, they should fuel you to keep going, to do more and keep the pressure on. Don't fear confrontation, in today's digital sphere people have a tendency to act in a completely different way than they would face to face. They will comment, unlike, offer a 1-star review, you know what I mean. Well, do engage, here's the thing encourage your followers to engage with them. At that point, you'll see just what an impact you are having in your sphere of influence. Don't fear the loathers when they turn up in your sphere with their own uncertainty, weakness, and loathing, rather see it as a mark of your progress. That you are resonating at such a level that they see fit to try and actively derail your progress.

**The Offensive Mindset**
When you step out to make your own progress towards your dreams and aspirations you will evoke the response from the doubters. The loving doubters who doubt your success from a position of love and affection and are probably happy where they are and think you should stay there too.
Then there are the loathers, those who actively seek your demise. Well welcome them, it's a sign you're on the right path and they have their own failings, shortcomings and weakness to deal with and you're now impacting

on them. When that happens and it will stay on track and ramp it up. Don't be afraid to challenge and evoke the response of your followers.

The most important point here is with your offensive mindset and not allowing these doubters, lovers or loathers to get inside your head. One other point here and one Brad Sugars has always challenged me with is to constantly be surrounding yourself with like-minded people.

As he is often quoted as saying:

Your success can be measured by the people you meet and the books you read.

### Scarcity versus Abundance in Thinking

Firstly, let's be absolutely clear, there is more than enough for everyone. No matter what you do, where you do it, there is enough business to go around. Thinking that there isn't enough to go around will impact on your ability to think with clarity, it will also fuel the fear and before long you will embrace the poor mindset. It will promote poor decision making and encourage short-term thinking.

Dr Ivan Misner, the founder of the Business Networking International (BNI) understands the power of the abundance mindset and its impact in a business environment. So much so, one of the first things you will learn when joining a BNI Chapter is the mantra of 'givers gain'. Have you ever been in a room of business owners where there is one person who is working the room in a bid to find business as quickly as possible, not interested in you or what you do, just wants to give you their business card and move on? How do they make you feel? Or have you been that person? How did it work out?

These are the 'hunters', always looking for the next kill, not interested in anyone, just themselves. Now I'd be the first to encourage a business mindset and indeed I've spoken of dominating your digital market space. The difference here is the mindset. If you have scarcity as a driving force you're only going to focus on you, your needs, making the sale and moving to the next one. You're not going to be very giving, sharing or forthcoming to other opportunities of those with an abundant mindset. You're going to struggle to build rapport and make new acquaintances in the business context, your business will become a very lonely place.

In addition to this, you'll also likely to suffer from slow to no expansion and growth because you will hold yourself back. You'll be convinced you don't have enough time, money, resources or the ability. You believe that you can't, which links right back to self-sabotage. You will look at others who are growing and experiencing success and be jealous, and envious, you'll become a loather, seeking their demise, waiting for them to take a fall so you can jump in and sweep up all their business. The fixed mindset.

Scarcity thinkers will be precious about the value they offer, see it as a vital element of their business and not seek to share it or offer it as marketing collateral. I'm not going to give away my value for free. The knowledge they have, which can be huge leverage in lead generation, building trust in relationships and credibility in the marketplace.

There is real value to the 'givers gain' abundance mindset. Every instance of scarcity thinking and the abundance mindset realigns you and focuses your mind on where you are going and what you set out to achieve. Here's the thing, along the way you will be respected, admired and trusted. Yes, you will still have the loathers out there waiting for you to trip and fall, do you think they have an abundant mindset? Absolutely not. After all, as we said at the beginning there is plenty to go around and your investment in an abundant mindset will offer a return of investment 10-fold.

**The Offensive Mindset**
The scarcity mindset is quite frankly for losers. It serves no purpose and will only serve to distance you from the real opportunity out there. Having an abundance 'giver gain' mindset will give you a place of trust from which to deliver your business from. You will become a pillar within your business community, people will trust you and your advice and guidance and will want to be associated with you. The direct result will be the fact business will come in your direction, it will find you. Let's be clear it will take commitment and will take time but what a great investment in you.
Be willing to share your knowledge and don't be worried about giving too much away in regard to what you know. Clearly, there will be a balance, you don't want to be giving away the recipe if your business is built on that USP. What will surprise you is just what value you can freely offer and the impact it will have. Yes, there are those who merely seek free stuff, guess what they probably suffer from the scarcity mindset.

One of the key aspects to an abundant mindset is to always wear a smile and be thankful. If you think that sounds odd, stop right now and smile to yourself. Your psychology shifts toward a positive mindset. Smiling puts others at ease, it induces others to smile and can be the simplest way to make a connection. Abundance is about giving; don't worry about the gains they will follow. One cautionary tale here is to be authentic in your abundance, don't be shallow and think you can fake it because you can't.

**The Superhero Complex.**
No this isn't about turning up to the office with your pants on the outside, there are two aspects. The first is about you feeling you can do everything, make every decision, think of every new idea, deliver every aspect of the business and so it goes on when we come across the business superheroes. The second is a result of the first where you put yourself on a pedestal and start to indulge in self-importance, you become a legend in your own coffee break! You start to feel an overwhelming need to be the 'man' or 'woman', to be revered and admired. A need to be respected.

If you have taken the time already to carry out the actions from Chapter 1 then you will have a clear idea of where and what you want to achieve in life and in your business. That doesn't mean you have to be the superhero in getting there. Be clear in terms of what it is to be the best version of you, who do you want to be, why and does that mean you become a 'self-licking lollipop'?

Absolutely there will be a requirement to put the effort in, work harder and smarter. Yes, you are likely to be the busiest in your business for a period, whilst you set the conditions for your success, build the winning team to leverage your drive forward. It doesn't mean you remain at that tempo and it certainly doesn't mean you don't allow anyone else to help. Being the superhero is often a sign that there is limited trust. 'It's my baby!' Because you feel no one can do it as well as you then you won't actually trust anyone to do it. The reality here is you must surround yourself with those who are better than you and leverage their time.

Now when I talk of surrounding yourself with those who are better than you let me quantify that statement. If you found people that were better than you overall that means they will have your technical ability and business acumen, why would they need you? Rather as the business owner, you are looking for a technician who is better than you, a financial manager who has greater expertise than you, an experienced operations manager and so on. Where you have skills in many areas of your business you need to start to surround yourself with those who have expertise in specific areas of the business. Allowing you to relinquish time for someone qualified to take on the particular role.

If you want to be a superhero then focus on the one aspect of your business and then have others leverage your power through supporting in the other fundamental areas of the business. Trying to do it all will only result in your slow demise. You will educate your team, clients and prospects that they are not to talk to the minions rather talk directly to you. Just how sustainable is a business that revolves solely around you? You will soon find that you are working even longer hours and doing the work of your team, now does that sound like the type of superhero you want to be. If you educate them that way, guess what they will conform to your greatness.

Now whilst you may receive the accolade and recognition, look at me and what I've achieved, it's not going to be sustainable, I can assure you it will be short lived. What is almost certain to follow is resentment from the team and you'll start to suffer from overwhelming, short-term thinking because you don't have the time for anything other than and making bad decisions.

### The Offensive Mindset
Give others a chance. Whether you have a team right now or are growing a team allow others to help. If you are on your own and doing everything then take a look at where you place the value on your time and seek the assistance from someone external to the team, build an external support team. If you have a team then leverage the skills they have, hire people to leverage your time in areas where you are not the superhero.
Additionally, make sure you empower your team, internally and externally, to make decisions for the benefit of the business. A level of autonomy will always give others incentive, empowerment and most important purpose. We will pick up these areas later in the book in Chapter 4.

### The World Owes Me
There is no doubt that today that there is an ever-increasing growth in society that the world in some ways owes them. They feel they deserve to have their wants and needs fulfilled, should be entitled to privileges. Today entitlement serves only to fuel those who frankly won't get off their arse and do what needs to be done. They live life with a fixed mindset below the parapet, and we'll be exploring that in detail in Chapter 4.

Let's be really clear, the world, your family, your friends don't owe you anything. Yes, your circumstance will have shaped your world, your blueprint which will determine how you behave today. Let's be clear, whilst in this book, I would like to engage with as many as possible, right now I'm talking directly to you. You picked up this book for whatever reason and so by virtue you have either made a decision or are to determine your future, are you right now entitled to anything other than your thoughts? NO!

Sadly, we are all in some way in today's world responsible for the entitled mindset. Materialism is in fact everywhere, in many respects, we are bombarded with opportunity, shiny stuff, gluttony, dare I say greed and we all in some small or large way subscribed to it. When you see someone successful do you think well done for them or that should be me? When you see something shiny you want to do, do you get depressed because you can't have it and feel you should have it because you deserve it? I've been working for so long I deserve a rise. I've just got my degree I deserve a great job. I'm so old I should have that by now?

You can live the life you truly want, but here's the thing, you're going to have to work hard for it. In many respects, you may have to go without to achieve your dreams, make your vision a reality, quite the opposite of having it now because you deserve it. You will get what you're owed in the context that you will first have to work for it and when I say work for it, I really mean work. Let's be clear you are not owed anything at all, there is no entitlement, no privileges no special circumstances.

**The Offensive Mindset**
Understanding you're entitled to live the life you want, you're not simply owed it. We each of us need to go out there and apply ourselves respectively and in context to what we each of us want to achieve. Your offensive mindset requires that you gain clarity in what you want to achieve and then work out just how you're going to achieve it. Be really clear on what you want to achieve, what you want, where you'd like to go and then work out what you need to do in order to get it.
Whether your vision, your long-term vision and goals or your next holiday, don't think entitlement, don't get wrapped up in self-pity and bitterness towards others having what you feel you're owed, rather define what you're going to need to do in order to get it.

The final point on the entitled mindset is a clear understanding in all likelihood that you are almost certainly going to have to work far harder to achieve your dreams than you ever thought. You'll need to probably give up today in order to gain tomorrow. Always be clear on the end game, be clear in what you really want to achieve and then go after it. Go after it with vigour, focus, drive and positive commitment.

**The Subtle Art of Resistance**
There is no doubt our minds work in very complex ways, making decisions for us without conscious consideration, irrational feelings, ignorance in the forefront of our minds, limited attention, a lack of commitment to our

purpose and why. We seek the excuses, denial and blame in order to appease our inner failings and the negative feelings which follow. If we are supposed to be the most intelligent beings on planet earth, we are pretty stupid, short-sighted and seek to place roadblocks and barriers in our way in a vain attempt to live out a life of personal neglect rather than fulfilment.

We create resistance at every turn, whether self-sabotage, our limiting beliefs, a sense of overwhelm, an inability to think long term, irrational fear, being out of our depth, just plain bad decisions, listening to and surrounding ourselves with doubters, scarcity thinking or thinking we can do it all ourselves because we of course are a superhero. In all likelihood, you'll be suffering from a combination of resistance and quite oblivious to it as well.

Here's the thing we will all have experienced our inner resistance at some point in our lives, a sense of feeling sorry for ourselves. Feeling 'sorry for ourselves' serves no purpose. Essentially it makes you feel like 'shit', and then the resistance kicks in. It removes your motivation, it depletes your energy levels, triggers stress, brings out the worst in you and just gets worse and worse, a self-perpetual cycle.

Once again it goes back to the conversation you have in your head and that's all you. That voice isn't owned by anyone else, just you. You need to be aware that you are responsible for you, your thoughts feelings and emotions. So, if you're going to feel sorry for yourselves you are in fact resisting the future you desire. You resist the ability to engage within your circumstances in a manner and fashion you choose. Now if your reality is a tough one right now, there is no difference, you can still remain in control of your inner dialogue and how you interpret what's going on.

The very first step to overcoming resistance is accepting it is there, accepting that you are in all likelihood your own worst enemy. Ultimately facing up to and accepting that in life there will be challenges and it is your response which will determine how you defeat resistance. In Mans Search for Meaning (Frankl, 1959) Viktor Frankl, during the very worst conditions conceivable made a conscious choice to see the plight in the concentration camps as a challenge. He decided to interpret his circumstances as part of life's great challenge and not to be overcome, not to give up hope.

In another great example of not succumbing to inner resistance and ultimately giving up is the account by James Bond Stockdale in his Hoover Essay 'Courage Under Fire' (Stockdale, 1993). Commonly referred to as the Stockdale paradox, James Stockdale a US aviator at the beginning of the Vietnam War, in fact almost within the first few hours of the war was shot down. He spent 8 years in captivity, 4 of which was under solitary confinement, tortured, abused, crippled with a broken leg when he crashed yet was able to retain faith.

The Stockdale paradox, which is today widely understood in business, is the ability to maintain faith, stay true to the vision, the goal, whilst facing the brutal facts, is a key aspect in the success of the truly great. Think about that for a moment. If you suffer from your own resistance and as previously mentioned self-sabotage, then yes there are difficulties, things will be hard. The challenge is to accept the fact it is challenging and then to embrace it in order to drive through it.

## The Offensive Mindset
You need to get out of your way, you need to accept the need for an offensive mindset, taking charge, accepting control of your destiny and having a high level of personal commitment. Part of being human and having a high level of self-consciousness is accepting with it comes complexity and challenge. That's a part of our human existence. Indirect paradox is the fact that to overcome these challenges is in the simplest terms an acceptance of their existence and the counter activity required to overcome them, which we discuss in Chapter 3.

## BLUF – Bottom Line Upfront
In this chapter, we have only highlighted a few of the many and numerous challenges and potholes you will encounter on your journey to success. The significance of understanding what these potholes are and how deep some maybe will be your understanding of them. Your ability to identify when you are in one and what you need to do to get out of it. Awareness is the major aspect of staying on track, not allowing yourself to be derailed by any of the potholes.

Tough as it is, it starts with having the clarity of what you will achieve, whilst not allowing the influences of your inner dialogue, environment or others to influence anything less than total commitment to your life. Developing and maintaining your offensive mindset will ensure you are always seeking opportunities to ensure you succeed. Be prepared for the intrusion of negativity and seek always to combat that negative inner voice, deflect and counter the doubters and always be looking to the end goal to determine how you will get there.

Having an insight to just what challenges lay ahead or defining what you have encountered is one thing. In the next chapter we will look at developing the offensive mindset and the habits required to set the conditions for success. If you haven't gained a greater level of clarity at this point go back and read the chapter again. Make sure you commit to take action and list your actions from Chapter 2, the impact and commit to a date to have them implemented.

| My Action | The Impact | Achieved by |
| --- | --- | --- |

# Chapter 3 –

# Setting the Conditions for Success

Having talked about the potholes, barriers and challenges you will face on your journey to success let's now focus on just how to increase your self-belief. To start the journey towards being the very best version of you, to achieve your life's dream. In Chapter 2 I introduced you to my concept of the offensive mindset. Not allowing adversity to impact and derail your journey, avoiding the potholes. Rather being prepared for battle in your own head, dealing with your limiting beliefs, your ego and pride. Having an offensive outlook within your environment, knowing that you will face challenges from others who are less inclined to live their life to the full and as such want to see you fail will drive your resolve towards success. So, in this chapter, we will take a look at what I define as the success habits and the focus you need in order to succeed and by virtue develop a high level of 'pig-headed discipline' to live by the habits and thus set the conditions for your success.

I hope by this stage you will have already started to set the conditions for your success, let's face it, so far how many times have I told you and encouraged you to take action, answer questions, reflect, make a commitment to yourself, essentially, I've been trying to inspire you to take action. Now regardless of what your dream is, the vision for your business and who you aim to be in pursuit of the very best version of you, it all requires you to ACT. Assess, Commit to Traction.

> A – Assess. You should by now have assessed your current situation and established where you are now and where you want to be in the future. If you have engaged, made an assessment of where you are right now and where and what you want to achieve it should be relatively easy to then assess the next step. Don't underestimate your assessment of your life. You will intrinsically know the level of dissatisfaction you have versus your vision. So,

it is highly likely you will have already made the first commitment to act, your own assessment.

C – Commitment, to take action. Just how excited are you when you reflect on just what you have assessed and established? You should by now be experiencing both excitement and fear when you look forward to the possibilities of your future. Your level of commitment and ability to take the first steps will be in direct correlation to this. If you have really made a detailed assessment you will discover just what it is you want and will achieve. If right now at this stage you are still struggling stop and take a review, go back over chapter 1 and define where you want to go. Review Chapter 2 and determined what's holding you back and develop your offensive mindset. Let's be quite clear if, at this stage, it's not important enough there will be no commitment to action, nothing will change. And that's ok, however, if you are reading this book to help make a change, to make the shift you want and to get out of your own way, stop messing around get committed! You should be feeling the mix of anxiety tempered with fear and excitement and an urge to get going!

T – Traction, will give you the ability to stick to and control your committed path and the inner power, performance and resilience to stay with it. Essentially traction will give you a grip or control as well as power and motion in the direction you aim to head with the outcomes you desire. Look at the context of a formula one car. Without traction, you will lack grip and power which when combined, gives the performance to win the race. A lack of traction and you'll be at the rear of the race, performance will be lacking and may result in not even starting let alone finishing. Traction can be viewed as the ability to apply momentum consistently in the direction you are heading. Traction can be defined as the success habits you stick to, more on that in a moment.

**The Chemical Cocktail for Success**
Yes, that's right there are chemicals that in the right quantity which will ensure success and the really good news is you have them. In fact, you have had them all your life and they are critical to your survival. The challenge is so many use them in the wrong way, use vast quantities in the wrong situations, don't realise the impact they are having on you. Let me explain…

It all started 50,000 years ago, when the earliest version of us started to take our first excursions into the world, Homo Sapien man had emerged. Essentially our ancestors, where each and every one of us came from. Palo lithic time. Life was tough, they had to deal with the fact that for some predators they were dinner, danger hid around every rock. Their intelligence allowed them to adapted to thrive and survive. It is our ability to survive very tough times which has designed our physiology and it is the root of our intoxicating chemical reliance that we have today.

In addition to our inner instinct for survival is the powerful programming we have for social interaction. Our communal instinct, to share, care and protect each other also gives us today a significant advantage when confronted with danger. Simon Sinek in his book Leaders Eat Last (Senik, 2014) discusses the impact of palo lithic times in the overall abilities we have today. Interestingly a little understanding as to why you behave as you do now can help you be more accountable to where you are now and why and as a direct result make positive change and commitment.

We are immensely social animals and the need for community is a key aspect to our survival. The greater the social interaction the greater the sense of wellbeing and security we experience. Just think for a moment when you interact in a social group of friends or family. You have a fall out with someone in the group. You begin to argue about that point. Then an outsider starts to joins in with you and abuses your friend, how do you react? You protect your friend, don't you? It's in your biology, you defend your group, your social circles.

We are so hard-wired for survival on every level it still impacts on us today. Interestingly Simon also talks in depth of the emotions we feel and the survival impact they have. Of all our emotions, anxiety, fear, joy, passion it is happiness which offers the greatest pursuit for survival. For many of us today happiness can be induced through the offer of a reward, our behaviours manipulated to positive effect. Regardless of the level of awareness. Whether being given a gold star as a child and not realising what happens as a result of the happiness we feel or as an adult knowing the bonus will make us happy and it will also please the boss because we hit our target, it works. We get better results and it makes us happy. Happiness, positivity and indeed the feeling of negativity are all produced by the cocktail of chemicals we have to ensure our survival.

What are the chemicals which today we are so addicted and dependent on and help to make us happy, positive and content? Endorphins, Dopamine,

Serotonin, Oxytocin and Cortisol. These chemicals align with your ability to be successful and socially interactive. Rather they will, once you have a greater understanding of how they induce emotional responses in you now and why a shift in your habits will allow you to utilise your chemicals to your benefit and that of others. Now, just to be clear, these collective chemicals which induce positivity, joy, passion, fear, paranoia, trust and happiness are for your survival.

Let's take a look at the impact of each of these chemicals. It's also important to realise they don't work in isolation they have effect collectively. The chemical cocktail in the right mix will vastly increase your ability to live a fulfilling and successful life. Now, I am not a biologist or an expert in this field, although I understand and can determine the feelings associated with each of these chemicals within our bodies and where and how to maintain the successful chemical cocktail in order to be the very best version of me within my social circles. That may be within my family, my business, with those I coach and those I interact with. It allows me to be a better leader, team player, friend and lover.

Endorphin.

In the simplest terms, endorphins mask pain. Often referred to as the 'runners high' they mask the pain and stress we feel when we are under physical strain. Finishing arduous training often feels really good, a feeling of ecstasy even though the process has been painful. Humans in general terms have an extreme ability towards endurance and it is our endorphin hit which allows us to go that bit further. 50,000 years ago, we remained firmly on the menu for some predators and as such, we needed to have the endurance to respond, run, escape, fight. In addition, we needed to be able to travel vast distances in order to find food and then do the same again the next day.

A hit of endorphins makes us feel good, they increase our feeling of happiness give us a natural high. Interestingly, many drugs today try to replicate this by giving artificial highs (and can also give mind bending and damaging side effects). Endorphins don't have any damaging side effects and can be seen as a natural way of increasing a feeling of wellbeing and happiness. There is no downside to increasing and working towards having endorphin hits. The most notable access to increasing your endorphin hit is through exercise. Interestingly, it may already be one of your goals, so this is a real win-win. In addition, eating a healthy diet, laughing more, socialising and connecting with others will also increase the endorphin hit.

There are many benefits from increased levels of endorphins. It can reduce the effects of stress, depression and anxiety. It can help towards reducing the impact and risk of addiction. It can improve the quality and amount of sleep you require, making you feel sleepy and helping you feel refreshed when you wake. It can also improve and increase your brain or cognitive ability, which can help you function at a higher level. Most obviously it can assist with the reduction and perception of pain.

Dopamine

In the earlier versions of us, dopamine was a survival chemical which would give us a hit and feeling of reward for getting food, it felt good. Ever been so hungry (or not) and when you have eaten you feel really good. Maybe you like chocolate or if you're like me, cheese. Take a bite and there it is, a rush of dopamine. As visual being's dopamine is also linked to visual cues, seeing the food might be enough to get a hit, to gain stimulus from. Dopamine regulates the perception and experience of pleasure. It's no surprise why food and sex have long been high on the list of delivering hits of dopamine. It could also explain why we suffer so much from eating-related health issues, lust, infidelity and addictions.

Interestingly it fits with the biology of having visual triggers. Having a goal is one thing, having a goal written helps to really visualise it. To see it, to have the vision, links to our ability to be visually responsive. Achieving the goal and gain the feeling of winning or reward and once again we get a hit of dopamine.

With dopamine also comes to the warning and probably one which most will be both aware of and in denial of. Dopamine is highly addictive or rather the activities which you find addictive. There is an old saying that if the first thing you pick up in the morning is a drink then there's a good chance you're an addict. Well, let's put that into context, being an alcoholic, sex addict, hooked on drugs, a smoker or today a gamer or TV soap addict are some of the more obvious candidates. None of which serve us well and can all lead to health issues in their own rights. Well, what about smart technology today or the need for connectivity, instant messages, email, emoticons, social media, your phone. Interestingly these are all addictions. What's the first thing you pick up in the morning? If it's your smartphone you may be an addict.

Now dopamine isn't the villain, far from it. When in the right balance it boosts your drive, concentration and motivation. Think of that in the pursuit of a goal, it will actually limit distractions and give you clarity of purpose and higher focus. These all lead to the feelings of reward, bliss and even euphoria and when associated with the right activities can be an immensely rewarding hit. Let's also be clear without dopamine you will be starved quite literally motivation, suffer malaise, poor incentive and drive.

There's no surprise that the best way to maintain a healthy level of dopamine in your body is with a healthy lifestyle, good food and plenty of healthy activity. Additional activities such as mediation can be a boost, listening to music, human interaction, touch such as stoking a pet and one of the most interesting is a cold shower or open water swim. The shock of getting into or under cold water gives the body a rush which once completed results in a euphoric feeling.

The Selfish Chemicals

Interestingly, both endorphins and dopamine play a significant part in our very existence and survival. Both focus on self-fulfilment or selfishness. The need for our own feelings of wellbeing, reward and pleasure. The chemical reactions with the right circumstances evoke selfish behaviours, a want and need for them to be satisfied for no other need than our own pleasure.

There are no major issues with this fact as long as the balance is right. Where we allow too much emphasis on our primal instinct to be a social, a tribal animal is set aside we would then tend only to focus on our needs and fulfilment.

Serotonin

Referred to as the happiness chemical or more recently the leadership chemical (Senik, 2014) serotine delivers the feeling and sense of pride and status, our sense of purpose and confidence. Interestingly it gives us a sense of significance and all too often in its absence is loneliness and depression. When we receive recognition for a job well done, graduate from study, win an award we encounter the feeling of pride and status and is driven as a result of serotonin.

The interesting fact associated with serotonin is the fact it is a socially shared feeling, which will trigger the same feeling in others who share your recognition and reward. Think how a parent feels when they see their child graduate, at the point of receiving the graduation certificate the parent will have the same feeling of reward as the child. Recognition within a team and its coach, a teacher sees a pupil gain an award, the officer commanding awards a soldier or the employee is given recognition. In all cases the feeling is reciprocated, it's a social interaction which increases the tribe cohesion, the sense of trust and togetherness. Serotonin is a social chemical, which leads to a greater sense of shared trust and unity.

Serotonin will strengthen the connections and trust within an organisation. It's linked to the Alpha status within the tribe, the recognition of the status of someone else who is seen as the leader. When a tribe, organisation or team recognise the status of an individual, the Alpha or leader it creates the environment of trust. The key here is the fact that the recognition or status is gladly given and respected. From my service, the command structure ran far deeper than a mere rank and status, rather an understanding that as the leader there is an expectation to deliver under certain and more often than not extreme circumstances. The connectivity of the organisation is strengthened by that understanding. There is an expectation to deliver under extreme circumstances.

Hey, if you don't believe me, ask yourself when was the last time you had a meeting with someone who you didn't feel confident in front of? You weren't the alpha. In similar terms when was the last time, you had a meeting where you felt extreme confidence? Having the serotonin hit enables a communal feeling of self-confidence and meaning within the group. There's no surprise that the ethos within the Military Academy Sandhurst, where British Army Officers are trained, is Serve to Lead.

Oxytocin

The feeling of love, friendship and trust are borne of oxytocin, it is the feeling we experience when we are with our friends, with the one we love or in an organisation which has a strong sense of trust. It is a social chemical which binds us and over time gives us a long-lasting impact, unlike dopamine. Oxytocin is about being within the safe environment, knowing those you are with have your back and they have theirs. A real sense of trust. It is within these organisations we see real success and real sense and strong culture.

Touch increases the levels and effect of oxytocin, now that would be crystal clear for you all if I were to give you the example of intimacy. However, let's look at this from the perspective of a simple handshake. In many cultures, it is traditional to shake hands at the conclusion and agreement of a deal. So, how would you feel and react if when you offered your hand to 'seal the deal' it was declined? 'No that's ok let's just get on and sign the contract'. In all likelihood, you would no longer feel comfortable let alone confident to sign the deal, why because your brain hasn't physically sealed the deal, shown a level of intimacy to satisfy the social interaction you require to feel comfortable. It's about human bonding and links right back to the fact we are social animals.

Interestingly, acts of generosity also release oxytocin when we observe them or are a part to them. Although some more than others. If I were to give money to a great cause you would probably be respectful of my commitment although not overly impressed and engaged by it. If, on the other hand, I was to give up my Saturday to helping the same cause you would likely be really engaged and feel a greater sense of connectivity and probably a sense to offer your time. In this instance time, can be seen as a common and equal commodity and one which we can all conform to, a common ground and where we all feel the same connectives.

Stories also play a big part in building relationships and social interactions. With both, oxytocin and serotonin stories can have a major impact, through creating a much higher level of relatedness. Sharing intimate stories of hardship, inspiration and your life's experiences allows you to connect at the most intimate level and strengthens the bond within a tribe, organisation and team.

There are some major benefits from oxytocin within the social aspects of the tribe or organisation. It inhibits addiction, it boosts the immune system, it makes for a healthier life. With higher levels of oxytocin, you will be happier and statistically happy people live longer. You'll have greater connections, more relationships, trusted, far more productivity, be more creative and be able to solve problems with greater ease. Oxytocin levels take longer to build up, so require greater focus or relatedness.

The Selfless Chemicals

Together Serotonin and Oxytocin have a social focus on selflessness. They are impacted on our need for relationships, trust and togetherness. We understand that reward and recognition within the tribe set the conditions for our survival and success. In today's organisation's relationships and relatedness matter, more than they ever have before. Just take a moment to think today just how connected we are, the mere fact we now have the term social media suggests we are by our very being social animals, so we need to make sure we are in all the appropriate ways.

Where there is a stifling and lack of social interaction and trust, there will be a greater focus on self and a lack of wanting to help and assist others. In these situations, we will experience failure, we will fail as leaders and we will see leadership fail.

Cortisol

Linked directly to our 'chimp' or 'lizard or reptilian' brain is cortisol. It provides us with the necessary responses we require for our survival. I often refer to it as your spider-sense, it alerts you to danger. In my days on operation, we would often refer to it as the absence of the normal and the presence of the abnormal. Not always something you see or touch, rather something you would feel. No doubt if you have been in that position and experienced it you will likely have been correct more often than not.

When cortisol floods into our body it is responsible for the freeze, flight or fight response, it will increase our blood flow and heart rate, readying the body for explosive action. It essentially shuts down all non-essential life support activities and focuses only on those which are essential for survival. In itself, this is a good thing, in fact, a very good thing for short periods of time. Once the threat or perceived threat has passed it leaves the system swiftly and the bodies functions return to normal. However, in today's environment, the prolonged presence of cortisol can be extremely damaging and lead to anxiety, stress and major health issues.

Today, we often find that we can be exposed to long exposure of cortisol through working in an environment where there is limited trust, a feeling of anxiety; 'I know the boss doesn't like me', 'they didn't like my proposal', 'money issues' and the list could go on, you'll know where and what the issues will be. The prolonged exposure to a drip feeding of cortisol results in significant psychological and physiological poor conditions. Some of the more obvious ones could be weight gain, lethargy, isolation, anxiety, headaches and many more. None of which are conducive to becoming the best version of you.

Balance

Understanding what's going on upstairs and why is the first step to then ensuring your environment and mindset is conducive to your journey. Understanding why you may have a particular addition is the first step towards dealing with it. Building the balance between the selfless and the selfish chemical reactions will assist in determining your direction.

Biology has a lot to answer for, we have more to answer for when we decide to understand why and what we need to do. Creating stability, living a balanced and fulfilled life is a major step towards achieving your success in life and in your context. We are who we are and we have the capacity to be who we want to be, there are no excuses we just need to get out there and start to be the very best version of ourselves.

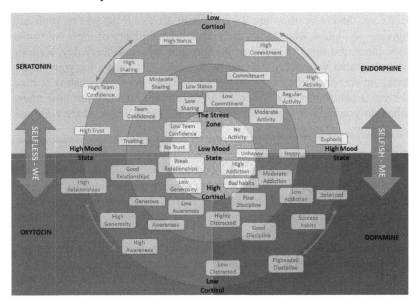

*EDSO*

## Success Habits
*"Winning is a habit, unfortunately so is losing".*

*Vince Lombardi*

It's worth taking a moment to understand that creating the conditions for success and being successful will require a commitment to new habits, which is to say you'll stop thinking, acting or behaving in one way and start to focus in a new way. Throughout the book, we have mentioned habits on a number of occasions, why because forming success orientated new habits will be a key part of realising your dream and gaining clarity on your vision. In this chapter, we will establish what your habits will need to be, in my humble opinion. In Chapter 1 we focused on your belief structure and challenged you to really determine what you wanted to achieve in life as well as your business. Chapter 2 then focused on just what it would take to get there. Developing your offensive mindset and highlighting what

123

potholes and barriers along your journey you are likely to face. Your willpower.

Before we go onto offer a series of habits to strengthen your resolve and develop your success mindset, it's worth understanding a little behind what habits are and why they are so important to us. Now you're probably thinking you know what habits are and will have plenty of them, sit in the same place, the same ritual when you prepare for work every day, walk or drive the same way every day, go to the same restaurants for your lunch, drink, smoke, have you ever wondered why you have certain habits or how to break a habit? Just take a moment to reflect and establish just how many habits do you have in a day, week or month? I'm going to share with you my 14 habits for success, my daily ritual.

Before I do I'm sorry to say there is no patch here, to suppress your urge to go back to what you know, where you were or are comfortable. Rather you'll need to take a robust and resilient focus to make the shift you want and commit to it. How often have you made a commitment to making a new start to achieving something different, to shift your mindset? In all likelihood, this book won't sit alone on your self-help or business excellence bookshelf. So, what is it to make a difference, commitment, which in the simplest terms is discipline. Still unsure go back and review Chapters 1 and 2. Otherwise, let's look at just how easy it is to make a shift in as little as 21 days.

In the 1960s Maxwell Maltz published Psycho-Cybernetics (Maxwell Maltz, 2015), a book which could be defined as the guiding principle of self-help as we know it today. Maxwell focuses on the power of the subconscious mind and how your image of yourself will govern the life you live. As we have discussed in Chapter 1 we now understand the role the RAS plays in empowering your subconscious. The challenge here is just how do we set our RAS.

Setting habits.

The definition of a habit as per dictionary.com is: *an acquired behaviour pattern regularly followed until it has become almost involuntary.* Here's the challenge, it's not easy to set habits as I am sure you will attest. Ironically, it's actually easier to start bad ones, even when your heads telling you this is a bad idea. In fact, it's bloody difficult, until you realise it only takes 21 days to set a new habit. It is widely assessed to take 21 days for someone who has undertaken plastic surgery to become comfortable with their new features. Essentially it will take 21 days for you to accept a new mental process, vision, acceptance of a new habit. Essentially to reprogram your brain. The challenge for many here is the mere commitment to 21 days is a bridge too far.

As you read on you need to be clear that there are no quick fixes, there is a need for commitment and resilience to set new habits. When you break it down 30,240 minutes or 504 hours may seem an eternity, when you look at 21 days or 3 weeks it's not long to make a really positive shift. As you read on and determine a course of action in direct relation to your desired dreams, vision and the goals getting started and having a positive impact could be a mere 3 weeks away. Think about that for a moment. Is the commitment worth it?

**Your Environment**
One of the most pivotal factors in regard to getting started and remaining committed and to stay on track is your environment. Your environment is where you live, it is in fact where you choose to live. You might not believe it right now when I say your environment could well be the one factor, if not the factors which are holding you back. Let's take a look at what the key factors are to make up your environment.

*'the social and cultural forces that shape the life of a person'.*

*Dictionary.com*

You and the Spirit of Success

The first point to note, you are the centre of your environment and determine its impact. So, when we talk about the influence your environment will have on you, the first factor is how you allow it to impact. If I have done my job so far, I hope I have heightened your awareness of what's going on in your head. The internal dialogue, just what you choose to listen too, how you choose to interpret your message and the behaviours you exhibit as a result.

Although tough to hear as a child, when our parents told us that 'sticks and stones will break our bones, names will never hurt us', they had a point. The major driving force is your spirit and just what you will endure to achieve success in your life as you determine it. In his book 'Mans Search for Meaning' (Frankl, 1959) Viktor E Frankl defined his world renown logotherapy theory which is founded on our search for meaning. His theory was founded on his personal experience when he was sent to a concentration camp in the second world war.

I highlight this because ultimately when everything was stripped away what really mattered was his understanding of the situation he found himself in and how he interpreted its meaning. With everything stripped away, living under extreme stress and fear he still maintained clarity in his mind. His search for meaning in his circumstances allowed him to focus on what would keep his focus. The love of his wife and looking forward to being reunited, recounting the feelings of love and happiness. Essentially no matter what his captors did they would be unable to affect his thoughts and feelings.

Now although this is a very extreme example of how you, your inner self can create your inner environment it goes to prove just what can be achieved when, if you'll excuse the pun, you put your mind to it. Throughout my military career, I have found myself 1000s of miles away from my loved ones for extended periods of time, months in fact. My circumstance, whilst not necessarily as dire as Victor, were none the less very bleak, tough and with a looming risk or threat ever present. Interestingly my thoughts in moments of quiet reflection would often focus on the happiness and love in my life, my wife Sam and later Quinn and then Phoebe when she finally arrived.

In the 1960s Maxwell Maltz published Psycho-Cybernetics (Maxwell Maltz, 2015), a book which, as already mentioned, could be determined as the guiding principle of self-help. Maxwell focuses on the power of the subconscious mind and how your image of yourself will govern the life you live. He highlights the impact a positive attitude and positive thought will have if committed to. The real power here is the actual shift of your internal beliefs, the uncommitted, uninspired will not achieve the shifts positivity can have when commitment to changing your blueprint is made. The power of a positive attitude isn't about feeling good, perking up, getting through tough times, it's about a consistent shifts in your subconscious to move you towards your desired self. Who do you want to be in realising your dreams, desires and aspirations?

The point here is you determine your environment, what makes you who you are and who you want to be. Having clarity on your meaning or as we could define it your why will give your environment the foundation from which to build your success and strive to achieve your meaning. Your spirit of success will be the driving force, the inner voice will give you the image of your ideal self and will turn you into that person, actually change your behaviours. This, in turn, will keep you on track, determine the quality of your actions and consistency. It will be the foundation of your belief structure that even if or when things do go wrong you have the inner strength and positivity to bounce right back and stay on track.

Your Success Society

Now this one maybe a little tougher and we already touched on it when we discussed the barriers to success, the doubters. Who do you hang out with? Who are your friends, your closest confidants, your advisors, coaches, mentors the people you cohabit with? Believe it or not, these people will have a direct influence on who you are and the actions you choose to take. Now let's be clear I have no idea who you hang out with, so in all likelihood, your society may already be empowering, may be a diverse mixture. What's important is your journey, that's why, you're reading this book.

If you surround yourself with people who question your dream or in fact, you don't feel you could share your dreams and aspirations, ask yourself why that would be the case? When we are out with our friends are they encouraging, supportive and excited when you share your aspirations. If not, why? How are you with them? Life's a mirror and we directly reflect and are a reflection of our surroundings. Most importantly, in this case, that means who you choose to hang out with.

If they have a poor mindset, how do you think they will respond to you having or developing a wealthy, rich and abundant mindset. However, if you hang out with those who have a rich mindset and are seeking their own success or are already successful what do you think the impact will be on you? Equally what impact will you have on them? This is a tough call, are your social circles helping you or hindering you. Take a look in the simplest terms, it's your life, you live it, you define it and only you can decide how it will turn out. Yes, it is absolutely important to have friends, be liked to mix in social circles and have interaction. It just needs to be right for you.

Ask yourself where do you find the people you really should be mixing with, those who will encourage you and from which you will gain social nourishment? Mixing with like-minded people will have a positive impact, it will give you inspiration and motivation to remain on track, committed and to go that bit further. Be in no doubt, your social interactions and circles have and will have a direct impact on your mindset.

One way to shift towards better connections is to create your sphere of influence. Who do you want to mix with, to meet to build relationships with? Start by building your personal network. Know where the people you want to hang out with congregate in mass, what events do they go to, where do they network, what do they read, who do you already know who can make an introduction for you? Then consciously start to build your personal sphere of influence, your network. Make sure you regularly pop up in the same places, comment on the same articles, seek to connect or gain an introduction via LINKEDIN or similar professional networking or social groups. Oh and make sure this is part of your RAS programming, who you rub shoulders with, who asks you for your opinion and advice.

You Want to Earn More You Need to Learn More

The mere fact you have bought this book and maybe others similar to it, means you already have a commitment to learning. It may be at the moment you're looking for that golden nugget or inspiration to make the leap towards your dream and vision. Whatever the fact, you need now to take your learning to the next level.

Having a thirst for knowledge will be a powerful addition to your environment, it will stimulate your brain, it will empower you, inspire you and once you have the bug you'll grow significantly as a person, business owner and entrepreneur. As to what you need to learn that really will depend on where you are heading and what you aim to achieve. I would say, however, challenge yourself to learn something completely new, a new skill or sport maybe associated with a hobby, try learning a new language or what about learning to play an instrument?

You'll find learning an extremely stimulating experience and one which will enrich and nourish your life. Just think for a moment where, how and what you spend your time doing. There will be 6 – 8 hours sleep, probably 8 or more hours working leaving 8 – 10 hours a day. What are you doing? If the answer is gaming or watching TV think for a moment just how mundane that existence is. Yes, there will be those who will resist this notion, the fact is you don't get any of that time back and you reduce the health of your brain, there's a reason for the term couch potato! Get out there and learn something new, make a commitment right now.

Now with learning, there is a great outcome, other than the increased knowledge, wellbeing, and mental stimulation you have the opportunity to teach others. In the 7 Habits, Steve Covey strongly recommends the single best way to embed your learning and knowledge is to teach others. So, whatever you are learning start to share, offer others your experience in terms of teaching them. It is also extremely rewarding to share your learnings with someone else.

Physical

Now, this may sound a little daft, that your physical surrounding will have an effect on you in a positive or negative manner, the fact remains it will. In terms of your physical surrounding, this could be your home, car, office, desk even what's on your PC desktop. Think for a moment what you could do to improve your surroundings, are you an ordered person, are you a creative, does your space give you the space to focus, does it inspire you, is it ergonomic, is it healthy for you? Take time out to assess just how your home and work environment makes you feel. If you don't get anything from it, or it is simply depressing what do you think the impact will be. Certainly not positive or inspiring.

Take the time to make the space your own, personalise it, make sure it reflects who you are. Making your space personal to you will be a reinforcement of your vision, where you are heading and what motivates you. Whether it's pictures of your loved ones, dream board, digital photo frame, the right furniture, colours, it should make you feel empowered and at home. Take the time to make sure your environment is right for you.

**Habit 1 – Self Value-I-sation**
Don't be the busiest person in your business. All too often when I visit a business the business owner is by far the busiest. Working the longest hours, the default setting for every decision deals with the clients foremost and primarily, always seems to have to put on hold their priorities in order to assist and help the team. Why? Namely, because they don't value themselves in the business and in their life in general. In this habit I've invented a new concept of self value-I-sation. Knowing and acting your worth.

Placing a value on your time, understanding what every second, minute, hour, day, week, month is worth will help you determine the impact of wasting time or having your time wasted. When you reflect at the end of a day and say to yourself 'what did I actually achieve' and are unable to offer an answer, that time is lost forever. We each of us get 24 hours a day, yet so many waste them, so don't. Gain a true value on your time. Both in life and your business be clear of the value you are able to achieve with your time. Don't undervalue yourself, be clear that you are priceless and as such should invest in yourself because you will gain a wonderful return on your investment.

All too often, in business, it boils down to a poor comprehension of the value of your time. Whether you have your own team or you have an external team or a combination of the two you need to have a real understanding and comprehension of the value you bring to your business. Have you ever stopped to establish the real value you bring to your business or should be bringing? You need to ensure you focus on where you bring value and then leverage within your internal and external team to allow you that time.

Now, this isn't about abdication it's about delegation and your team understanding and being given the autonomy and empowerment to work without constantly seeking permission, advice, direction or consent from you. You will immediately start to notice that you have time on your hands and are able to focus on the pursuit of value adding. This is about allowing you to focus on the business, the strategic thinking to determine the direction, maintain a commitment to the plan and achieving the goals.

Your team can then focus on the tactical delivery of the day to day business fundamentals. You will have a great ability to know the responsibilities you have in tactical delivery and in the course of time as the business grows you will then be able to redirect these responsibilities to additional team members. You must first truly understand where your value lies and then make sure you have time to apply yourself accordingly.

This habit is one of reflecting constantly as to your value, making time for the things that matter in your life, the habits we are going to cover, the time you need with your loved ones, for yourself, the areas you offer the greatest value in the business. Remember it starts with 'self-value-I-sation' and you'll receive a great return from the investment you make in your time.

**Habit 2 – Health**
How many times have you been asked what's the most important thing to you in your life? What's your number one value? Now it wouldn't be a surprise to hear many of you saying my loved ones, my family, wife, children and so on. Now here's the thing, you're all wrong, yes that's right you're all wrong. I have no doubt that your loved ones are important, what's more, important is you. Let's face it, primarily it's about being there and with your family and loved ones which is important. So, the real focus here is doing all we can to prolong our presence, to do everything we can to extend our stay and your health is really the number one issue when you look at it in that context.

In addition, health gives us vitality, it invigorates us, makes us happy, reduces stress and increases a sense of wellbeing. However, today it's also a real challenge to actually make sure health is on the agenda, to look after ourselves. With so many distractions it can be very difficult to make the commitment because let's face it some of the healthy stuff can seem like hard work, tough, not very enjoyable so how do we make the commitment? Ask yourself the simple question here, when you look to your ideal self-image, does health play a part? Are you as fit and active as you would like to be, are you at your ideal weight, do you pursue the activities you'd like to and do you feel energised each and every day?

Here's an interesting point for you, in the animal kingdom how many fat animals do you tend to see? The answer is none, well not too many anyway (Hibernation may be an exception). Essentially animals in the wild eat in order to survive, protect and nurture their young. They don't tend to comfort eat, eat for pleasure, eat even when they are not hungry or as a past-time. Oh and they don't tend to be seen smoking and drinking. We do. As a result, one in every 4 adults in the UK is obese, that means they carry more body fat than is healthy. Let's be clear this one area of health which is always very topical leads to a significant amount of life-shortening health problems, high blood pressure, heart disease and stroke, osteoarthritis, gout, gallbladder and gallstones to mention a few.

Then, as we have discussed there is your brain. What do you do to invigorate your brain to exercise your capacity to think, problem solve and expand your learning capacity? You have to look after your brain as much as you do your body. We used to always focus in the Army that the ideal position was to be fit in mind and body. To be able to have the mental agility on the battlefield and the physical ability to respond. So, your health is absolutely key to your success and living a truly fulfilled life. How much emphasis do you place on it?

Defining your health habits will be key towards becoming your ideal self, to achieving your goals and aspirations, to living your life to its full. So, what do you need to do, how can you create your health habits. Start by asking yourself how committed to you, you are and are you significantly worthy and an important factor in your success? From there start to make the lifestyle changes you need. As easy as it is today to be overtaken by the poor health habits it is as easy to focus on your own good  health habits. Buy a device or download an app to assist in your health monitoring, from measuring your steps to your calorie intake.

Focus on your health every day, be active, eat well and exercise your brain. If you truly want to enjoy your life then you absolutely need to make health a daily habit. In fact, take a moment now to establish what your health goals are, where are you now and where would you like to be?

| Health focus for | Currently | Target |
|---|---|---|
| My weight | | |
| My BMI | | |
| My muscle mass | | |
| My cardio ability | | |
| My energy levels | | |
| What exercise level | | |
| What diet | | |
| Drinking | | |
| Smoking | | |
| My Attentiveness | | |

In order to enjoy what you are going onto achieve, you absolutely need to focus on your health if it's currently not a focus on your agenda. For me, it's a simple focus that my health is a direct correlation to living a wealthy life. No point in being rich and wealthy if you're dead!

## Habit 3 – Centre Yourself

All too often our lives seem to run at 100 mph, we go from one thing to the next with hardly a moment's thought. Just take a moment now and think, when was the last time you programmed in thinking and reflective time? Having time to centre yourself is a key addition to your focus and managing stress. This is about allowing yourself reflective time, a moment to centre yourself each and every day. The greatest challenge most will face on a daily basis is the stress they feel, which is often self-induced.

Prolonged exposure to stress will limit your ability to make the right decisions, increase the feelings of fear and anxiety and limit your ability to think with clarity. It's true we want to limit stress, although not remove it completely. Stress is actually, in controlled doses a good motivator. The cortisol stress creates works best in small doses and those doses help to motivate. The challenge is many of us are unable to manage stress and allow it to take hold and derail us, too much cortisol. This is where getting centred and remaining aware of the need will greatly help and maintain the focus of our activity.

One of the biggest challenges in maintaining the levels of focus and commitment you're going to need, to remain true to yourself and disciplined to do what needs to be done will be your state of mind. Whether you take time to meditate or focus on mindfulness there are a plethora of different techniques and apps to guide you through the process. Ironically it can be really confusing to establish what's going to work really well for you.

For me, there is a simple process which I have taken from Dr Jack Lewis (Lewis & Adrian Webster, 2014) GOM time. GOM is the Tibetan word for meditation. In his context of taking GOM time, it's a case of pressing pause and taking a few moments to relax and focus on what lies ahead. In simple terms find somewhere quiet, take some deep breaths and focus on what it is you need to do or to visualise your future or recall a relaxing environment. The essential element here is to allow a few moments to centre yourself.

I have also found guided meditation extremely useful and plan a quiet period towards the end of the day to declutter the mind from the day's activities. Whatever you decide on and by the way do decide on something, take your mental health seriously, meditation, mindfulness or GOM time isn't fluffy, it's about you staying on track achieving your goals. Your mind is a powerful element and will require you to look after it, centring yourself and taking a few moments every day will help.

Laughter also negates the effects of cortisol and reduces the levels within your brain. So, in addition to taking the GOM moments make sure you are having fun, your office should be a fun place to work. Prescribe yourself laughter throughout the day, clearly don't allow it to become a distraction, or you'll never get anything done and likely not to be taken seriously. Remember this habit is about creating your success environment with the aim to assist with optimal performance. And interestingly you'll find it also impacts positively with those you associate with.

Having enough sleep is also another stress-reducing factor. So many business owners I have worked with are unable to sleep well, wake through the night, at the point their heads hit the pillow stress and all the associated feelings take hold. It's like being awake in a nightmare. One of the key essentials here is to limit the activity in your brain at least an hour before you go to bed. Don't allow your brain to be too active, don't be working until the moment you go to bed, don't exercise just before you hit the sack and save the shower until the morning or have it well before you retire. Essentially your centring focus should be in that hour leading up to sleep, it allows the stress levels to be reduced, clears the mind and helps you prepare for sleep.

Maintain the habit of consciously centring yourself throughout the day, making sure fun and having a laugh is an active part of your routine and being prepared for sleep will allow you to better control stress, which in itself will improve your productivity.

**Habit 4 – Tell Your Face**
It's a funny thing when you watch people about their business and daily life, most have a very solemn, stern, serious look to them. In fact, more often than not it might be difficult to see the difference between that and a sad face. Why is that? Because we are so engrossed in ourselves! Life just isn't exciting enough! There is nothing to smile about! Primarily it is down to a simple lack of awareness and our programming.

I've already mentioned the impact a smile can have when discussing with you the power of the offensive mindset. So, I'd like to now challenge you to make it a habit. I want you to actively smile both inwardly and exhibit one, in other words, whatever you are doing tell your face. Yes, it's that simple, you can lift your spirits by simply telling your face you are happy and smiling. There is a fact that happiness increases your level and quality of productivity.

But Steve there are occasions I generally don't feel happy! Yes, there will be and when it's a truly sad occasion, which warrants true sadness then you have a choice. Fake it or don't turn up. Sorry if that sounds a little stark, but then these are success habits. Let's try an experiment right now, take a moment and smile, strike a big fat cheesy grin, right across your face. Lifts your spirits doesn't it? We chose to be sad, as we choose with most of our emotions, it's really about making the right choice for you. Now sadly, I have had to say goodbye to many along the way, attended many funerals. Each and everyone has been a solemn occasion until the wake. At which case the only way I can really explain them is 'fun for all', a celebration of life.

Now I raise the issue of funerals because they are probably one of those occasions where we feel sadness. I'm fully aware there is a myriad of reasons we feel sadness, anxiety, fear etc, my point here is to make a decision. What emotion serves you best? Happiness, so tell your face, smile and make a positive shift daily.

## Habit 5 – I Am

This habit focuses on you and your internal dialogue, actually through externally verbalising, to reinforce your belief structure and by that, I'm referring to your RAS. These are known as your 'I AM' statements. In Think and Grow Rich (Hill, 1937) Napoleon Hill states the need to speak out loud when you rise in the morning and when you retire for the night your desired financial goal. The principle is the same here and the good news is you've already done some of the work towards determining what they are.

If you go back to Chapter 1 and review Your Dream, the Be, Do, See, Have, Go and Share. I asked you a number of questions in relation to what your dream is. These will form the backbone of your I Am statements. To establish your I Am statements let's imagine it's 10 years or 20 years from now and you are looking in the mirror, who is looking back at you? What type of person are you now? What are your values? What are your priorities? What are your living circumstances? What now matters to you in your life? What is your level of focus? These are just an example of who you may see. The point here is to determine who is looking back at you, from here you can now define your I Am statements.

Verbalising your I Am statements will feel awkward, silly, daft when you get started. Once they start to come true it doesn't feel quite so silly. This is all part of your level of commitment, be committed and you will open up new opportunities. Why? Because you have spent the time to reprogramme your RAS. Remember your subconscious mind is extremely powerful. Your conscious mind has limitations, so verbalising your future self through a daily habit of saying out loud your I Am statements will programme your subconscious to tune into those small opportunities when they show themselves. That subliminal niggle to check something out, read an email, meet someone, speak to someone you vaguely recognise across a networking room, ask a pertinent question and so on. All opportunities your subconscious is constantly surveying your environment for. It's like programming your personal warning system to alert you to opportunity.

So, what are your I Am statements? Let's take a look here at just what you are going to write. What are your desired traits, your behaviours, in general, the person you want to be? Remember this is about your future and tuning yourself into it. Your I am statements reflect you and your desires, to help here are some suggested areas to look at.

I am......

A great husband, father, friend, son, daughter, partner. Number 1 in my ..... Have financial freedom, security, stability, income of.... The owner of .... The pillar in the community, business community. Full of confidence, happiness, excitement, motivation. A successful business owner with passive income. A successful investor with passive income. A successful property investor with passive income. The owner of a business which runs without me. Healthy, fit, happy. Able to take holidays every.... The founder of.... The owner of..... The developer of.... The inventor of .... The investor of .... The leader of ..... The manager of ....

These are just a few suggestions, take some time to define yours. Once you have your list the important part is to reinforce them every day. Have the list printed out, frame them put them on a wall, have them on a card in your wallet, stick post it's to a mirror. The important part here is to have a daily routine to recite them verbally every day. For the sake of 7 to 10 minutes to take a timeout to really get in the zone, find a space where you can go through them with confidence, Loudly to yourself, with purpose. Close your eyes and visualise yourself in the future as the person you aim to be. The more clarity the better. Remember this all goes to programme your RAS and tap into the power of your subconscious mind.

### Habit 6 – The Power Hour

From the moment, you wake how much time do you actually invest in yourself? In all likelihood, none to very little. In his book, 'The Miracle Morning Hal Elrod (Elrod, 2016) offers a great insight to really kicking the day off to a great start with a focus for you. All too often life is so busy and hectic we barely have any time for ourselves. Often, we will commit to read a book, partake in fitness and exercise, for our affirmations (I am statements) or meditation. Great intentions although never seem to commit to consistently.

Well, the power hour habit can and will change all that. In the simple terms, you're going to get up an hour earlier than you do now. You are then going to spend an hour focusing on you and setting your success mindset for the day ahead. Just think what you're going to be able to achieve in setting your mindset with 60 minutes to focus on you each and every day. Take a moment to contemplate the habits we have highlighted and what you will be able to achieve committing to your daily I ams; centering on yourself and seeing the real value you're going to offer today and being thankful for what will come today; reading for a short period of time, having time to start the day with exercise and a healthy breakfast.

If you have read through these habits so far and been wondering how will I be able to find the time, we just did! The biggest problem will be your ability to wake up an hour earlier and get out of bed. The fact of the matter here is that thought process you have in the morning to wipe the tiredness from your brain is a mere 40 seconds. That's how long it takes for you to kick your legs out of bed and wake up. The reality for so many is the fact they hit snooze, and for the sake of a few more minutes still wake unrefreshed and into the daily rush to get out of the door. Give yourself the power hour, define what it is you can focus on each and every day to empower yourself and kick the day off to a fantastic start. As Hal defines the hour you can spend:

- 5 minutes' silence or meditation, centering yourself.

- 5 minutes on affirmations or 'I am' statements.

- 5 minutes of visualisation and value-I-sation.

- 20 minutes of exercise, being healthy.

- 20 minutes of reading.

- 5 minutes of scribbling in your learning journal.

Start the day with a smile.

Think the next time you wake up and before you hit snooze, what would you prefer, to kick the day off feeling empowered, centred and excited about the day ahead or rushed, unprepared and like every other day? This will take time and it will go back to one of our opening points of committing to 21 days to make it a fully-fledged habit.

**Habit 7 – KISS, Keep It Simple Stupid.**
The height of stupidity is making things far more complex than is required. The real art of complexity is simplicity. Why is it we tend to over complicate, over think and purposefully make things difficult? Often things are merely over complicated to demonstrate someone's intelligence, a form of self-indulgence. More often than not they will lose credibility, distance themselves from their team and friends. For every challenge, task or activity

there is a simple focus to be gained and outcome to be had. Let's face it life is complicated at the best of time. So why make it even more difficult?

I believe it was Albert Einstein who is quoted as saying if you can't explain it to a 6-year-old you don't understand it well enough. It's quite a good lesson to bear in mind when you are planning, contemplating action or reviewing any situation. Will it be deliverable, could I explain my intention, what I mean or what I want to achieve in simple terms? No matter the circumstance don't you owe it to yourself to seek the simple options. It's interesting when I look back to math lessons when I was at school and often remembered the teachers telling us for any equation there is a simple solution and a complex way of getting the same answer. Yet so many of us always seem to find ourselves toiling over the complex option.

Some areas to focus your simplicity to build the habit will be:

• Why use 10 words when 1 will do. All too often we overcomplicate dialogue trying to say too much, just say what needs to be said. In the military, there was an absolute necessity to be succinct with brevity in communication. If you need to send a radio message it needed to be kept short, it was no place for lengthy discussion if another call sign needed to send an emergency message. Frankly, complexity would risk lives in this situation.

• Be humble, not too hard on yourself. This isn't about being a genius, having to be the font of all knowledge. Frankly, even if you don't know, who cares.

• Apply KISS to any situation, ask yourself or others what is the simplest solution here?

• Focus on one thing. All too often the complexity may not come from a single issue rather from the overwhelming activities and tasks to be completed. Let's be clear you can only relay focus on one thing at a time so do simply that. Focus on what needs to be done and then do that.

• Why email when you can call, why call when you can meet. All too often we make communication far more challenging than it needs to be. When you can communicate with someone directly do!

Choose to make your life simpler in every way you can. Don't get bogged down in complex and over complicated issues. Don't allow your business to become sluggish through overthinking processes, procedure and delivery. Think 'what is the simplest way to achieve my aim', 'how can I answer these questions and apply a process with simplicity'. Don't be stupid and make your life and business overly complicated. Keep it Simple Stupid.

**Habit 8 – The 7 Ps, Prior Preparation Prevents a P___ Poor Performance**
I hope by now you'll either have or starting to understand the value of time and how you decide to spend it and an insight to looking at the simple option or solution. It never ceases to amaze me just how ineffective we can be owing to a real lack of preparation. Earlier I mentioned the average time we potentially have on planet earth, 84 years or 30, 660 days, or 4,380 weeks. It's not an infinite number, there is an end and we are all heading there second by second, minute by minute. Yet we waste so much of our time, often living in regret at the end of a wasted weekend, having slept for too long and then realised there was no time for the enjoyable stuff. So often there is much regret once that time has passed and there is still so much to do or I haven't managed to achieve what I set out too. STOP IT!

Start to really focus on just how you are going to invest in your time, your life. Use that focus to make sure you allow time to prepare for action, being ready, committed and focused. This book has been about getting into action, taking your life to the destination of your dreams and having your business facilitate that journey. So, let's stop arsing around and start to get focused on how best to use your time. Habit 8 is about getting focused on your time (Habit 1, value-I-sation) and the requirement for being prepared, here are some simple principles to make the most out of each and every day.

1.      Plan tomorrow today. At the end of each day plan out in as much detail as you can what you will be doing tomorrow, define what will happen and when, what are the priorities and what you will absolutely achieve by the end of the day. Take a look at the activities you will undertake which move you closer to achieving your goals and make sure they are planned for.

2.      Plan for procrastination. It's a funny thing, procrastination is suffered by so many and it's not surprising when you look at the level of distraction which we are bombarded with today. My advice here is to take control and plan short periods where you can step out and procrastinate. That's right, allowing yourself the time to procrastinate. In this manner you

remain in control, you keep on top of your time efficiency, it doesn't take over.

3.      Get the important stuff done. Make sure important issues are dealt with whilst they remain important, don't put things off. If you do, before you know it they become urgent and you increase your levels of stress and pressure you unnecessarily, at which point your efficiency goes out the window.

4.      Work to a default diary. Have a structure in your life, have a programme of what you aim to do on a daily basis and when. Essentially having a timetable for your daily activities will create efficiency and keep you on track. It is always wise to make sure you have flexible and free space in the diary in order to allow for the unknown.

5.      Eat the frog. In his book Eat that Frog (Tracy, 2001) Brian Tracy makes reference to eat a frog daily. When he talks of the frog he refers to an activity you have been putting off, avoiding and sees it as the most distasteful activity you need to do. Where he refers to eating a frog daily it's about doing a distasteful task each and every day and what's more he suggests it's done first. Eating a frog daily will improve your efficiency and also helps to avoid the urgent stuff ever turning up. Oh, and if you currently have a number of frogs, which is very likely, start with the biggest first.

Getting into the habit of asking yourself and setting the 7 P's will vastly increase your productivity, motivate you and the team with clearly thought through agendas and plans. There will be far greater consistency, the quality of your work will improve and you will generally start to get more done at a higher quality.

**Habit 9 – Prepare to Learn**
This is about expanding your knowledge, learning and the application towards your growth. Although I have already highlighted this within your success environment, it deserves additional comment because having a learning focus should be a habit. We also highlighted it in Chapter 1 the impact and focus you'll need to have on learning, which you can go back and review.

It's about taking a good look at yourself and understanding where your strengths are and what you are good at and then applying it. As you focus on learning you'll see your self-belief improve, merely through realising just how much knowledge you can assimilate and apply.  Regarding the habits here are a few additional suggestions to make learning a part of your success oriented habits.

1.      Start a learning journal. One of the best ways to internalise your learning is to write it down, just think back to school and all your exercise books. When we write down our learnings it significantly helps to embed the learning, file it away in the subconscious. You will also have a rich reference which you can refer to in the future.

2.      Exercise your brain daily. Today with the massive advancements in technology we all have a sense of 'need it now', why learn something when I can find the answer at the request of a simple google search. We become lazy and don't feel the need to commit to memory or learn. If you're not using your brain it will become redundant and your ability to problem solve will decrease. Exercising your brain will increase and expand your capacity to learn and assimilate knowledge. On average we are able to remember up to 7 items in our working memory (Lewis & Adrian Webster, 2014), however, with practice, you can increase your capacity which will lead to a far greater ability to deal with complex problem solving and retention.

3.      Be creative. In the simplest of terms, the two sides of the brain left and right, are responsible for different functionality. The left is logical and the right creative. Interestingly it is stated that long-term memory sits on the right side along with creativity and short-term memory with the left and logic. You could see here that long-term memory would be better served on the left side with logic and short-term with the right creative side. What's interesting is how we can maximise the whole potential of the brain by engaging both sides simultaneously. Some simple methods to tap into both sides would be to make your learning fun. The use of diagrams, drawing and pictures helps to tap into both sides. What colour pen do you use? I'd bet it will be black or blue. Start to write your notes in different colours, create multi-coloured notebooks, move away from being monotone. Each of these will help to engage your brain more fully, to lock in the learnings and to allow you to develop and maintain your brain function.

4.      Know your VAK. Do you know what style of learning you prefer? Are you a visual person, maybe someone who listens more and audible or hands on a kinesthetic learner? Whichever you are it's worth finding out, so you can maximise your learning accordingly. If you're hands-on then it may be a practical course

you need, which has a hands-on approach, it could be that an audiobook will be a preferred method, or it could be that watching a video or reading a book would be preferred. Best of all here is to use multisensory techniques, really tap into all levels of learning.

5.      Have a learning agenda. With the focus we have gained from Chapter 1, there will be plenty to learn in order to get to where you want to. So make an agenda, set your learning goals, decide what you want and need to learn and in what sequence, then commit to it. Within the agenda will be the need to apply your learning, where and how will the new knowledge be applied?

6.      Learn to speed read. On average, I'm reading and completing a book a week, that's 52 books a year. Learning to speed read will offer you the ability to really devour information and grow your knowledge base significantly. Speed reading isn't as difficult as it sounds and in many respects, is just training yourself to read in a new way. You don't miss any information, you don't skip over the content you are merely tapping into what you and your brain can really do. Not sure if you'd be able to do it, just ask yourself, how many books did I read last year? What would happen if I was able to read a book a week? Would I increase my knowledge base and by how much?

7.      Sign up for a course or two. External validation really does increase your confidence in learning. It's never been so easy to learn new stuff, not merely asking Google for the answer, actually join a course and actively have to apply yourself to learning. Whether you participate in an online course, distant learning, attend a workshop or course you'll find a great reward from actively participating and gaining external validation.

**Habit 10 – Try New Stuff**
One great way to expand yourself is to try new stuff. This will be a sure way to expand your horizons and ensure life remains a journey of challenge. In concert with learning, you'll come across things you have never tried, and this will be a chance to really expand who you are and what you are able to do. It may be it's a skill you have yet to try, it could be beneficial to what you aim to achieve or just something you have always wanted to have a go at. Whatever it is be open to trying new stuff. Don't just say no, because that's what you have always done or because it takes you out of your comfort zone. As a famous sports brand says…..'just do it'

Right now, what hobby you have always wanted to have a go at, haven't committed to because of a lack of time. Go back over your bucket list and have a look at what it is your aiming to achieve in life, is there an activity you could make a commitment to today? Get out and be bold, find something new today and make a start, you'll also find it helps your creativeness and offers something different to focus on.

## Habit 11 – Do What You Ought

Who are you? Habit 5 highlighted the need to set your RAS, be clear on who you are and who you want to be. Getting focused through the 'I Am Statements' on a daily basis. Well, authenticity is about you being you 100% of the time. Aiming to act out the I Am statements. If you aim to be a great husband and father, then do it. If you aim to be confident, then start to behave in a confident manner. Always be true to yourself and never try to be someone others want you to be, or who you think they want you to be. Constantly strive to be the best version of you.

The challenge with being less than authentic is people will see through any façade, if not now than in the course of time. And it doesn't take long to smell bull shit! Even when you are trying to please others, don't be someone you assume they want you to be, it can damage your credibility because unless you are a very good character actor it's not going to work. Have you ever come across that person who completely changes when the boss comes? They have a completely different character in front of the boss, often referred to as a 'kiss arse'. These take the lack of authenticity to an extreme and in my experience, are more often than found wanting. Interestingly this level of inauthenticity is a conscious choice, actively trying to be someone they are not and often for self-gratification, self-indulgence and personal furtherment. None of which are good character traits because often it will be at the expense of others.

Now being authentic has its challenges in its own right. When we look into the mirror and our future self-looks back at us without any of the challenges, fears, concerns, limitations we have right now, how do you respond? It may be that person looking back is more controlled, reserved or not so keen to be heard. Has skills, knowledge or ability we long to have. You get the idea. So, how often does that inner voice (you know the one we have referred to throughout the book) pipe up when you are being anything less than authentic?

Being authentic is a journey of discovery over a lifetime and can be extremely challenging and scary. To help with your journey let me share with you one of the most valuable lessons I learned from my service in the military, a Commanding Officer once said to me…

'Always seek to do what you ought …

… Not what you want.'

Taking a moment to ask this question will ensure you reflect before committing to an action. It can make the difference between making a decision which will help you, your family, friends, the business or the team or making a bad decision with consequences. Just think about it for a moment. How often are you faced with a decision and there is a want to respond in a particular way. Maybe a response which is self-serving, selfish, conceited, self-indulgent or just wrong. The urge to respond in a way you know isn't a true reflection of you or who you aim to be.

When you seek to respond as you ought, it forces you to look at the true outcome from your decision. It is likely you'll start to feel better about yourself as you start to make decisions which are in essence close to being your authentic self. The habit of doing what you ought not what you want takes self-discipline, commitment, self-authenticity and a consistent approach to remain true to yourself.

**Habit 12 – Gratitude and Celebration**
Have you ever walked in a crowd and taken notice of the solemn, non-descript, in some cases miserable expressions? People seem to walk around in a constant state of what I can only describe as solemn discontentedness (see Habit 4). Here's a great habit to maintain the focus on your success by sharing your happiness with others. It's also the simplest way to show gratitude and to celebrate life. Sharing a smile is the very best celebration of life being good. That's right the simplest way is to offer a smile. A smile is infectious and changes your psychological state. A smile we already know it actually makes you feel better, it lifts our spirits. Take a moment to try this experiment, share a smile right now, catch someone's eye and smile, it will be infectious.

Taking it to the next level is the principle of feed it forward. In this case, it's the simplest act of kindness to someone else, a complete stranger. A great example would be offering someone that illusive £1 when they are looking for change at a parking meter. Checking their pockets and they don't have the change, you do. Give them the pound. When they seek to repay you merely say the best way to pay me back would be to 'feed it forward' offer a random kind act to someone else today. I have to say there is something quite fulfilling about random acts of kindness, they really do make you and those affected feel great.

The other area we should mention here is that of celebration. We tend to only celebrate on a few occasions a year, birthdays, anniversaries etc. Take the time to celebrate the small wins, for you, your family and team. It doesn't necessarily have to be a major celebration, mere recognition, a small gesture. A random celebration of thanks to another person for just being there, supporting you or helping you. It makes a difference and fuels your commitment and drive. In essence, it feels great to be a nice person. I can assure you in my life I have witnessed and had my fill of those who are not nice, in fact at the other end of the scale. So be gracious, show gratitude and celebrate.

### Habit 13 – When is Now a Good Time to Get Started?
No, it's not a typo! All too often we have good, no, great intentions which we will get started tomorrow! It's interesting so many will defer until tomorrow, well let's ask the question has tomorrow arrived yet? If you keep putting things off, you are less than committed to then make a shift right now, make the commitment to get underway right now. Take a moment, what have you been putting off getting started? What has been the driving force behind not starting, especially if the outcome is going to offer you growth, enrichment, betterment, progress you to the next level or generally just make you feel better? In all likelihood, just being lazy, non-committal, feeling sorry for yourself, allowing that inner dialogue to stop you from being who you are destined to be.

This habit is about making a commitment as soon as you have decided the course and what you want to do, get started right now. Whatever you need to do to get underway get started now, don't put it off. This does take courage, commitment and consistency. The courage to get underway knowing it may take you out of your comfort zone, the commitment to your journey and achieving what you want and the consistency to then remain on track to complete what you set out to achieve.

Right NOW is the best time to get started. So, what's stopping you?

### Habit 14 – Daily Margins
The spokes of the wheel, the element which keeps all the habits securely in place and progressing towards success or that never-ending pursuit of continued success. Richard Moore, in his book Mastermind, highlighted the impact Sir Dave Brailsford had on the Sky Cycling team as the head coach. One of the most widely spoken about areas was that of aggregation of marginal gains, the focus on minor shifts in the pursuit of success for the Sky Team. Making small changes 1% here, 1 gram there, 1 second

reduction all of which when compounded together made a major shift had incredible results.

Today many sports teams, businesses and corporations have a focus on the marginal gains. It is the same for you in the development and commitment towards this cycle of habits. Working on all the habits will, of course, be overwhelming when you seek to make major gains in each. The point here and the reason why focusing on daily margins will be the habit which will move you towards success is a simple one. If each day you are able to reflect and say you have made a marginal gain in all of them or a number of them or the ones you define as important will have a positive effect.

The point here is, regardless of the amount of shift, small or large you should have a constant aim to hold yourself accountable every day to review your habits. By making a difference each and every day do you think you'll move towards your goal, your vision? In short yes, of course, you will. In this manner, you can hold yourself accountable on so many levels. By reviewing your activity at the end of every day you will be able to determine the level of gain you made. What does that look like, feel like across all the habits? What is the impact on the quality of the action? What traction is it creating? What shift are you seeing? Throughout those first 21 days, this will make the difference between internalising your habits or merely letting yourself off the hook.

**BLUF - The Cycle of Habits**
Setting these habits isn't about just getting to a point and then thinking all's good no need to remain so focused. The whole point of the habits is to shift you towards a better business to ensure you live the life you deserve. And remember you define what that will be. If you have the discipline and focus then you do deserve the results, let's be clear your dedication and commitment will pay off. Your success habits will pay dividends over time.

Habits by virtue in time don't become a chore, rather an unknown competence, just what you do, a self-prophesying prophecy. Interestingly this is the challenge, it's getting to this stage that most will fail. All the time you are consciously having to make the shift, to embed the habits you will have that internal battle, that inner voice asking whether it's really worth all this heartache, this is tough, there must be an easier way, is it really worth it? Well, that's for you to define.

Having shared with you what I believe are the success habits, certainly, they are for me, there is a natural cycle to them, almost the cycle of priority and then the cycle of reinforcement, essentially the cycle of success. Now I can't offer you any empirical evidence other than as a professional coach each of these habits when embraced and nurtured improve results, shift people and improve life. Below I offer the cycle of success, the cyclical nature of the habits with the hub being the ability to make the daily marginal gains. Putting the cycle into context it starts with valuation, first understanding your true value, having clarity of your worth and then defining it. From here you'll take a look at your health and then take a tough view of how long you want to be around. Because you'll influence and increase your longevity.

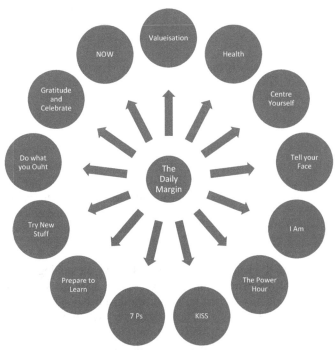

*The Cycle of Success*

Taking time to then focus on yourself and manage your inner dialogue, not allowing it to derail you or impact your ability to maintain your offensive mindset. This will lead to a natural inner peace and calm and ultimately happiness, which you'll be able to display with sincerity.

With inner belief and a stronger sense of contentment you'll have the foundation to determine with authenticity your I Am Statements and internalise them thoroughly. With these habits, you'll be able to conduct your power hour, your daily ritual to kick and boost the start of each day.

You'll have a KISS focus each day and always seek to apply the 7Ps to being organised in all your activities and reduce overwhelm. With this approach, your willingness to learn and try new things will enrich your mind and soul and further reinforce your being.

Your discipline will drive the right decisions, recognising where you are doing well and where others are worthy of recognition and celebration. Essentially improving the sense of well-being in yourself and those you influence, employ and rely on. Having a focus on NOW will keep you on track, determine just what the next focus should be and the quality of ACTion.

Combined with the daily focus on marginal gains across each of the habits will ensure you remain in positive motion. Making the small shifts every day towards your end state, ultimately living the life you want.

Did I Power

Marshall Goldsmith (Goldsmith, 2015) in his book Triggers talks extensively of our inner power, how we all of us respond to triggers, both positive and negative. As we have discussed there is much in our lives and surrounding our lives which will either impede or accelerate change. It's really easy to let yourself off the hook, to go easy on yourself, to not be fully committed. The challenge here is the fact these result in evoking and reinforcing your bad habits.

Marshall refers to 4 specific magic moves. Firstly 'the apologies'. For the vast majority of us when someone offers an apology we will offer forgiveness. An apology is the first step towards a behavioural change. The second is when we 'ask for help', once again very few will refuse a sincere plea for help. The third Marshall mentions is optimism, the belief that everything will be alright. In this case, people are drawn towards those who are confident, have the inner assurance that everything will be alright. The fourth is the magic move I want you to focus on from this point. It will majorly assist in making and sustain your shift, establishing the behaviours through habits to achieve success in your life.

The fourth magic move is 'active questioning' the act of self-questioning, the first step towards self-coaching. In the same light as apologies, requests for help and optimism the act of self-questioning acts as a mechanism to encourage behavioural shift. Asking ourselves questions is one thing; the most important aspect is the questions we ask. Marshalls' extensive research found that when we ask ourselves a question in regards to our performance, commitment or motivation, essentially what we want to have focus on, there was a significant improvement.

Having also evoked the self-questioning as a daily ritual, a habit in my day it has made a significant difference. It further programs my RAS, raises my awareness. Interestingly I have measured my responses for a year and when I have low-performance periods, lower levels of motivation and happiness, there is a correlation to asking if I had completed my daily questions. This is truly about you holding you accountable, actively seeking to 'get out of your own way'.

In relation to the questions you ask yourself, well that's going to depend on what and where you want to focus, to make the behavioural shift. You can focus on the habits we have highlighted here and ask yourself each day to what extent did I remain focused. You may wish to focus on very specific activities. Essentially you can determine just what questions you aim to ask; a significant key is how you ask the question. Marshall has a very simple focus in the manner to ask the questions, 'did I'. Asking a 'did I' question allows you to reflect in such a manner to be truly reflective on the aspect of the question which aims to make the difference.

In asking 'Did I' you hold yourself accountable to the level of your commitment on a daily basis. As a sample, here are my 'Did I' questions I asked throughout 2017:

1. Did I do my best to be a great husband today?
2. Did I do my best to be a great father today?
3. Did I do my best to enjoy today?
4. Did I do my best to avoid procrastination?
5. Did I work on my book today?
6. Did I add value today?
7. Did I complete my planned agenda and goals for today?
8. Did I coach in a challenging and courageous way?
9. Did I do my best to be abundant today?
10. Did I do my best to be healthy today?
11. Did I engage in learning today?

Your questions don't need to follow my example, they need to be relevant to your focus, your future and what you need to do each and every day to achieve your dreams. What's really great about setting your questions is the fact you can't fool yourself, you actually can't kid yourself, there will always be your inner voice which will know if you are trying to kid yourself.

**My Action**    **The Impact**    **Achieved by**

## SEE YOU IN 21 DAYS

I want you to now focus on you for the next 21 days. I want you to put the book down and put the habits in action. Over the next 21 days, you can gain clarity on your dream and focus the vision. Set your goals and the learning agenda and then determine the plan.

Decide which habits you need to establish. Understand clearly the impact they will have on you and your life and your business. The next 21 days is about developing your 'Pig-Headed Discipline', you can choose to go easy on yourself or to make a major step towards the future you desire.

Write out your 'did I' questions and set a daily reminder to ask yourself them. Remember these questions will hold you accountable. There is no value in lying to yourself, so by virtue if you remain committed you will see a change in your habits.

After you 21 days' I want you to then return to the book. At that time if you have made the shift you will be a great place to act. Through Chapters 4 and 5 I will then give you insight to remaining above the parapet in both your life and business. Thereafter I will introduce you to the concept of business rhythm.

Date
Today:

| Habit | My Chosen Habits | Yes/No |
|---|---|---|
| 1 | **Self Visue-I-sation** | |
| 2 | **Health** | |
| 3 | **Centre Yourself** | |
| 4 | **Tell your Face** | |
| 5 | **I Am** | |
| 6 | **The Power Hour** | |
| 7 | **KISS, Keep it Simple** | |
| 8 | **The 7 Ps** | |
| 9 | **Prepare to Learn** | |
| 11 | **Try New Stuff** | |
| 12 | **Do What You Ought** | |
| 13 | **When is Now a Good Time to Start** | |
| 14 | **Daily Margins** | |

**Did I Questions**

1

2

3

4

5

6

7

153

8

9

10

11

12

13

14

15

17

18

19

20

21

Pick up the book on …….. / …… / ……

# Chapter 4 –

# Business Above the Parapet

Welcome back, if you did, in fact, take the 21-day challenge, great job. What is business? In the simplest terms, a business is a viable commercial operation which offers services or products of value to a defined consumer for a profitable outcome. So, this requires the business to have the ability to service and supply their consumers and find new ones to remain profitable and grow. Sounds easy, doesn't it? In essence supply and demand, establish what it is you would like to supply find enough demand for it and grow your business, ultimately go on to live the life you desire.

What was it that encouraged you to get into business in the first place? Most likely the dream of being your own boss, getting out of the rat race, tired of others making all the profits from your hard work and knowledge and likely to be a plethora of other similar drivers. There is likely to be one common denominator you had skills in a particular field and wanted to turn that into your business. Essentially you were the technician, the expert, had the skills and knowledge. We've already touched on this in Chapter 2 when we discussed being out of your depth.

The point here is to be clear that a business cannot be built, sustained and grow just because you have a technical skill which you want to make profitable. In all likelihood, you probably already know that or at this point, the light bulb has just gone on. Having spoken to 1000s of business owners I have seen this played out 100s of times. The technician is the owner and spends most of their time being the technician. Hard working in the business. The electrician is installing circuits, the IT specialist is building computers, the building contractor is on the tools, the butcher is preparing joints of meat and on and on it goes.

There is the second level to this, once you have a team you may go directly from the tools to being the default setting for the service you provide for your team and clients. They seek your advice, guidance and direction to being the technician. Resulting in you having no time to run the business. In both cases, the fundamental aspects of running your business begin to be impacted on business. Poor management, poor sales pipeline, inefficient marketing, constant worry about the business finances and so on.

In the Chapters leading up to here, we have, I hope by now to have defined the need for clarity, resilience, vision and motivation which combined will be required to establish your business and the elusive supply and demand model. With reinvigorated purpose and frame of reference having an offensive mindset we now need to focus on the business. This will be a challenge for many of you who are currently working in your businesses as the technicians. Going from working in your business, being your own employee or merely owning a job will be the first major step. Developing your focus on the business will, in fact, be the first major step to true growth and ultimately success.

The growth of your business will require a true understanding of where you are heading and what you aim to achieve. So, let's take a little time now to determine just what a successful business looks like. Here's the definition I use to describe what a successful business should strive to achieve:

A Commercial

Profitable Enterprise

That's Works

Without You

To put this into context I'm going to break it down and explain each part of the definition.

*A Commercial* – Being a commercial business may sound obvious unless you are the technician in the business and busy doing a technical stuff. In itself would probably suggest there isn't a commercial focus within the business and most likely a limited understanding of what it takes to be commercial. Having a commercial focus within the business is about profitability and growth. Seeking to generate a profitable return in exchange for your products or services. This results in the business having and adding value.

Right now, if you were to put a price on your business what would it be worth? In all likelihood, it won't be worth quite what you think or it maybe you would place a significant value on it right now. To have a commercial business means you have a business which has value, it has a worth in the marketplace where other parties would be interested in buying it. In many respects, it is this point which makes owning a business really exciting, having the opportunity to sell a business can offer an incredible return. Maybe have a business which is replicable or franchisable.

However, there will likely need to be a significant amount of focus in the business in order to make it a truly commercial opportunity. Take for instant when you buy a house, high-ticket items. What do you contemplate when looking about the marketplace? What state of repair is it in, how tidy is it, is it nicely decorated, where is it situated etc. Interestingly each of these have an intrinsic value proposition to negotiate the sale. And with each one you are able to determine the increase in value if you are able to make the changes. Essentially adding a commercial value to it.

In a similar context, your business is the same. There are a number of areas which will determine just what the value of your business is right now. Essentially you can measure your business against them to determine what the potential value is now and where and how to focus activity to increase the value.

- Customer retention.
- Financial stability.
- Profitability.
- Business scalability.
- USP and brand positioning.
- Team autonomy.
- The business reliability on you.

Interestingly as you read on we'll be adding a little more detail to some of these points as they intrinsically help to define a successful business.

**Profitable Enterprise.** The purpose of any business is to make money in order to make a profit. Without profit the business will not survive, it will not grow and is not sustainable. Hence the focus on the commercial aspect of the business. Being profitable isn't just about the margins, although that's a major point, it's also about where you retain and invest your money. How tuned into the fixed, variable expenses and the level of detail in direct reference to the cost of goods sold are you? Profitability is knowing your numbers and how to make them work for you.

Additionally, profitability relates to the use of time and how productive your business is. Having a team will be one of the most significant investments, buying other people's time. Are they productive, do they increase the profits or start to absorb them? As we will see later in this chapter profitability is a key component to the success, longevity and sustainability of any business.

**That Works.** Having a functional business might seem obvious, although in many businesses they don't work as efficiently as they should or could. Any business needs to have systems, processes and procedures in order to deliver their product or services. Let's be clear here, a system does not reside in the mind of the business owner. The business owner should not be the default setting for delivery of the business. In all too many cases, the business owner is the default setting, they are the one who deals directly with the customers, are the expert in all the businesses systems and are likely to be the one who makes all the decisions and complete the major administration processes in the business. All of which stifle growth and result in the business owner remaining an immovable entity from the business.

It's not just about how embedded the business owner is within the business in addition or alternatively it is about the efficiencies of the rhythm of business. Essentially the business owner should offer direction, focus, inspiration and strategies as to the direction of the business. The team should be focused on dealing with the customers, the customers result in the business and the business owner can continue to develop the growth. A working business model in its simplest terms. More on this in Chapter 5.

**Without You.** The ultimate goal here is to be able to remove you as the business owner from the business entirely and for the business to continue to grow. Now I would be surprised to hear many of you state that my business already works. Now if that were the case we would be at chapter 3 and it shouldn't have taken this long for the penny to drop. So, let me put this into context. A business that works without you, the business owner means it works without you, period. This isn't about being able to take a couple of weeks off here and there without impact to the business. This is about your business not depending on your influence, technical ability or need to make the decisions period. It works without YOU!

Let's say you went into the office today and told the receptionist you were going to be away and not contactable for the next 3 months, what would happen? Would you be able to walk away from the business with the knowledge and comfort that it will survive and prosper without your leadership, intervention and guidance? For the vast majority of business owners, it wouldn't.

**Being Above the Parapet**

Being above the parapet is about waking up to the real opportunities your business presents you each and every day. Aiming always to be the business owner and moving away from owning a job. In military service one of the scariest things you'll ever have to do is 'put your head above the parapet[1]', essentially looking to the line of fire. Today its defined as having the courage to voice an opinion, say what needs to be said, stand out, do what needs to be done, put your team first, challenge and stretch the boundaries. For me putting your head above the parapet, above the parapet takes courage.

Now in the context of the field of operations, if you don't get your head above the parapet you'll never be able to identify the objective. You won't see the obstacles in front, you won't be able to react to the movement of the enemy forces. You certainly won't gain the big picture, gather all the available information to complete the mission to deny the enemy and to successfully complete the operation. In context, you won't have any responsibility, limited if any accountability and certainly no ownership.

So, in business, getting your head above the parapet is about having a clear look at what's going on in the marketplace, team efficiencies or new opportunities, gaining the big picture. Getting your head above the parapet, getting your business above the parapet results in a significantly high level of responsibility. You will take account of what's going on right now and ultimately, be in a position to take command, lead to assume ownership.

Conversely, keeping yourself safe, staying below the parapet, remaining below the line of fire will result in blame, excuse and denial. I wasn't in a position to see what was going on, I wasn't told where to go, what vantage point to take up, I wasn't given instruction by higher command; blame. I didn't have the time, resources, skills to observe what was going on, it wasn't my fault, excuses. How was I supposed to know I was responsible for observing what was happening, no one told me I didn't know; denial!

Now if the military ran operations like that we would have significantly more travesty on operations and the battlefield. Frankly, the military would fail to function, to perform at the consistently high levels of operations that it does, to maintain the tempo of operations. Yet, in my experience, we

---

[1] A protective wall or earth defence along the top of a trench or other place of concealment for troops.

often hear and can relate to blame, excuse and denial in business. From business owners not taking responsibility for their business, to disengaged and unempowered teams. The story is often the same.

Getting the business above the parapet, or more precisely getting business owners and their teams above the parapet, into the line of fire we need to understand the hierarchy moving from denial to ownership, getting your business head, your mindset, above the parapet. Let's start at the bottom of the trench with denial.

Denial

Ignorance is bliss, isn't it? Choosing to ignore what's going on, knowing you are able to have plausible deniability makes us feel good. Well, that's what we'd like to think, although we all know it doesn't in reflection. More often than not you know, it really is a choice you've made, to be ignorant, oblivious or unaware. How can it be my fault if 'I didn't know', no one told me! Ever come across that, or maybe you've been that person?

Interestingly denial is often residing in the area of our subconscious which is just out of earshot until it is required to protect us. Even though we may have all the information we require, the means, the ability the knowledge even then we can deny our true believes. Irrational isn't it. Yet at some point, we will have all found ourselves in that position. Only when brought into focus do we then seek to deny what our hearts desire. Goes back to our ability to self-sabotage even without consciously knowing.

There's a great example of denial being played out within our education. What's fascinating with this example of denial is the significant impact it has had on what on the face of it are educated, intelligent students. Having attained a degree, I can contest to the focus and commitment students need in order to complete the rigours of attaining a higher level of education. Yet even among these young scholars, there is an underlying current. What if I fail, what if I don't get the results I need?

Yet there will be many students who unwittingly sabotage their own study. Now students are well versed in the art of work hard play hard. Yet some take the play hard to the extremes. They remain in denial in regards to the work they need to submit, the exams they have to take and as a result find themselves with less than acceptable results. All through their education, they remain in denial as to the impact and effect of a major miss balance in their extra curricular activities and lack of focus on their study.

Many will merely walk away with less than satisfactory results and will often have no accountability as to the reason. They will remain in denial and walk away with their student loan and a less than average result.

In business, today, it's not good enough to merely stick your head in the sand and plead ignorance. That's not going to grow the business, generate profit, increase sales etc. Ignorance will ultimately destroy your business. Ever heard those words, sorry I should have known better? Well, in short, you should and your team should. Denial is the root cause of limiting beliefs and can therefore directly lead to business failure. And it all starts with walking backwards into the future. What's the difference between these two pictures?

*Figure 1 5th Avenue New York 1900 - 1913*

Here is a picture of 5th Avenue in 1900, and you'll just make out a car circle bottom left. Conversely 13 years later you can just make out the horse drawn carriage amongst the cars.

This picture demonstrated the impact Henry Ford had with the introduction of the 'Horseless Carriage' the automobile. The sceptics were adamant the car would never replace the horse and carriage. Well, we know how that story turned out. The fact that there was a complete denial that such a machine would ever replace horsepower.

Interestingly the denial remains rife within business. In his book Denial, Richard Tedlow (Tedlow, 2010) describes how denial ultimately killed one of the most renowned minds and physicians, Sigmund Freud. In itself a paradox. Freud, who was a heavy cigar smoker ultimately died of cancer, knowing his cigar habit had given him cancer of the jaw and palate, he remained an avid smoker. He ended his life in 1923 with assisted suicide owing to the manner in which cancer plagued his life. The ironic context of the story was Freud's' definition of denial; an unconscious defence mechanism against external realities that threaten the ego. Interestingly it remains a strong interpretation of deniel today.

For me, one of the most interesting aspects to denial is that of it being an anaesthetic. Whether subconsciously seeking anaesthesia or through our own protection programming we choose to filter out offending information. Denial protects us from offending and harmful information. Think about that for a moment. You choose not to look at what's in the bank, check the cash flow, look at the order sheet, look at the activity in lead generation and the list goes on. Sadly, as a result denial can be the most damaging element of choice. Choosing ignorance, oblivion being unaware. Think back to the student, literally feeding the oblivion with the good times.

Let's be quite clear denial is an overwhelming inconsistency in your ability to interpret what's going on in your business and life. The reluctance to interpret or see facts for what they represent, the truth. Facts should offer you an insight into what is actually going on and offer you the options to respond, act and deal with. Ignorance and the concept 'that it will never happen to me' is a fallacy and a road to disaster.

Now it's important that you have a full understanding of denial, remember as a coach my job is that of raising awareness, now you have to take responsibility. More on that in a moment. Your understanding will also equip you with the knowledge to identify denial in others giving you the options to confront it. Blissful ignorance will not serve you well, it will not protect you and will only serve to deny you the opportunities and options you should pursue in the bid to achieve all you can in life.

Excuse

Now we enter into the hierarchy of living in the trenches, staying in perceived safety below the parapet. Denial will naturally lead to excuses. It's almost a natural next step. If you have been in denial and ignorant at the point awareness brings it firmly to the forefront of your mind you're going to engineer excuse. Just ask yourself how many times you have offered excuses for your inactivity, lack of commitment, poor focus or failures. Been able to have some form of reason as to why it really wasn't your fault. Deniability is one and often leads to excuses naturally; 'I didn't know!'

In chapter 2 we discussed the impact of FEAR, here we can start to see the direct impact of it and just how it manifests itself. Excuses are a safe way to avoid the areas you fear, to make irrational decisions contra to your true potential, drive and ability. Excuses confine us to the comfort zone, the safe zone, the zone where there is no growth, no achieving your true potential, the zone where ultimately you will remain average or worse below average. Live your life to less than your true potential.

Excuses become a self-fulfilling prophecy, they become your reality or at least the anchor to which you are shackled in your current safe reality. Your comfort zone. You'll exist in an illusion of security, that is until it goes wrong and then, guess what, you'll have an excuse as to what happened, why it wasn't your fault and that's ok, isn't it! They become a manner in which we are able to look at situations, opportunities, respond to others in a rational way. The reasons why we become confined to our comfort zone of inactivity, inability and missed opportunity.

Interestingly once you start down the path of making and accepting excuses you will prevent yourself from reaching your true potential, you will be the reason for your own limitations. Opportunities will pass you by, even when they are presented to you directly. Sadly, you won't even have sight of what you can really achieve. The good thing is it's not going to be your fault, is it? You'll be able to quantify why because of the excuses you live by.

Interestingly, as a coach, there are certain excuses which always seem to present themselves time and time again. Almost a common theme for those individuals who are 'head down' below the parapet. Let me share a few with you, give you some insight and as I do ask yourself if any of these are or have been excuses which have hindered, prevented or remain in the way of your growth and true potential.

- I never have enough time. The age-old excuse of never enough time, well we will be discussing time shortly. Suffice to say here, we all have the same amount of time every day, 84500 seconds to be precise, so why is it some people seem to be able to get so much more done? Self-discipline.
- I don't have enough money. In Chapter 2 we discussed the impact of having the poor mindset and here's how it manifests itself. If you believe you don't have enough money, then you're not asking the right questions or focusing on the activities which will directly impact on the money you require. It would also suggest you don't have or at least haven't unlocked your desire,

determination and commitment to make money. If you have now defined your dream and have clarity in regards to what you want to achieve then you should now be establishing where and how you'll be able to finance your dream.

• I don't have the resources. As an excuse, this one often reeks of self-pity. The bigger companies have all the resources, they have the ability I don't, is such BS. In the same light as money is a resource, so too are the other tools, people, systems you may feel you require. You are your primary resource in the very first instant and one which you need to put to work and hard work. This is really about inaction and inactivity, you don't need huge resources you need to get into action. Build from the bottom up and develop the resource you require as you grow.

• I need to finish some other stuff first. Really, now isn't the best time to make the commitment and get going. I often come across this excuse and more often than not it is a simple way to remain uncommitted. To stay in the comfort zone to shy away from your dreams and passion. If you have ever used this excuse or you are using it now then ask yourself just what needs to be completed, how vital is it for you to engage in your future, and how often has 'stuff' been the reason you remain where you are now? There will always be something else to do, something else which will get in the way, so ask yourself just how important your dreams are. Oh, another one here is the thought of long-term focus versus that short-term gain. Yes, in all likelihood you'll need to give up on a few things in order to reach your aspirations, and that may mean giving up those short-term hits.

• Now isn't good for me. In short if not now when? Think about this......When is NOW a good time to start? Think about that for a moment.

• It will never work. Wow, what an excuse, not even willing to get out there and give it a go, giving in before you've even got started. If you truly believe it won't work, then you're probably right! What's more, you'll live your life always questioning whether you should have done it. And if you do then you already know the answer should have been to give it a go.

• What if I fail? What if you fail? The more important question here is what if I live my life in regret for never having given it a chance, having a go, getting out there and doing it. If this is one of your excuses go back to Chapter 2 and understand the impact of FEAR and be clear just how it is holding you back.

When you also look deeply into the fear aspect, what exactly is it you are fearful of? What gaps do you need to fill in understanding, ability and commitment to overcome your fear? Be clear on specifically what it is you are fearful of, then rectify it.

- I lack the knowledge, skill or ability, I'm just don't have the ability. This is a great example of a complete inability to have the confidence to learn new things. To stretch your mind to develop new skills and ability. In the very simplest terms, you are not willing or have the belief you can learn new things. Really, pick up a book, research online, go on a course or attend a conference it's never too late to learn.

Interestingly with excuses, we are at least now recognising why you shouldn't, couldn't or won't follow your dreams. That's a good thing because at least it is now firmly in your mind's eye and we can now do something about it. As mentioned a number of times so far in this book (22 to be precise) awareness is a key responsibility I have as a coach. Now you can actively do something about the excuses, once you accept you are making them.

Blame

It wasn't my fault. Have you ever uttered those words by way of offering yourself silent consolation or verbalised to others? Had a moment when you were aware of what you should have done and didn't and your self-defence mechanism stepped in and allowed you to blame something or someone for your failure. When we reside below the parapet, in the bottom of the trench in our perceived safety, not getting above the parapet our actions become increasingly about self-preservation at all costs.

It's interesting to watch the dynamics of a body of people and observe the behaviours when things go well and there is success. Conversely, it's sickening to watch what happens when things go wrong, who are those who then go directly into self-preservation mode, looking out for themselves and seeking to lay blame on others. It shifts any responsibility away from us, and as with excuses allows us to remain safe in the comfort zone. It's not a good quality and whether you have experienced it or been guilty of it, the only focus here is self-preservation and being self-servient.

So why are there occasions where it feels right to lay blame elsewhere or on others? In fact, is there an occasion where it is ok to lay blame and protect yourself? In short, no, blame in my view is a despicable habit and one which will keep you firmly below the parapet. It will not allow you to embrace situations in a learning context, have the ability to grow in stature to develop and learn from mistakes, failure or inactivity. For me, blame is quite simply cowards in action.

Staying in the comfort zone, staying safe below the parapet in the bottom of the proverbial trench means we don't have to face our true ability, get uncomfortable or ultimately face our fears and grow. Think of it in the very simplest terms, getting out and maintaining a healthy regime can be tough, especially if you have to work hard at it. So it's far easier to blame circumstances or someone for inactivity and not reaching your goals.

When I was the Regimental Sergeant Major, a lofty rank and one where you have a significant responsibility to the maintenance of the 'Regiments' values, to maintaining the discipline to encouraging excellence throughout a battalion of over 600 there were those who fell into the trenches. Most notably on a Monday morning, there would be a collection of those who had found themselves in trouble, been in contra to standing orders and bringing the Regiments name into disrepute. More often than not as a result of a few too many alcoholic beverages.

Now in any large organisation, you'll have some who get themselves into trouble, innocently, as a result of poor judgment or just because they were bad apples. The fact is in the Military we had the regulations and the follow up disciplinary rules in place to deal with these indiscretions. Most businesses don't. Now the point here wasn't so much about the individuals rather one of the Company Sergeant Majors.

I would always be assured a call from Iain, C Company Sergeant Major if ever his troops stood outside my door on a Monday morning. For me, he had the utmost integrity and would never allow blame for his troops poor, inappropriate or bad behaviour anywhere but at his door. He would always call me and apologise for what the soldiers, not to lessen their dressing down or punishment, rather accept that as their Sergeant Major he had a duty to ensure they behaved in a manner befitting to C Company. He was quite simply revered by his company and unsurprisingly C Company had far fewer issues. He never laid blame on the individual he always sought to assume responsibility.

So, what are the circumstances where blame comes out and is prevalent, here are just a few:

- Status – a protection mechanism, to avoid or deter our name from being brought into disrepute. It protects our stature within our social circles, doesn't allow our reputation to be damaged and maintains our higher acclaim to the status we perceive we have within our social groups.

- Feelings – We don't generally want to feel bad and so laying blame away from ourselves protects our feelings. In essence, we can effectively make ourselves feel better by blaming others or circumstances. We also tend to feel better projecting our bad attitude towards others so laying blame makes us feel better, in a manner it appeases our feelings and reinforces the blame mindset.
- Attack and Defence – What about the situation where someone blames you, have you ever immediately retorted with a counter blame? Or maybe you have gone on the attack in the first instant and attacked someone else, blaming them in order to defend against being blamed.

Conditioning for Below the Parapet – The Fixed Mindset

Earlier in the book we discussed the mindset and how it will impact on our very being. Be under no illusion that if you have resonated with below the parapet fixed mindset you will or do blame others and circumstances for your failings and shortfall. If you recall in Chapter two we spoke of your blueprint, with regards to the abundant or poor mindset and the need for the offensive and growth mindset. The fixed mindset will not serve you well in seeking the life you truly desire. Understanding your blueprint and how it was imprinted on you, now is the time to make the shift away from it.

As we will discover when we discuss the mindset above the parapet, sticking your head above the parapet and the growth mindset, the first step to making the positive shift through self-actualisation. Become aware of your mindset and how it impacts, encourages, limits your thoughts and beliefs.

So what defines a fixed mindset? The following statements will offer a relatively simplistic and paradoxically detailed understanding of the thoughts a fixed mindset will evoke more often than not.

- Talent is not enough.
- Intelligence is static, you can only assimilate so much.
- Tell me I'm smart
- Failure is to be avoided and limits my ability
- If you succeed I feel threatened.
- Talent is the gift of aptitude.

167

- My potential is predetermined.
- I'm either good at it or not.
- I like to stick to what I know.
- I avoid challenges.
- Give's up easily.
- I don't enjoy being out of my comfort zone.
- Responds badly to feedback.
- If I don't try I will protect my dignity.
- It's not my fault, it's something or someone else's fault.

The fixed mindset will limit potential, even create glass ceilings and true belief that they are unable to break through. Their true potential will never be reached with a fixed mindset, whether in life, love or relationships. Interestingly as you read this what's your reaction? Has it shone a light on the fact you're more fixed than growth orientated? Are you even reading this in denial of the fact you seem to be predominantly fixed in your view of the world around you? Hey, that's ok because no one can hear what's going on in your head right now, you are the only audience. If that is the case, as you read on and as we start to explore the growth mindset be open to the infinite opportunities it offers.

You'll now start to see how being below the parapet will link directly to an individual's blueprint. What was the environment they grew up in, was there a general acceptance and focus on solutions and not blame excuse and denial? Just think for a moment, what was your circumstances and how has that gone on to impact you? In an ironic paradoxical twist, this is almost an opportunity to establish blame as to why you may reside below the parapet, and a review of the circumstances. If this is the point the penny drops, you then have no reason to remain with a fixed mindset and you need to start to redefine your blueprint, who do you want to be?

I guess in today's environment it is tough to face the mirror and take responsibility for who's looking back at you. We live in a world where blame excuse and denial are prevalent. Let's face it there is an entire industry built of the notion of 'where's there's blame there's a claim'. Every time you turn on the TV it seems someone or something is being blamed for our inadequacy, poor self-discipline or, poor results. We blame the health service for being unhealthy, yet we eat all the wrong things and don't exercise. We blame education for not preparing us for a working life, yet we won't study. Blame is almost the default to laying blame elsewhere, because it ratifies us, makes us actually feel better for a short period, helps us to make sense and accept our lot in life. The point is you have a choice and that choice defines who you are and what you want to achieve. The great news is you make the decision.

If you don't want a positive mindset that's ok, have a negative one.

If you don't want to live a healthy lifestyle, that's ok be unhealthy.

If you don't want to be happy, that's ok be unhappy.

If you don't want wealth, that's ok be poor.

If you don't want to have freedom of choice, that's ok be restricted.

If you don't want to have fun, it's ok to be bored.

If you don't want to be educated, it's ok to be ignorant.

If you don't want to find love, it's ok to be unloved.

If you don't want to be committed, it's ok to be uncommitted.

If you don't want to be successful, its ok to be a failure.

Now my guess is you probably do want a life where these things matter. So, make the choice, decide if you're willing to go after them with vigour, to get your head above the parapet and take a long hard look at what's going on and what to do about it.

Whatever your circumstance, wherever you work, whatever your position, conduct a review today regarding your circumstances, your blueprint. Are you faced with below the parapet activity and responses walking amidst others at the bottom of the trench? Are there a few who reside at the bottom of the trenches and as a result always seek the easy below the parapet way out and in the course of doing so infect others and start the blame game. Are there those who attempt to infect you, the organisation and your environment?

Check to see if there is a general feeling of being stuck in the past. A sense that things are the way they are because it's always been that way and it works just fine. Does it? Or is there a real resistance and avoidance of change in any way shape or form. There will be no circumstance where certain individuals, family, friends, members of teams or departments will embrace any change rather seek to stop it, deter it and just not accept it. They quite frankly have absolutely no interest in growth.

169

What about the language you use? We have a tendency to be very lazy with the use of language, not very engaged in how best to respond to our own ideas, those of others or communicating in general. There are a group of words which seem very innocuous, just words which we use daily and on the face of it probably words you use with some regularity without even contemplating the limitations they set. The damage they do to your mindset or how they impact on others. Yes, whilst these words can be used in a context which has none of the above impacts, in my experience and having now spoken with 1000's of business owners and leaders they have a major limiting effect. It's also one which will last until something is done to balance out your vocabulary.

No

But

I Know

Now, I have already touched on the impact of language in direct reference to limiting beliefs and decision making in Chapter 2. I would like to now give you a far more in-depth understanding of the impact of these words and more importantly how to effectively manage and replace the use of them.

If you recall we have spoken about the power of the unconscious mind, the fact that we tend to only use 5% of our mind in conscious thought whilst 95% of our brain is unconsciously working in the background. What's interesting here is the impact your unconscious mind has on the language you use and its context. No, is a great example of your unconscious mind in full flow. When, in discussion with someone an idea, suggestion or thought is shared and when you respond the very first word out is NO, what do you think your unconscious mind is saying? Regardless of the context of what follows, it's NO.

When we respond with NO first we are subconsciously saying that we don't agree, with, support or like the idea, suggestion or thought being offered. Regardless of the following words and statement after NO, even if they are a positive response, your subconscious mind is saying NO. By way of an example:

Friend – *I have a great plan to deal with the problem we have and you're going to love it.*

You – *No, that's sound very interesting what's the plan?*

170

Do you think the plan is interesting as a proposition and you'll love it? You don't. Quite the opposite, you probably don't want to hear the plan and you've already decided that you are not going to love it. Now, believe it or not there is a level to just how much you disagree with, dislike or oppose when using NO at the beginning of a sentence. No matter how affirming or positive the response thereafter. If the sentence is started with a double NO. *No, no, that's sounds very interesting what's the plan? Or. No, no, no, that sounds very interesting what's the plan?*

It would be unusual if right now you're a little sceptical, I never use NO at the beginning of a sentence and I certainly haven't heard anyone doing it, let alone do it yourself. You're probably right after all, your brain does have the ability to filter out elements it doesn't want to interpret, especially when you are being given a positive response. Listen for it over the next few days in yourself and others, it's there.

The next is the use of the word BUT, which we have highlighted already in Chapter 2 when we spoke about limiting beliefs. In both your inner and external dialogue if you use BUT you are holding yourself back. Now there will be the linguistics out there telling me that but has its uses and they are correct, not in my vocabulary though! I'm doing my very utmost to absolutely eradicate the word from my vocabulary and I'm not doing too badly. At this point in the book, you will have now read a little over 62000 words, of that BUT (not including this one) has only been used 20 times, and that's not bad, in fact just reflect on your use? The point is to be clear on the language you use and to listen carefully to how it impacts on you. It should never limit your beliefs, actions, behaviours, thoughts or desires.

Now I'm a retired officer so I would like to also share with you the posh but; HOWEVER. When we seek to use BUT and I suggest we should change it and maybe use AND, as previously suggested, it's not unusual to hear however creep into the conversation. Now I can tell you with some confidence having had many conversations with senior generals when I was in the Officers Mess that however is a posh version of BUT.

Captain Gaskell – *General I have a great idea and plan which you're going to love, sir.*

General Dogsbody – *No,no,no, that's a wonderful idea, however .........*

Whether you believe me or not, your vocabulary will reinforce your limiting beliefs, it will hold you back and you're going to be too lazy to realise it. Just tune in today to see if you suffer if you are a BUT Ninja!

My last insight into our laziness when it comes to language is by far the most expensive. I KNOW. In business, these two words together cost business owners, leaders and managers a fortune every day. I would love to be able to give you statistics as to just how much these words cost businesses in general, unfortunately, it's a case of taking my word for it. Let's put it this way within the 1000's of business owners I've spoken with it's going to be millions of pounds. Sadly, I recall a number of businesses I have previously approached to open discussions to explore the potential impact of businesses coaching, some of which knew best, sadly, some are no longer here today. I Know was a symptom and it cost them.

It never ceases to amaze me the way in which some allow their minds to work. Let me put this into context. You're ill, you know you're ill, you know something isn't right and you know what you must do. Visit the doctor and discuss the embarrassing ailment. You don't, it gets worse, you take more painkillers, then one day it's just too late. Sound familiar? Probably not, you're educated, intelligent people, aren't you? You would go to the doctors in good time and seek prevention rather than cure! Wouldn't you? And yet it seems today there is so many who die knowing they needed to visit the doctor.

Having engaged with 1000's of business owners, now clearly, they didn't all come on as clients, would have been nice! During that conversation, I met with those who were open to exploring coaching, those who engaged with coaching and those who already knew everything they needed to know! In simple terms, they were where they were. More often than not, actually not where they wanted to be. As I raised awareness with them, discussed just what they needed to do, or how they needed to do it or offered a simple insight to where and how things could be better. What do think the response was? I KNOW. They knew where, what and how they needed to move forward, to grow, to get out of the rut, yet in many cases long after I had engaged with them they didn't.

Here's the thing, I KNOW is a barrier to growth and to grow we need to learn, develop, adapt gain experience and try new things. Having the 'I KNOW' attitude merely hinders and slows, if not halts your growth, and if you're not growing your dying. 'I Know' serves no purpose in your business, within your organisation or within your team and certainly not in your life. Just think for a moment what has been the impact and response for you when someone else responded to you with 'I KNOW', how did it make you feel.

As I have mentioned on a number of occasions throughout this book we are generally lazy with the language we use. I know offers another lazy tendency and it is one of the fine distinctions of knowing and having knowledge. Many circumstances when we use 'I Know' there will be recognition in what we are hearing, in all likelihood limited knowledge. The fine distinction is understanding the difference between recognition and knowledge. In business, it can be costly. Not gain the available knowledge because we know or recognise what is being said can deprive us of valuable information and knowledge.

There simply is no excuse for 'I KNOW', slamming the preverbal door in someone's face! It's not very nice and certainly won't encourage personal development, growth in you, the business or team. So why do we use the phrase the gap filler, or barrier so much? I sense once again it's just about having lazy and bad habits when we come to use language, it's probably an automatic response. Might be we don't want to be challenged, haven't enough time, don't want to be seen as not being the all-knowing oracle, or just simply rude. Whatever your reason one thing you can be sure of it's costing you.

In the first instant, you need to fully engage with the idea that you don't know everything, you don't have all the answers, you aren't the oracle and no one has the ability to see the future. This is about having an open mind, accepting the next best idea may come from the most surprising place or person. You need to take 'I KNOW' out of your daily vocabulary and shift towards a response like 'ISN'T THAT INTERESTING', keeping the door of opportunity open.

Now, this isn't about being all woolly and fluffy, not being the boss, the leader or manager. It's not about undermining your ability to need to take decisions, to have to define a particular course of action and get on with it. This is about allowing yourself access to knowledge from wherever it may be presented. There will be occasions where the information you are receiving you know and that's ok. The point here is being smart about how you respond, don't slam the door in their face. Let them know you understand, you have the information already and maybe you don't agree. The point here is to acknowledge in such a manner to expand opportunity not limit it, for both you and them.

With a below the parapet fixed mindset there is a high possibility that your circumstances, your beliefs are re-enforced through asking poor questions. Asking judging questions. In life, every encounter, every interaction, every conversation offers us a learning outcome. The ability to walk away knowing more, gaining more knowledge and by virtue expanding your personal understanding and knowledge. Yet we so often miss these opportunities, through ignorance and lazy use of language, as we discussed. So, here's the thing, stop asking judging questions.

Judging Questions

So, what is a judging question? Judging questions are those which evoke an emotional, below the parapet response. For me the most often used and least understood question is the use of WHY! So often why is used in conversation as a lazy response to understand the circumstance which has led to a less than favourable outcome or situation or failure. Why did that …? Why did you do …? Why didn't you do …? Why are you …? Why has the ….? Why would …? The challenge with why questions are they more often than not evoke an emotional response. Rather than the focus on process or procedure, they are either targeted at an individual or the response is taken at a personal level.

A great example, so often misunderstood and misused would be the well-established and know, 5 whys root cause analysis. In the book, the Rockefeller Habits, Verne Harnish (Harnish, 2006) offers the simplest example when he explains the 5 whys and their use. Let me explain. It's not about the analysis it's about the questions you ask and how. When you ask 'why' what type of response do you think you are going to get? Above or below the parapet? You'll get a below the parapet response, think about it for a moment when you are asked why how does that tend to make you feel? The point here and one highlighted by Verne is the why question works only when it is focused on process and procedure. Don't ask a why question of an individual, it generally won't end well, insofar as to their external or internal response.

You may be given verbal blame, excuse or denial or they may harbour an emotional response which damages the relationship or their future productivity and motivation, long-lasting damage. Pursuing that focus and asking another 4 why questions in order to gain insight to the root cause doesn't evoke the greatest of responses from the person being questioned. I would suggest in the majority of cases it would steadily drive the person further below the parapet. Now in principle, the 5 whys work and works really well in the context of establishing the root or true cause when we focus on process and procedure and not people.

So, you can see for me as a coach that WHY is a judging question and lazy? I'm not a fan as a coach of using the 'why question' in any context. In fact, I avoid it at all costs. In a coaching session, it adds no value and merely demonstrates a simplistic and lazy questioning technique.

Learning Questions

As a coach seek always to ask 'learning questions'. Seeking out the root or true cause in a manner which encourages a greater deal of thought in both query and answer. 'Why' will merely have someone answer in a rear-facing manner, looking to the past, it will be a canned and hollow response and most damaging it will be a response which they believe they should make, which is what they suspect wants or needs to be the answer. It's also more likely the chimp in response because we are tapping straight into an emotion.

Being lazy when it comes to the use of language (have I mentioned that already!), always seeking the simplest solution. It's very easy to ask a why question, there's no need to think about it at all, you merely pass on the responsibility to the other party with no thought as to the effect on them. The fact you will be limiting the true response, the deeper meaning which is certainly where there will be a rich source of meaning and learning.

In order to uncover a deeper meaning and enrich the questioning or conversation, we need to be focused on dialogue through questioning. 'Learning questions' take thought, they take a moment's contemplation to ask yourself 'what is the best learning outcome' in this situation? In this situation, what would the best outcome be for interviewer and interviewee? It means we have to process what's been said, we have to take a moment to understand. Where we would have normally have moved onto the next why we must contemplate the answer before the next question. Take a moment's reflection.

Learning questions also force us to listen and listen intently, as Steven Covey states (Covey S. , 1989) seek first to understand. Listening or more critically effective listening means you need to be present, fully present. Think for a moment to the questions you ask now and the manner in which you ask them. Do you wait for the interviewee to finish their point, give them the space to complete their point of view and in a suitable environment? Or do you have an agenda when you start to ask questions, have you one purpose to reinforce your position and status or make sure you are heard, and your point of view is heard? All of which will reinforce a below the parapet fixed mindset response.

Furthermore and in addition to the learning outcomes, it will also increase the level of accountability in the interviewee. There will be a process of reflecting which will lead to greater outcomes because they have to search deeper for the answer, not just an excuse, denial or blame. In order to start a path of asking and more importantly focusing on achieving a learning outcome these are some techniques you could use:

- AWE? In his book 'The Coaching Habits' (Stanier, 2016) Michael introduces the concept of AWE, 'AND WHAT ELSE?' I'm a big fan of simplicity and this is the archetypal solution. Once you have opened the query and questioning 'and what else' keeps the response alive. It encourages deeper thought, greater self-awareness, uncovers greater possibilities and ultimately leads to a far greater learning. And what else is by far one of the most powerful and simple questioning techniques.

- Encourage a story. What's the story behind that? We all love stories, we love being told stories and we love telling stories. Encouraging a storytelling response will encourage a greater flow in their response.

- The five solid gold questions, as Alan Pease (Pease A. ) highlights in his book Questions are the answer are a very useful series of questions to ask. In outline the questions are:
  o What is/ was your No 1 priority/ focus/aim/the desired outcome?
  o You picked that one because?
  o And that's important to you because?
  o What are the consequences of not having the opportunity?
  o That would worry you?

- Your question will need to be specific. So often we are asked questions and not actually understand just how to answer it. Have you ever been asked a question and not really understood what answer to offer? Ensure your question is clearly understood and specific.

- Avoid the drive to interrupt the answer and offer your insight. Merely demonstrating your understanding. It is ok to interrupt to reinforce your understanding; 'so I'm clear you mean ..', 'what your saying is ..' Etc..

Asking a learning outcome should focus on a learning outcome for both you and the interviewee. Avoid asking leading questions, they will ultimately result in your impacting on the ability to offer an authentic and unbiased response. This isn't an opportunity to or about demonstrating your level of intellect. A good learning question will promote deep thinking and critical reflection. It will really engage the brain. Interestingly this will be the case for both parties.

One aspect of asking a learning question is being confident to go deep. As the questioning progresses there is an opportunity to gain a deeper understanding. This is where we are able to apply the principles of '5 Whys' without ever asking why. Through this process, you can uncover the true cause and have a significant long-lasting learning outcome. The true outcome for a growth mindset and above the parapet outcome.

**Above the Parapet**
Now, shifting your mindset and taking a look above the parapet takes a strong sense of purpose, self-awareness and personal courage. Just because you're getting above the parapet doesn't mean life will suddenly become rosy. You'll be faced with the same challenges you had the day before. Problems don't simply disappear. The stresses and pressure of life will remain, the difference will be the manner in which you deal with them, the manner in which you view and focus on them. The sense of challenge in facing them will also, in a paradoxical way, strengthen your resolve and commitment.

So where does the development of an above the parapet mindset begin? What are the progressive steps and habits you're going to need to embrace and constantly develop to remain above the parapet and make the positive shift in your life? The first step is about perception, understanding that it is you at the centre of your universe, it is you who reacts and responds to your interaction with life. It is you and your mindset who interprets and decodes your experiences. If you have a fixed mindset tendency, which will determine your response, actions and behaviours you will need to make a significant shift. So, the first step above the parapet, the first glimpse you take above the parapet will be to take responsibility.

Responsibility

This is the first major step to take complete uncompromising responsibility for your life. It's your life and you are responsible to live it. Responsible for every element of it. At the very basic level, no one else is going to live it for you. Some will try and influence your life, some will try to have you follow a specific path. The fact of the matter is you will have made a choice and decided to do or don't do. If right now you have been following a life's agenda which is not yours then make a choice to change it. This is probably the most important part of truly getting and remaining above the parapet, sticking your head right over the parapet, is to acknowledge it's your life and you'll choose how to live it.

In all probability, you've picked up this book because you want to improve the potential and future of your business. Well, the great news is that as a business owner you made a choice when you launched it to take responsibility. It's probably the impact of the challenges since getting underway which keeps you in the trenches or reinforces a fixed mindset. I guarantee, the same applies, your business, your responsibilities! Here's a simple notion, everything which goes wrong, is difficult, tough or fails is your fault. Let me say that again, IT'S YOUR FAULT!

Tough I know, there you have it. Now the first major step in this transition to taking responsibility is a realisation that you count, you matter, your business matters and your thoughts, ideas and actions matter. That's why you're in business. At some point, you decided to take responsibility for your path and decided that you could do whatever you do in business to such a level that you'll succeed. And then it got a little tough, hard work maybe, made some mistakes, failed even and then found yourself in denial, offered excuses and blamed everything except yourself!

So, in all likelihood, you've come from a place of responsibility to now find yourself in a place where you feel reluctance to step up once again. Let's be clear here, no matter what happens you have choices, even when things happen out of your control you can decide to learn from them, become stronger and move on. Choose a path of productivity, contribution, believe what you think matters and what you share will assist others. No matter how small a contribution be responsible in all I think, do and commit to.

It's further likely that you have boundaries and limits to your responsibility, probably unconsciously as the technician in your business you focus only on your technical ability. Probably the reason you started the business in the first place. Having already discussed the 3 elements of the business mind, the technician, manager and entrepreneur (Gerber, 1995) here we will often see first-hand the effect. Now, this isn't a bad thing, it's merely a fact that we need to widen the sphere of responsibility.

Let's take for instance the 3 elements of the business mindset for a moment and ask ourselves just how much responsibility we have taken for them? In all likelihood, you'll have a great deal of focus as the technician, having a great deal of knowledge is what you do and how to do it. Have a detailed and comprehensive understanding of what you do in your business it is highly likely you'll have a very high level of unconscious competence, you don't realise just how much you know because you just do it naturally.

It's unlikely you'll be able to say the same for the management of the business. The normal tell-tale signs would be outstanding debt, backlog of quotes, poor follow up on leads, poor invoicing, inefficient administration etc.. The fundamentals of what it takes to run a business might not be so fluid. You as yet haven't taken responsibility for these functions and it's likely you don't see them as important because it's all about the technical focus in the business and keeping up with that!

Then we have the entrepreneurial element to take responsibility for, where is the business heading what are you aiming to achieve? The same applies here, with little or no sight of what you aim to achieve we move from one job to the next, hand to mouth. It's isn't unusual here to have completely lost sight of why we first got into business. What is it we aimed to achieve in the first place? As we assume responsibility across the whole of the business we start to see the bigger picture and steadily move from self-employed, owning a job towards being the business owner.

I would be surprised as you read this, having already read about blame, excuse and denial and having referred to the fixed mindset traits that you, even at this point have an inner voice shouting BULL SHIT! Still refusing to see how your choices have shaped where and who you are today, right now. If this isn't you I'm delighted, we have progressed. As a coach, I understand these thoughts, feelings and behaviours can and are often deep-seated, not easy to shift. Well before you move on, take the opportunity to realise and accept you own them, no one else. Realisation that your thoughts and their impact are yours and yours alone, will be a major step in the right direction and paradoxically taking responsibility.

If that voice, at this stage, is still there, then go back to chapter 2 and understand the root cause of your limiting beliefs and determine which habits you need to adopt. With realisation comes the choice, you can simply choose to stay as you are or make change. Actively move towards a growth mindset towards personal and business growth. I certainly don't know anyone who wants to harbour limiting beliefs or who wants to be negative and prefers to remain unaccomplished.

Now the great news with taking responsibility is that you'll soon discover that solutions will avail themselves. You'll start to see the wood for the trees. You will attract success, steadily. Essentially, you're going to encourage a positive growth mindset. You'll start to actively take responsibility across many fronts, from your circumstances to your team's mistakes, to losing customers or not making the sale and with this level of realisation and acceptance you'll grow, learn and develop robust coping mechanisms. It will essentially lead to a comprehension and awareness, which is that next step in the journey above the parapet. It will also vastly improve your self-esteem and sense of empowerment.

Review your learnings so far, go back and remind yourself what the dream is, what it is you want to achieve and the vision of getting there. There is no surprise I have already challenged you to complete these exercises, they will focus the mind on your life and how you want to live it. Know who you are, who you want to be, what you want to achieve and stop making excuses, blaming others and being truly aware and out of denial result in a high level of responsibility.

Accountability

With the focus on taking responsibility you naturally become responsible and with responsibility comes clarity, of mind, purpose and where you are heading. In turn, this leads to heightened accountability. With increased accountability, you tune into your life at a higher level and you tune into to new opportunities which would certainly have been missed had you not taken first responsibility and then become more aware. Let me be clear here, we are focusing on a level of accountability which will improve your life, business and pursuit of the life you seek. You become account*able*.

Having discussed the virtues, well the negative virtues of being in the bottom of the trench, below the parapet, it's about your perception. Whilst you will be aware of your surroundings it is your perception of your circumstance which will reduce the level of accountability and encourages a deeper sense of blame, excuses and ultimately denial. Our perception might suggest we are not responsible, we don't take responsibility for our circumstances or the factors we own within the business. Our level of accountability is masked with a distance between what we experience and our perception of it. When we step up above the parapet we also shift our perception and having taken responsibility for where we are, what we have achieved and maybe what we haven't we are able to increase our state of awareness towards being truly accountable.

We can, therefore, begin to see the natural progression from responsibility to accountability. As the business owner, you'll become aware of the wider context of what you need to focus on and how you can become a better business owner. Having taken responsibility for the technical, managerial and entrepreneurial elements within your business your awareness of what now needs to be done starts to come into clear focus, you take an account.

It isn't unusual at this point to have overwhelm creep in. Suddenly we go from a paradoxical blissful ignorance to suddenly being confronted with potentially many additional areas of responsibility. Your awareness increases significantly as you now start to piece together the areas and factors within the business which need to be addressed. Interestingly with each, there then comes further depth of knowledge and the realisation of what needs to be achieved. This can seem to be a significant challenge becoming accountable towards just what is required, what should be acted upon and the ability to then deliver it.

Taking account is the first step towards acquiring knowledge, determining just what it is you need to know in your business. This is a significant step towards taking ownership. You become responsible for the choices you make, with this comes need, necessity and learning. As an example, you take responsibility for the fact your business is lacking new business. You take responsibility and now seek to understand what the cause has been. You now realise the need, increased lead conversion, whilst there may be interest in what you are doing in the business you haven't been converting. As your analysis gets underway you then establish what is necessary to make the shift. From here you then become accountable in terms of what you haven't been doing and what you should have been doing; you have taken account of the situation and accountability for it.

It is said knowledge is power and when you think about it there is truth to that. In my opinion, knowledge leads to power only when the knowledge is applied. There's no point in having a wealth of knowledge and doing nothing with it. Being aware of just what we need to understand, learn and develop is first preceded by the need to be aware of just what the learning agenda needs to be. I rather hope as you have read this book you will have encountered a number of BFO's. I mentioned Blinding Flashes of the Obvious at the very beginning of the book, to set your mind to receive, to make sure as you started to turn the pages you had a level of expectation to potentially find the inspiration or insight you are looking for.

A blinding flash of the obvious is a great example of accountability in play. By virtue of reading the book you have taken a level of responsibility, you have told yourself that it's time to take control, to shift, that there must be a better or more effective way. You've taken responsibility. As you have read the book, you have encountered a number of BFO's, well at least I hope you have. So, what is the anatomy of a BFO?

As you read the passages there is a trigger.

WoW that's a great idea

Your psychology shifts

You have a feeling of excitement, interest maybe positivity

There is a heightened awareness

'Why didn't I think of that'

You look to where, how and what it will impact, you take account

You begin to establish the 'what ifs'

'What if I do this then this will happen' you have taken account

You have started the learning process

Analysing just what the likely outcome could be

There may even be excitement to the point of wanting to get started now

You now have a significantly higher level of awareness

What was, what is and what will be

Accountability is a significant step towards having a success mindset and embedding the success habits. It enables you to have a clear focus on where the opportunities are, what you need to do and the application of doing it. Your realisation regarding the need for greater lead conversion leads to your BFO that you haven't been disciplined with following up the leads as they have come into the business. You become aware that you lack the skills and confidence to pick the phone up (interestingly one of the most irrational fears in business). You determine what the learning agenda needs to be and get underway, with the excitement of foreseeing what the impact is going to be on the business. Sure enough, you start to follow up with far greater regularity and your conversion rate increases as does business. You have taken account and become accountable.

There is also a deeper level of accountability, remembering on average we are only utilising 5% of our brain power when we are awake. Through a greater level of being accountable, we can now actively programme our subconsciousness. This relates to the setting of your RAS, which we discussed earlier. Being truly accountable will allow us to programme our consciousness or more accurately our subconsciousness. We can actively write the programme of who you want to be, what you want to achieve, what opportunities you seek and start to shape what your tomorrow looks like. Being tuned into a far higher level.

This level of accountability and awareness directly links into the 'Law of Attraction' and having the focus to ensure you focus on a positive vibe and by virtue allow yourself to tune into positive opportunities. The focus on setting goals will shift towards attracting what you seek, actively focusing on attracting the outcome of the goal.

So where are you right now, what level of accountability have you? I'd rather hope your level of responsibility and accountability will have significantly increased as you have read this book. It will certainly increase in the final chapter when we explore some of the fundamental areas in business you should and need to have a handle on. As for right now what do you know already?

What do you understand in direct relation to your experience to date?

What have you already achieved?

What have you learnt from the mistakes and failures so far?

What do you know regarding the current trends in your business or industry?

What commercial accountability do you possess currently?

It's an interesting factor when we truly start to tune into a greater sense of accountability off the back of heightened responsibility it can be the catalyst for significant change. Having taken responsibility for where you are now and what has been achieved focuses primarily on factors which have been presented and are being presented. This, in turn, leads to accountability.

The entire principle of raising awareness as to accountability will result in decision making. Interestingly one which is as simple as to respond to it or not. I have experienced many who have chosen the latter, essentially to actively remain ignorant of the situation. Even knowing they should be accountable. When questioned there is a profuse use of 'I Know' and 'But', which merely goes to frustrate and infuriate the individual when seeking a rational reason for not acting. The point here is accountability on its own is one thing being accountable is another!

You can have all the awareness in the world, in fact, be the all-knowing oracle, the fact remains the choices it then offers are where positive shift happens. It is, for this reason, the ascendance from responsibility to being accountable is key. Essentially if you haven't taken responsibility you can and likely will choose blissful unawareness! Yes, that's right you will choose not to respond and that's the recipe for disaster.

So, we can see that there is an ascendance from responsibility to accountability, thankfully the true result of getting above the parapet comes with the ultimate consciousness and realisation and that is taking ownership. Through your accountability, you will also begin to focus on what needs to be managed. The managerial process will be a significant step toward systemisation and process within the business. You will take account of what needs to be systemised, what requires process and what requires to be monitored and measure your KPIs. We will pick up on these aspects in some detail in the final chapter. Key now though is the ascent to ownership.

Ownership

When we truly ascend to the height of getting above the parapet, truly surveying all that is happening on the field of operations in business when ownership is embraced and engaged with. Ownership means simply that, owning the challenge, an opportunities the problems, being the 'Captain of the Ship'. Taking ownership can only result in better things because there is a drive to do something with that knowledge.

Let's look at this with the analogy of 'owning a ship' becoming the captain. When we have responsibility on board, it's likely we'll have a crew members mindset, a technical responsibility and that's what will be focused on. Having the technical ability was the reason you entered into business in the first place. To move away from being an employee and having others reap the rewards of your skills and ability towards you gaining the benefit. And so, it was when you entered into business and got underway you the technician went about delivering your service, what it is you do.

Here's the challenge when you're on your own ship you can't just be the technician, because you have a ship to run. You have the various functions on board which you need to be able to maintain. Taking ownership means you have to maintain all the aspects of your business. In the course of time, you will undoubtedly build a team who will, in turn, have responsibility on board your ship. It means you'll be on the bridge running your ship, leading the business. Able to set the course, determine the speed at which you want to progress, build the team and remain on the bridge leading your business.

Now you may be thinking that there is no room or current capacity to grow a team, in which case you're probably right and your ship is a single engine cruiser. Here you'll need to remain all things to your business and that's hard work, you'll need to remain on the bridge and when you need to deliver and or maintain the other functions you'll have to slow or stop the ship to conduct that function, and that's ok as long as you remain in control. In the course of time, you will establish where you grow your team, which may first be the external support elements, your accountant, IT support, marketing or your coach. This will, in turn, lead to your internal team at which point you'll be able to spend more time on the bridge navigating the business waters ahead.

There is a euphoric feeling which accompanies ownership, a sense of doing things right, being able to focus on what will ultimately grow your business. Significant change and shift happens when we embrace and gain ownership, the understanding that you are truly in charge of your destiny. It will often be the first time for many business owners when they truly step into the realm of being a true business owner, have moved from employee, to self-employed to manager to business owner. It is the start of being able to truly focus on business growth and not business survival.

*The Pyramid of Ownership*

Conditioning to be above the Parapet – The Growth Mindset

I'm really clear as you read this, whilst you may feel invigorated, inspired maybe even excited there is a kind of utopian pursuit living above the parapet. Seeking always to be responsible, have gained accountability and taking ownership. The challenge right now for you is the fact you are living in your personal habitual circumstances, probably doing what you have always done. In many respects blissfully unaware of your true potential. In order to start down this course, you'll need to implement much of what we have discussed in chapter one, getting out of your own way and determining where you want to get to. Removing your barriers. You'll need also to develop your offensive mindset as described in Chapter 2 and the shift your habits towards those defined to create and support success, Chapter 3.

Feedforward

It is at this point I'd like to introduce you to a concept I first came across when I was fortunate enough to have been coached by one of the greatest coaches in the world, Marshall Goldsmith. Now you will all know and have a view on giving and or receiving feedback. Giving feedback in many organisations is a requirement for appraisals and performance rating, quite often in a downward manner. Although today there is a focus on 360 appraisals thus enabling an upward contribution to feedback.

The point here and one Marshall made extremely succinctly is where we gain feedback from. The past. Feedback focuses on what has already happened and the critical point here is there is nothing we can do to change that. We talk of learning lessons from the past and in the vast majority of cases that's ok. Nonetheless, it remains a very static and limited method to offer an assessment. Feedforward conversely focuses on the future and here lies the enormous magnitude of its impact, there are infinite opportunities tomorrow offers. The decision we make today can have a dynamic and exciting consequence and results.

Offering feedforward requires a focus on what could be, advice and guidance on what you should or could do tomorrow. Now subtle as the shift is from feedback to feedforward the impact of offering actual insight into how to improve and where to improve is immense. In many respects, this links closely to the law of attraction we discussed in Chapter 1. We aim not to focus on the negative aspect of what has happened, the fact we can't do anything about it and our inability, poor performance or whatever is being reinforced. Rather we focus on the positive aspects of what to do better and where to focus from this point.

Clearly, feedforward can be based on our learnings from the past, we are just not going to anchor ourselves there or deliver the advice in past context. We will focus on the future, that which we can influence and impact on, where we can make a difference, be better and offer improvement. Feedforward, when embraced and delivered in this manner has a dramatic impact and can really create a positive shift for individuals, the team and organisation. It resides firmly with a growth mindset.

You can see there has been a good reason in developing the structure of the book and getting to this point, there is much you need to develop, new habits you need to embrace. Cease old habits in a bid to design your new redefined blueprint, a blueprint for success. Essentially making a positive shift to define what will be your growth mindset. Now, this will take time and effort and the ability to modify your thinking in reinforcing what you want to achieve, by when and in what manner. In the same context, as with the fixed mindset, you'll start to resonate with some of these statements as you develop your growth mindset if you're not already:

- It's not about talent, I can learn anything new I want.
- Intelligence can expand and grow, I'm like a sponge.
- I appreciate my abilities.
- Failure offers a learning experience.
- If you succeed I'm inspired.
- Talent is a life pursuit.
- My true potential is untapped.
- Good is part way on the journey of great.
- I like to expand upon what I know.
- I embrace challenges.
- I am resilient.
- I aim to expand my comfort zone.
- Uses feedforward rather than feedback.
- Nothing ventured nothing gained.
- I am accountable for myself.

In my experience, there is no quick fix. Very few if any wake one morning and have made a shift from fixed to growth. That said and as mentioned at the beginning of the book there will be occasions where the BFO's are so profound as to encourage a significant shift from one state to the next. You may have experienced some already. You need to be aware that in order to make the shift, assuming you want to, you will experience and encounter difficulty. Interestingly it is this difficulty which often results in giving up because it's all too hard. What's critical here is expect that difficulty, even embrace it, understand that your true ascent to ownership through responsibility and accountability will require it. To take true ownership we need to experience and get through perturbation.

**Perturbation**
Now in all likelihood, you may understand perturbation to mean anxiety, mental uneasiness; feeling perturbed. I'd like to explain it in reference to its definition *'when a deviation of a system, moving object, or process from its regular or normal state or path, caused by an outside influence'*. It is this application and context of perturbation which I'll focus on in reference to making a change and gaining ownership. To explain perturbation, we need to be reminded of a fundamental lesson in science. Making steam.

Firstly, we need to understand that in order to achieve ownership we will need to change. Think of that for a moment within your circumstances, if you have resonated with getting above the parapet, then in all likelihood where you want to be, what you want to achieve will require a shift, change to think and do things differently. Maybe even significantly shift your knowledge towards becoming a better version of you. Embracing change is key to making a meaningful embedded shift.

So back to making steam.

As we know steam comes from boiling water and it is that moment that the water molecules make the shift from being a fluid to become steam that perturbation is achieved. Perturbation is the impact of the external pressure which triggers the change from a solid to gas. In the case of boiling water that's heat. When we place a pan of water onto a source of heat we will soon start to see agitation. The water begins to heat up and we start to see bubbles forming and the water begins to boil. It is at this point, at 100°C, that water makes the shift to becoming steam, perturbation. The external pressure is significant enough to create the shift from one state to the next. Water to steam.

In your life and in business it will be a fact that to get to where you want to you will need to make a shift, to change and that will require your perturbation. Now if you think for a moment, in reference to perturbation, it is primarily the change in your emotions, your response to the changed situation, circumstances and cause where you will experience the change. A shift in mindset. The way in which you responded will absolutely determine the outcome. Will the shift result in fixed or growth emotional mindset outputs?

188

To allow benefit from the change it will require a growth emotional response, an understanding that shifting from one state to the next is positive and will result in a positive outcome. Seeing it through, remaining committed to the outcome you desire, even when it may not result favourably maintaining your resolve to work it out, take ownership. The growth response to perturbation is the manner in which you need to have made a prior commitment. Having the understanding that you will experience perturbation will allow you to pre-determine your reaction and response.

What's the alternative, clearly the fixed mindset onset of perturbation. How did you react the last time you were faced with a difficulty or unsavoury situation? Did you step up to the mark or opt for the course of least resistance, maybe somewhere in between, or it may have resulted in a 'head in the sand' moment. Essentially procrastination in its primary function. It is likely you experienced a fixed response and rather than experience the growth opportunity you simply protected yourself from the difficulties which you face through the experience.

The external pressure will evoke a response which will, in turn, impact your emotional state, what you feel. The growth or fixed mindset response. In many cases, at this point, I have witnessed the chimp running rampant, defining the outcome because this is so much harder than I thought it was going to be. Sadly, the outcome in these circumstances is all too often to give up because it's getting too difficult. In attaining true ownership and being in a place where you are truly above the parapet will require, in all likelihood significant change from where you are now to where you want to be and that means growth. An emotional shift in your ability to deal with, respond to and act upon change. Your inner self really needs to be in charge, that side of you which is driven to get to where you want to be.

It is here where there is a significant realisation on a number of levels; ever had the thought 'I never realised I had it in me? Did I just do that? Was that me?' In each case and in all probability, you wouldn't have thought it possible to do, act or respond in the manner you did. Whilst these by context can be described as a fixed response, paradoxically you have experienced a growth outcome reviewing what was achieved. The external pressure often brings out the best in you merely because that's what we are designed to do under pressure.

By virtue of experiencing perturbation, your body and mind will almost certainly experience stress, the release of cortisol. As we have previously discussed for short periods this offers a heightened state of awareness and ability to physically act. Understanding this is a natural response is the key to having it work in your benefit. The risk here is seeking a hit of dopamine, which will result in a fixed mindset response, this will come in the form of procrastination, wanting to avoid the tough decisions, seeking the course of least resistance, looking for the 'quick fix'. All too often will result in your staying where you are, not growing, not developing, not moving towards your goals.

Getting through perturbation is not easy and will take significant focus, commitment, pig-headed discipline, higher level responsibility and awareness may present itself as you experience growth and the associated growing pains. You will already have an idea what the barriers are going to be, that will give you a good idea of just what you need to break them down. To make a breakthrough.

In Chapter 1 I had you complete an exercise to determine where you are now and where you aim to be in 12 months to 3 years from now. Go back and remind yourself or maybe complete it, if you skipped over it. The point here is one of taking responsibility for where and who you are right now and where you aim to get to. What is your BE right now? Understanding you, how you react, your behaviours, knowing your values and what's important to you are key to your growth. These directly correlate to the quality of your activity, your doing, your current level of unconscious or conscious incompetence and competence (Chapter 1).

When we start to collate who you are and what you do we can then start to determine a strategy and focused growth mindset, which always focuses on the destination, your ideal self and how you determine your future. Let's be really clear and remain on track with the overarching theme of this book, getting above the parapet is ultimately about you taking ownership of your destination.

As a coach, I focus on this journey in mind and body through the formula for life's abundance.

**The Formula for Life Abundance**
The formula for life's abundance in its essence seems simple and a paradoxical journey of self-discovery and realisation is Be x Do = Have. I first encountered the formula having been coached by Brad Sugars. He offered this very simple formula in direct relation to the wise words and lessons of Zig Ziglar to achieve success. Today this remains one of the most simple and productive formulas to achieving success and being who you

want to be and achieving what you want to achieve. The simplicity as a formula boiled down to the sum of the two halves Being and Doing resulting in Having more, as I will go onto explain.

Throughout the book so far, we have focused on the formula. The book kicked off with the end in mind and challenging you to gain clarity on your destination, what you really want to achieve in life. You should have by now determined who you need to be in order to get to your destination. In order to better understand how all our learnings now start to come together let's take a look at the success mechanism, you all have access to in your minds. In the book Psycho-Cybernetics, Maxwell Maltz (Maxwell Maltz, 2015) explains how each of us are already hardwired for success. Lets see if I can offer my insight here.

**Your Success Mechanism**
Believe it or not, we are all pre-programmed for success, being goal oriented and driven. We each of us have the instinctive drive to pursue goals and targets. In fact, it is this very level of consciousness which really marks out from every other living creature on the planet. In general terms animals have two primal drives; self-preservation and procreation. They have essentially no other inner drive than those two aspects and every instinctive drive they have relates directly to those.

My pet dog, Casper, is a great companion and family member, but when it comes down to it, we are his self-preservation. We feed him daily and make sure he lives in a safe environment. So, it's no wonder he lavishes affection in our direction, responds to commands we give him when he thinks there's a treat waiting for him. Now take you. Whilst you will also have those primal instincts what sets you apart is the fact you have the ability to apply creative thinking and an instinct to achieve goals, which is your success mechanism.

Taking all we have learnt through the book to this point you have probably determined that where you are now, the version of you currently is not who you want to be. You have a clear picture of your ideal self. That version of you doesn't as yet exist in your conscious habits and interactions, although there are the thoughts, feelings and emotions being developed to make the shift. When you look in the mirror you can now picture what your future you looks like.

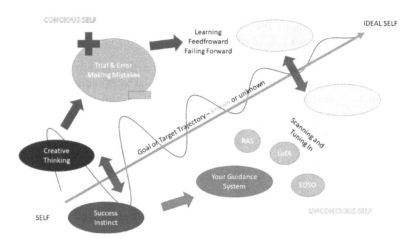

*The Success Mechanism*

The ideal self has been created through your imagination, thinking creatively about what could be. As you further solidify that vision, through internalisation, verbalisation, visualisation your success instincts can now start to kick in. You begin to programme your vast subconsciousness to tune into your new course. In effect this becomes your guidance system, keeping you on the trajectory for your goals and targets. You understand the impact of the Law of attraction, your RAS is set, and you understand some of the biology behind how your brain and nervous systems functions.

With your trajectory set, you will likely be in pursuit of a goal which could be determined as known, it exists now. That might be a promotion, a destination, a sum of money etc. In which case, your success mechanism will maintain your course, keep you on track. Where mistakes are made there will be development and learning which can then be applied in order to achieve the goal or target.

When you have set a goal or target which is as yet unknown, maybe creating significant wealth, attaining a new level of learning to develop a new skill or ability, maybe setting up your own business although not knowing in what. In these cases, your success mechanism allows you to tune into new opportunities, scans the path ahead seeking out the opportunities for the goal and target you have set. The system will always be scanning what's ahead on a wave trajectory looking for and tuned in to every opportunity to achieve your goal and hit your target.

Whether you are aiming for a goal or target which is known and exists already or you have yet to determine the fine detail of what will actually be achieved to discover the goal, you have the ability to engage your success mechanism.

As with everything I have written and shared with you in this book, responsibility and awareness are a mantra of every good coach. You need to understand you have the inbuilt ability to engage your success mechanism, to get creative with your thinking, learn from mistakes and maintain the conscious momentum forward. To also make sure you make every effort to have your success instincts primed, programmed and ready to be constantly scanning your environment for every opportunity. To be tuned in and ready to apply yourself fully when progression towards your goals or target appear.

Now sadly for 97% of you, there will be a failure to comprehend overcome. Your success mechanism, if you've programmed it will kick in, your formula for an abundant life. Ultimately along your journey you will encounter failure or failing forward. The one fundamental challenge you will face and is the key reason I challenged you to develop your own offensive mindset and switch your success mechanism on. Why you need to be aware of what will get in the way to then have the confidence to overcome it and continue on your journey.

For a vast majority, the focus and application of this formula (BE x DO = HAVE) is often applied in reverse. Think having will allow them to do what they desire and be the person they want to be. Sadly, today that can be all too easy to achieve in principle but very rarely in practice.

When you apply the process, you create a sustainable progression along your journey towards your destination. Here's the challenge and the part most people struggle with, it takes time. In a world, today where we need self-gratification now and it is on offer everywhere, where our attention span is dramatically reducing it's all about now. I want success now, I want riches now, I want a dream home now, I want a dream holiday now and so our self-indulgent impatient list goes on.

Our impatient response to what we WANT and WANT NOW is one of the key aspects to why so few truly live the life they were destined too. Why so few have the resolve, the determination the discipline to stay the course is because they want it now. Let's face it, in so many respects you can have it now. You can be given large lines of credit in order to buy what you want when you want it. Interestingly you will often then fall foul of the need to pay it back, guess what that takes time.

And so, there is an additional aspect we need to apply when engaging with this formula, TIME. Let's be really clear, you can't shortcut time. You can't go around it, you can't bypass it, you can't condense it and you certainly can't speed it up. When you look for those who have achieved success it has taken time, in fact rather than the cliché of offering a bunch of names look to your circle of friends, your community who has achieved success? How long did it take them? How committed have they been?

Yes, I know, there are those looking to create the next Facebook to rock the world, take Mark Zuckerberg, he remained committed to first get into Harvard and then to pursue his idea, his vision. If you asked Mark he'd tell you about how he remained committed to his vision, how he was disciplined to achieving it and now how he remains so today.

With this in mind let's look at the formula with the addition of time. It's vital to understand the success doesn't happen overnight. To live the life you desire, to attain the heights you seek you will need to be committed to the time it will take. Time in both the hours of hard work you are willing and will require to apply and the length of time it will take, which in all likelihood will be measured in years.

**BE x Do x Time = HAVE**

Be

Who do you need to be in order to achieve your goals? The one thing that differentiates us from all living things on the planet is our consciousness. Our ability to see the reflection in the mirror and have a view of who we ideally want to be. In the formula, the primary focus is on who you need to be. By now, if this book has had the desired effect, you will have a better picture of who you want looking back at you in the mirror. Your being. This will trigger your success instincts.

Now I have no idea what it is you want to achieve, what I am certain of is you will need to focus on aspects of who you are now in order to shift towards the version of you, you want to be. Bearing in mind when we focus on your BE you will need to focus on who you need to be now and in the short-term future, maybe to achieve the impending goal. You will, by virtue, also then be focusing on who you want and need to be in developing your ideal self in the long-term. This will be an area which will develop as you grow and uncover your BE, your true potential.

Your BE will focus on:

- BEliefs – Your belief will directly influence just what you will be able to achieve. If you believe it's all too hard, guess what? It will be. What you believe to be true in your life is because you believe it. If you start to believe there are bigger and better opportunities if you believe you can learn new skills, if you can believe you can achieve more then you will be empowered to do just that. This, in turn, links to your being....
- BEing – Your being relates to your inner self, who do you need to be inside, activating your success instincts. If your inner dialogue is a challenge now, what self-development exercises and habits do you need to undertake to change the inner dialogue? If you have a negative outlook, how do you shift towards a positive one? Let's be really clear, the thoughts you have are your thoughts, you own them. They will give you the drive and commitment you want. If you think success, if you host a successful internal dialogue you will tune into the success opportunities and in time success itself. The key from being will be to translate the thoughts into actions, your behaviours....
- BEhaviours – belief in yourself and embracing the true version of you in your inner being will naturally start to translate into actions and activity. We discussed the success habits in Chapter 3, these will reinforce your ability to truly engage with your true inner being. Who you truly want to be. Start to behave in a manner befitting to what you aim to achieve and who you truly want to be.
- BEhold – In short as you activate your BE you will behold the new you. You will start to act and respond in a way aligned with what you seek to achieve, your goal or target.

Why your BE is a high requirement for success revolves around the focus of the person you actually strive to want to be. Reinforcing your being will heighten the success behaviours. The physical aspect of your being. As you become more comfortable with your success behaviours you will find your confidence grows, which in turn will empower you and strengthen your self-belief.

*The Behaviours Cycle*

With a higher self-belief, you reinforce the values which will support your behaviours and so the cycle goes on. With every cycle you grow as an individual, you move towards your ideal self. That ideal self is where you ultimately find your success, where your dreams were born and where you can see yourself in your vision.

DO

By virtue of being and activating your success mechanism, you will then need to act or DO. Your ability to carry out the activities and the actions are vital to achieving your goals, in having. There is no shortcut, this is where the hard work resides, where it will require effort and commitment. Being able to focus on what actually needs to be done.

A significant point here relates in direct application of your being. By virtue of focusing on who you need to be the congruence, quality, consistency and commitment will match. If you have a focus on being the very best version of you in your business and marketplace when applied to the level of doing, then you will operate at a much higher level. It is a self-fulfilling prophecy from this point. The better you think and behave the better the actions and activities you produce.

A key connection and why successful 'doing' is intrinsically linked to your BE is the consistency and quality of your application. Essentially when you define your being and have focused on applying yourself your performance in doing will vastly increase. The following performance cycle highlights the drive and commitment:

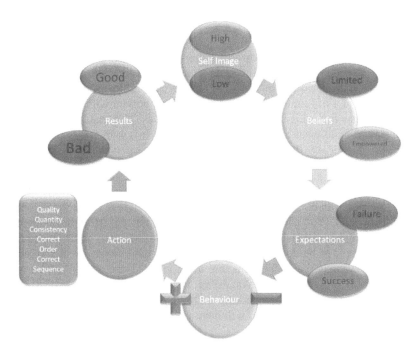

*The Performance Cycle*

A high-level focus on our being, our self-image will increase our esteem. If you encourage and engage a high level of self-esteem, the net result is a significantly higher level of self-belief. Having a greater belief in yourself, regardless of outside influences will result in empowerment. You will have a far greater sense and feeling of empowerment. This, in turn, will limit the impact of any limiting beliefs you may have harboured, fear you have held, anxiety and thus the impending sense of doom and failure. You will by virtue have tuned your success instincts.

This is then directly portrayed in your behaviours. A positive output in all you do. Even when things may be a tough, difficult, challenging if you have a positive focus you are far more likely to benefit from the experience, to be more proactive in the need to be adaptive. Your actions or 'DOING' will have a far greater impact. Interestingly in these circumstances when mistakes and errors occur there will be a great success outcome due to the response and reaction to them. In general context success is far more likely to be the outcome, thus reinforcing your self-esteem and self-image.

Time

There is no definitive scale towards gaining success and in the digital age with the exponential growth in certain areas you could achieve success in a relatively short period of time, whilst other areas and focused commitment may result in a life-time's journey. There is one constant with time and that is once it has passed it is lost. You cannot go back, you cannot have more, you cannot undo what has happened in that time. It is with this in mind you need to understand that time is an intrinsic element in your formula for success.

Primarily if you are committed to success in gaining your 'HAVE' you must be committed. Setting out to achieve a goal will take commitment and application on your part. Are you prepared to put the effort in, are you prepared to forgo all else in order to achieve your goal, are you dedicated to what will need to be done, hour by hour, day by day, month by month and ultimately year on year? There is one thing which I can assure you of on your journey to living the life you desire, it's hard work, bloody hard work. In fact, for some of you embarking on your new business venture it will likely be the hardest work you will have ever undertaken and with little or no reward for a long time.

Success is in its rawest form boring because it requires you to wake up each and every day and do just a little better than you did yesterday. It is those incremental improvements which will compound together to ultimately define your success. It takes a great deal of personal discipline along the journey to success and to also stay the course, to have the patience and commitment to understanding it will take time.

Know it will take time is one aspect there is another. Are you prepared to reassign time, to give up time in order to succeed? If today you are coming from an employed background and entering into owning your own business do you have the focus to work 7 days a week, put more time in, all the while knowing it may be some time before you reap the rewards? Are you of the mind to 'put the time in'?

As a coach, I often find that time is one of the greatest challenges and we will take a detailed look at how to get more productive in the final chapter. How clear are you on what you aim to achieve? Take a broad look at what it is you want to achieve by answering these questions and then applying the timescale and you'll start to see the length of time you are going to need to commit:

By When/How Long

What is the big picture of the Dream?

What is the timescale you think it will take to get there?

What's the vision and have you defined the vivid vision 3 – 5 years from now?

In that timescale what are the top 4 goals to be achieved?

In order to achieve the goals, what are you going to need to learn and develop?

What's the plan of action and associated timeline?

Time needed to succeed: ...............

Now, this isn't to dampen your sprints, rather show you it is possible with the time you have. Remember it will be relative to the perceived time you have. If you're a late starter your timescale may look different than someone in their early twenties, to someone who is a teenager. The point is you have the time available and in order to get to your destination, you have to be committed to a higher level of consciousness when it comes to your time.

So now we can start to see how focusing on who you need to BE in order to evoke the appropriate and higher capacity in DO will lead to a far higher focus on productivity and efficiency when it comes to your TIME. All of which leads to HAVE

Have

The results of Be x Do x Time is you get to have the life you desire. Sounds simple enough doesn't? Well, the reality is the opposite, as we have discussed in Be, Do and Time there is one constant element which will be required and we've only mentioned it a couple of times in the book. So now is the time to ensure you are crystal clear in understanding that without this element you will not reach your destination, frankly, you will fail and in some cases, will fail to even get started. Discipline or to be more defined pig-headed discipline.

When we look at Pig-Headed discipline you will start to determine what has likely been getting in the way so far in your life. You have probably picked up by now that there is no shortcutting your journey to success and sustained success at that. I have no doubt you have clarity on who you are right now. Whether you are seeking to start your own business, are a start-up or business owner the context is the same. There is a distinct correlation between who you are and what you have achieved now and what you want to achieve in the future.

## Be x Do x Time = Have Quadrant...Where are you?

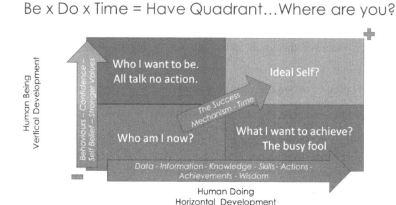

*The Be x DO x Time = Have Quadrant*

When we look at Pig-Headed discipline you will start to determine what has likely been getting in the way so far in your life. You have probably picked up by now that there is no shortcutting your journey to success and sustained success at that. I have no doubt you have clarity on who you are right now. Whether you are seeking to start your own business, are a start-up or business owner the context is the same. There is a distinct correlation between who you are and what you have achieved now and what you want to achieve in the future.

When we look at the top left quadrant, who I want to be. If you are the type of person who has all the ideas, reads all the books, knows what you need to do but always fails to get into action you are 'all talk and no action'. The challenge here is the frustration of failing to start time and time again. Your likely to be the type of person who will set your New Year's resolution only to have failed before January is over. Now this may sound quite harsh and I guess it will if I'm describing you, here's the thing, this book is about education and action combined. Which after all is the key focus and theme of Be x Do x Time = Have. Don't let this be you, use the habits in this book,

200

combined with the offensive mindset to act, start doing. Just think for a moment about all the knowledge you have and the impact without action. Well, it's a trick question because there is no action.

When we look at the bottom right quadrant it's all about action. To succeed you just have to get out there and do stuff. This is where the technically minded always reside. They have the knowledge on what they want and maybe enjoy but no idea of what it will take to succeed. No idea of what they will require to learn in addition in order to take their life and business to the next level. It's merely a focus on work hard and keep working hard. As I term it 'the busy fool'. Is that you? Does it sound like someone you know? For these people life's a hamster wheel, it takes great effort to stay on track, to be focused on paying the bills each month, to constantly be worrying about cash flow and then never getting to the point where you can actually send out the invoices. Essentially action and activity without the application of their learning.

Activation of your success mechanism over time combined with a progressively high level of being and doing will result in success, your ideal self. You will need to develop yourself and you will need to be clear on what your learning agenda will need to be. As mentioned in Chapter 1 this is your journey to gaining wisdom. Oh, and here's the thing with learning, it never stops, you will always be learning, in fact, you will always need to be learning because this process never stops. Just take a moment to picture yourself standing in front of the mirror 5 or 10 years from now, the ideal version of you. Who will you be looking back at you? What will the journey look like for you to become your ideal self? What will you have mastered, what wisdom will you have gained and what will you be seeking to learn next.

Have Do Be

There are those who will never really be able to truly achieve their potential because to apply the formula in reverse, juxtaposed to Be x Do x Time = Have. Believing they can shortcut success, enjoy the fruits without any of the labour. Sadly, you cannot.

Focusing on primarily having first, seeking to gain the treasures, the material items they desire. Sadly, today we live in a world where it is possible to have your cake and pay for it later. For those who believe having will in some way improve their ability to do and make them a better being are likely never to achieve their true potential.

Filling the gaps in their life with stuff, artificially achieve greatness through material wealth or bluffing their way to the top is shallow, has no deep meaning and is unsustainable. I have seen so many try to gain greatness through taking shortcuts, a lack of personal investment, using the success of others to further their pursuit of success, seeking ways to purchase success on credit. In every case, they have got to a point where they are found to be wanting. Alienated, lacking in the personal ability to apply themselves owing to a lack of learning, not being trusted. Frankly in many cases not being liked.

My point here is to not be that person, if you have taken anything from my writings so far it is this, to succeed you need primarily and in all cases, to invest in yourself, trust you have the innate ability to be the person you want to be. There is no shortcut to living an enriched and fulfilled life. The hard work commitment and effort is well worth it in the end.

### BLUF – Bottom Line Up Front
The ascent to attaining ownership is in actual fact a lifelong process, there will always be that next summit and in many respects, it can be aligned with the pursuit of excellence. Do we ever really achieve it? The point here is, for the most part, many will never realise responsibility let alone accountability. There is a blissful peace in dissatisfaction in our life pursuits. So many live their lives without ever truly attempting to achieve personal greatness however they would define it in their lives.

As a coach, what I find inspirational is the fact that business owners have taken a step to get above the parapet. After all, when you made a choice to start your own business what were the motivations, the dreams, the aspirations and the vision? Whether that was merely stepping out to be your own boss or a deeper driving force of aiming to provide financial freedom for your family or give something back to the community whatever it was, it drove you to step out and commit to a venture on your own.

Let's face it you set on a venture which, when you look at the failure rate of business is massive, 1 in 5 make it past 5 years. Yet you made the commitment. The focus of this book has been to offer re-engagement in your commitment and self-belief. We all have it, in one shape or another, I'm certain if you are a business owner you have experienced it first-hand. If you're starting a business, then you are likely experiencing it and having doubts. If you are employed, then you are likely looking for what it takes to get underway. Whatever encouraged you to pick up my book you needed to satisfy your curiosity. To re-engage or indeed engage yourself.

Well at this stage I have offered you an insight into defining your destination, challenging you to think outside the box to take a really good look at what you have the ability to truly achieve. To live a full and thoroughly exhilarating life as you define it. To achieve your full potential. I have gone to some lengths to identify and raise awareness of why even after reading this book you will still fail, feel scared, apprehensive, dissatisfied, have low self-esteem because that may be ok for others but they're not you. 'My circumstances are different, it's tougher for me, I wouldn't be able to achieve this because I can't. I know I should but, but, but'. Bull Shit!

If the smallest part has resonated with you then you need to apply the success habits. And here's the thing the success habits are those taken from many different sources of success. From the many coaches who have coached me in my pursuits and why I am writing this book. Why I strive for greatness in the coaching world. Why I aim to be a coach within the global arena in order to help as many as I can in my lifetime. So, apply the habits, make a conscious decision to shift and start to program your unconscious self.

This Chapter should have helped to piece together the insights, lessons and learnings so far. Now you need to activate your success mechanism and applying it step by step, goal by goal towards the pursuit of the life you live and the life you will live. To become the very best version of you. It's all about choice so what do you choose? Go back to Chapter 1 and read your commitment statement, what did you agree? What did you commit to before engaging with this book? In some shape or form, you would have made a commitment to getting above the parapet. It just wasn't in context at that point. Well, it is now, so what are you going to do next?

Having given you the success habits, you need to set them in motion, to have made a commitment to apply them to your everyday existence, to make them your habits. I assure you when you do, you'll start to see, react and act differently. You'll unlock your true self and actually start on that journey towards your ideal self. You'll start living your dream.

In the final Chapter, I'm going to introduce business rhythm, the means to set in motion the fundamentals required to have your business or businesses be the vehicle that will transport you to the life you want to live. We'll look at what foundations you need to have for the business to be successful and where you need to apply pig-headed discipline. The essence of setting momentum in your business towards creating your profitable enterprise which will work without you.

| My Action | The Impact | Achieved by |
|-----------|-----------|-------------|
|           |           |             |

# Chapter 5 –

# Business Rhythm

Throughout the book I have challenged you to reflect and commit to action and activity without, as yet, offering a structured approach to its application in your business. In this chapter, I seek to offer you my insight into that structure, to define for you effectively, what I will refer to as 'Business Rhythm'. From the onset of developing your business plan, the strategic context of what you want to achieve, by when and the tactical delivery within your business it is now time for action. Essentially the transference of what you have taken from the book, the knowledge, to its application. Whilst also ensuring the balanced approach to your focus ON the business and the working IN it. There is a rhythm to a successful business, its harmonious function. Not necessarily the same thing day in day out, rather a harmony of delivery, growth and pinpointing the success factors within the business.

Being a business owner is tough, it can feel a very lonely place to be, there is often limited support in the decisions you need to make both strategically and tactically. At both levels, it is often down to you to make the decisions, which will almost certainly have consequences. You shoulder all the burden. You have to deal with and pre-empt high levels of uncertainty. You may be the hardest working in the business, working ridiculous hours in and on the business. Although more often than not in. You have to deal with all the resistance that comes with being a business owner. You have to have the offensive mindset in order to succeed.

Business Rhythm is my interpretation of 'Battle Rhythm' the driver of military operations. Battle Rhythm is the routine and cycle from which officers and soldiers, activity and knowledge remain synchronised, thus increasing productivity, the ability to pre-empt and respond. The process is utilised for future and present operations. Now, this isn't going to be a direct correlation of bringing military doctrine to the business world. This is rather highlighting the concept and characterises within the business context. Giving you the structure to be tuned into your business. Attain the knowledge and decipher its meaning in order to impact in all areas of the business. To ultimately create a highly functional team delivering business and highly leveraged whilst being managed at an optimised level.

Business rhythm is underpinned with the focus of developing and maintaining a 'commercial profitable enterprise which works without the business owner, you'. So, what is business rhythm? First, let's be clear about rhythm and its impact in everything we do. We are intertwined in rhythm; our lives are driven by rhythm. Indeed, the planet maintains rhythm in its never-ending orbit of the sun and is the source of our rhythmic existence. Rhythm is not just fundamental to our existence it is in many respects life; our growth is born of rhythm.

The changes in the ecology, the weather are all driven by the rhythm of the seasons, the changing temperatures and daylight. Then there is the circadian existence we and every living organism on the planet abide by, day and night. Which we often see as the physiology and behavioural existence we all adhere too. This continual living rhythm inspires growth, encourages existence. Whilst we can comprehend the infinite opportunities tomorrow offers and our ability to choose a certain course the fact remains there is always a tomorrow.

Having no business rhythm will ultimately result in a course leading to demise and at the very least never really realising your true potential. Business rhythm will encourage the development of routine and vastly improve a consistent approach in all aspects. Reflect for a moment on the discussions you will have had so far throughout the book. Review your offensive mindset and commitment. Have the 14 success habits and how to function above the parapet resonated? Ultimately what are habits if not a rhythmic approach to your positive mindset?

Rhythm is also self-perpetuating. As you build on the fundamentals we will discuss and introduce you to where and how you'll experience growth in yourself and your business. There is the matter of consistency, to create a self-perpetuating process the maintenance of rhythm is key to the motion. If for whatever reason you step out of rhythm and draw to a halt you cease to grow, cease to have forward momentum and by virtue, start to die.

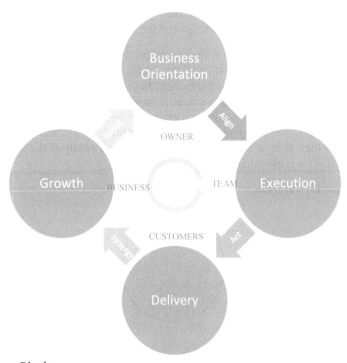

*Business Rhythm*

At the core of Business Rhythm is the cycle of business. The owner is ultimately responsible for everything in the business and all too often is the busiest in the business as a direct result:

- The owner deals with all aspects of the business and decision making.
- The owner is the default setting for the team, directing how, what, where, when etc.
- The owner is on speed dial to all the customers and more often than not the first port of call.
- The owner deals with all the business administration, debt management, invoicing, customer administration etc.

The owner essentially is the default for all aspects of the business. Interestingly initially by choice as the business grows, then becoming trapped as the business becomes overly reliant on them and the team and customers are educated that they are responsible for everything! The owner becomes the owned! There is no wonder that they then have no focus on the business, the direction it needs to go and the long-term aspirations.

Business Rhythm focuses on the development and the cycle of business functions. It underpins just how to create a commercially profitable enterprise that works without the owner. In the simplest terms, the business owner invests in where the business is heading, the strategic thinking, in order to give clarity to the team and empower them to deliver and deal with the customers. The customers, in turn, ensure the business and the business owner is then able to focus on further growth as a result of the increasing business. This is essentially Business Rhythm.

**Business Orientation**

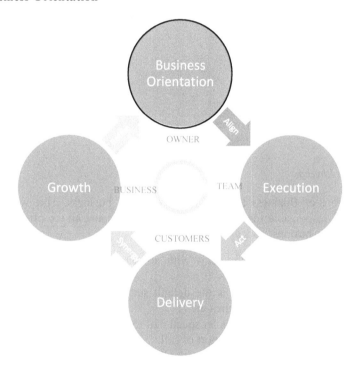

By now you should already have defined the destination of the business, in Chapter 1, we paid particular emphasis to the process of defining your future.

Dreams x Vision x Goals x Learn x Plan x Act

We also touched on both the need for strategic and tactical planning. A key aspect of Business Rhythm regards the need to remain oriented to the strategic aims of the business. In terms of the destination, the need for the journey in the first place. Orientation is the ability to constantly be checking your current position in direct relation to the short, medium and long-term destination.

Business orientation is the constant necessity to remain in the correct position in direct relation to the strategic objective. This is where you define where the business should be on the journey in relation to where you are, the actual and budgeted position. Key focus is the clarity on what the strategic, big picture, objectives need to be, or need to be defined as. Business orientation is about being tuned into the business, 'business awareness'. Constantly building 'business wisdom', striving to excel in your industry.

As we will go on to discuss, gaining wisdom is one thing, 'application' is another. This will create 'strategic agility', maintaining correlation to what has happened, what is happening now and what is likely to happen and how to pre-empt, respond or act. To be change ready, in other words not dogmatic about what's going on in the business rather have a mindset for change and by virtue growth. To always be seeking to improve your business wisdom, essentially the master of your industry, to be an industry leader.

There is also the interesting issue of what drives the need for a continuing focus on business orientation. During operations from my military days at the strategic level, there would always be a focus on the best, probable and worst course of action (COA). What course of action would be followed if certain circumstances were met on the field of operation? You would then be able to follow an alternate pre-planned course of action towards the desired outcome.

In this manner, if your business has determined a set of criteria in direct relation to the businesses current course the same level of constant orientation can be maintained. The business becomes far more agile in its ability to set a refined direction. Donald Rumsfeld was famously quoted when he was the Secretary of State for Defence in the USA for saying:

*"There are known knowns. These are things we know that we know. There are known unknowns. That is to say, there are things that we know we don't know. But there are also unknown unknowns. There are things we don't know we don't know".*

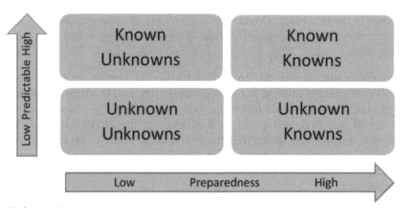

*Unknown Knowns*

Unknown Knowns

Interestingly many people thought he was talking gibberish and laughed at his comment until they listened to what he actually said. Now whilst he was relating to the WMD in 2002 and the Iraq crisis the focus of this table gives a great outline of just what you need to be predicting and prepared for. There is a balance when we look to the ability to strategically apply ourselves within our chosen businesses and sectors. As experts there is also a need to be tuned into what you know and may as yet not know.

Draw out a blank table and see if you are able to predict what will happen in your business sector in the next 90 days. Then from there what assumptions can you make?

Let's take a look at what defines business orientation:

- KPIs
- Business Wisdom

- Strategic Agility
- Application

The Cycle of Orientation

## Key Performance Indicators (KPI)

Take a moment to reflect on your business, where it is now, how far have you have come, what have you have already experienced and achieved? If you're starting out where are you heading, what have you already discovered you need to know and indeed what you may not know? In business, there are many moving parts. KPIs isn't about remaining in one place, it's being tuned in, seeking wisdom ultimately having heightened awareness in the business environment. KPIs allow you to maintain a high level of business awareness, which in turn will enable you to respond to what's happened, what's happening and what may happen in the future.

Key Performance Indicators or a Business Scorecard are the key measurements towards achieving success in your business. What gets measured gets managed. Understanding what the key metrics you need to measure will enable you to actually manage growth. Let's be really clear here if you're not growing your dying. Think for a moment the impact of driving a car without a dashboard. How confident would you be? Not knowing the speed of travel, engine temperature, the revs all of which offer an insight into how efficiently it's running. What about the fuel gauge, how much is being used and how quickly? Then there are the engine warning lights, which warn of impending problems. Frankly, you wouldn't feel confident to travel any distance.

Interestingly I come across businesses running without dashboards regularly, which is ludicrous. Not knowing metrics in your business is foolhardy and cavalier. It will stifle productivity, efficiency, profitability and limit your ability to predict opportunity and threats for the future. Business owners are often embroiled and overwhelmed in the day to day running of a business. There will be many occasions where they need to make important decisions and will often focus on the tactical rather than the strategic direction of the business.

For the large part, I find most businesses I talk to are reactive, at best. The 'tell' is often the quantity of time a business owner spends IN the business, versus ON the business. Focus on being employed in your own business will impact on your ability to react to situations and changes which benefit the business. The reality here is your already behind the curve, you've already missed the opportunity to have an impact.

Ensuring you have KPIs set within the business, the business dashboard will significantly improve growth. Establishing your KPIs will have a significant impact throughout the business.

> • Communication and informing – having the ability to share the metric in a timely and clear fashion will create high levels of engagement. Actively watching growth happen can really motivate both yourself and the team.
> • Diagnostic – being able to diagnose the metrics or a series of metrics from across the business enables you to make informed assumptions and decisions. You can observe business, regional and industry trends, allowing strategic decisions to be made often in good time.
> • Learning and decisions – You will learn more about your business through observing the KPIs, what's trending, what's not, what's working, what's not and what you may need to learn as a result of what your numbers tell you.

In terms of where you focus on the KPIs within the business right now, there are 6 key areas:

> 1. Marketing and Sales. When we look at the KPIs you need in relation to the marketing and your sales pipeline there are numerous areas where you could focus. In today's digital age it can seem somewhat overwhelming. Just take a look at the analytics you have access to today, click rates, impressions, site visits, likes, etc.. In the simplest terms think of the purpose of your marketing

and sales, to gain and retain customers, whilst gaining maximum wallet share.

2.      Financial. Now for many business owners, they will be adamant they have a close handle on their business financial KPIs, insofar as they know what's in the bank account and what's due out. The reality is starkly different. There are many levels to having a sound set of financial KPIs in place. It goes beyond the bank account.

3.      Operations/Production. Productivity and efficiency are key KPIs to have in place. If you need to establish just what needs to be measured, then ask yourself just how reliant is the business on you right now. The greatest leverage comes from investing in other people's time and have them deliver the process and procedure. To ensure the highest levels of efficiency and productivity there needs to be some clear metrics in place.

4.      People. In this instance, it really revolves around the level of engagement.

5.      Suppliers. Interestingly we often miss the external team, those who you rely on and require paid services from. Let's be clear they provide you with a service and as such should be accountable to your KPIs. You need to ensure you gain the very best service you can against the investment in them.

6.      Innovation. Growth requires innovation and in turn, we should be measuring the results from our innovation. Just how well are we doing in terms of actively seeking to forge into new territory or ground.

It is highly important to ensure we have a clear set of KPIs in place in order to actively measure our growth and ensure high levels of accountability to the numbers. One final note on KPIs is the regularity which they are assessed. More often than not, there is at best a quarterly review of the numbers and then only because we have taxes to pay. Or in the worst cases, it is a once a year occurrence when the annual report is prepared for compliance reasons.

The various KPIs should be measure daily, weekly, monthly and annually. Think for a moment if you merely measure yearly. What would the impact be if you started to measure those numbers monthly, you'd move from once a year to 12 times a year or what about monthly to weekly, going from 12 to 52 times in a year. Ask yourself what impact would that have on your business? Having a set of KPIs you measure, review and respond too weekly. I'm sure you will start to see a dramatic shift in your responsiveness to delivery.

You need to make sure you have full awareness throughout the business, become really tuned into what's going on. Have the ability to pick up on the opportunities and the threats and be able to respond. Interestingly this awareness links directly to a 'business above the parapet' through ensuring you are tuned in. Keeping your head above the parapet will also help to develop you as a business owner. You manage and lead your team with ever greater efficiency which will, in turn, increase productivity. This, in turn, will also allow you to encourage greater anonymity in the team, allowing your focus on the business to increase. More on this in a moment. Throughout you will also assimilate a far greater understanding and comprehension of business, all the elements it will take to run and grow your business.

Let's be really clear on the importance of KPIs. Without KPIs, you cannot run your business above the parapet because you will have no in-depth awareness of what's going on. So, an intrinsic element of having a business above the parapet are the KPIs. They offer the business owner access to information critical to business growth. We already know that right now as the business owner you are likely to be the busiest person, have many distractions, be required to make many decisions. KPIs allow you to reflect and remain aware and tuned into the key aspects of what's happened, happening or about to happen.

Critical to this is the requirement for quick decision making or having the speed and velocity of responsiveness. If you only have limited information from which to make decisions, how good are the decisions likely to be, if and when you make them. What if you have no information, you certainly can't guess your way to success. So KPIs vastly speed up the decision-making process and reduce the consequence of poor decision making. Essentially where limited or no information, metrics are available, no KPIs, then all you can hope for is the ability to be subjective. You'll only be able to base your decisions on what you feel. Now whilst I'm a fan of following your gut instinct in the right situations, it's not a strategy for sustainable growth.

With KPIs in place, having a system to record and deliver the key metrics will allow you to have an objective view. Essentially your number will give you the insight you need to make informed and timely decisions. Objectivity doesn't leave the growth, development, productivity or direction of travel to chance, it means you are able to respond appropriately. Yet so many businesses fail to observe the significance of having key measurables in the business.

The other aspect here that will become apparent when we discuss delivery is that of the strategic and tactical decisions being made. Primarily as the business owner, you want ultimately to be in a position to be making strategic decisions and not tactical ones. The team should through your leadership and strategic focus be able to respond at the tactical level.

Implementing, Setting and Maintaining KPIs

Understanding that KPIs are critical to the success of your business it is now important to ensure we have them implemented and active within the business. The following is a 5-step cycle to implement and maintain KPIs in your business. Determining the strategic direction; Audit any existing measures in place; Revised measures; Analysis and reporting; Continuous development.

The first priority is to understand where the business is right now, what is the strategic direction, where is the business heading? Now at this stage of the book, there is a good chance you have a far better idea, if not already a clear vision and plan beginning to take shape. So, if you have taken on board what was discussed in Chapter 1 then you should be able to determine the business vision, review the plan of action and have clarity on the business's mission.

*The KPI Cycle*

From this what are the goals the business has set? What are the most important objectives for the business? What are the elements which you can now clearly define as the success criteria? From these, you start to determine just what the drivers should be for the results you are looking for. A critical discovery at this stage will also be where and what the limitations and barriers are or could be. You also ensure the team are aligned, which we will cover shortly.

Understanding your strategic direction allows you to take a critical view of where you are now. What existing measures do you have in place? At this point, it's important to have a good look at the strategic fit to the business. What are you doing or not doing now? You'll also need to determine what data is available and its validity. Where and what is the source of the data, its accuracy and the timelines. In the course of this, it will also determine and identify the gaps.

In turn, you will then be able to ensure that the data being collected, the KPIs are relevant and any identified gaps or limits in data are bridged. It is vital that the KPIs implemented must reflect and be true measures of performance, progress and the growth of the business. The need to be quantifiable and measurable indirect relations to historical information, budgets, goals and trends.

Most critically the collated and recorded KPIs will need to enable you to act upon the data. In simple terms, the KPIs and the data being collated needs to be simple to analyse and interpret. Easy to read reports, one page is always optimal as you will need to ensure all the salient and important issues are highlighted without white noise. A pictorial representation, charts, graphs and tables will allow the information to be understood at a glance.

| Marketing and Sales | <ul><li>Market share</li><li>Leads</li><li>Suspect to prospect conversion</li><li>Profit per transaction</li><li>Number of transactions</li><li>Number of customers</li><li>Average retention</li><li>Life value</li></ul> |
|---|---|
| Financial | <ul><li>Revenue</li><li>Profit margin</li><li>Gross margin</li></ul> |

| | |
|---|---|
| | • Return of Investment (RoI)/break even |
| | • Debtor days |
| | • Earnings before interest, tax, depreciation and amortisation (EBITDA) |
| | • Profit and Loss (P and L) |
| | • Cost of Goods (CoGs)/Services Sold. |
| Operations/Production | • Cost per unit/session |
| | • Number of employees |
| | • Current capacity |
| | • Response time |
| | • No of complaints |
| | • Work in progress |
| | • Labour hours |
| | • Downtime |
| People | • Number of employees to managers |
| | • Absenteeism |
| | • Employee training hours |
| | • Output per employee - sales/productivity |
| | • Core values and behaviours |
| | • Employee engagement |
| | • Quality of output |
| | • Skills matrix |
| Suppliers | • Responsiveness to payment |
| | • General service |
| | • Competition v cost |
| | • On time delivery |
| | • Overall satisfaction |
| | • Credit terms |
| | • Number of suppliers |
| | • Defects (number or %) |
| Innovation | • Revenue from new products |
| | • Revenue from a market segment |

| | |
|---|---|
| | • Revenue from new geography |
| | • Number of new customers |
| | • Time to market for new products/services |
| | • Research and development expenditure |
| | • Time spent on research and development |

*Key Business KPIs*

The key aspect is to then ensure that the collated data offers relevance through interpretation. It is this interpretation which ensures continual development. Development of the overall plan, review or new goals and being SMART with it. It also offers the focus to actually track data, essentially observe growth, decline or changing circumstance which you need to act upon.

The focus throughout delivery is to ensure the pig-headed discipline and systems are firmly in place to ensure you are able to collate the numbers. In addition, we need to determine the regularity in which we assess the information being collated. Are they daily, weekly, monthly or annual KPIs. The point behind KPIs is to enable responses, as we will go on to discuss during the growth element of the cycle. The idea here is to remain constant in delivery whilst focusing on the predictability to constantly seek to improve delivery in your business.

A key focus here relates back to Chapter 1 and my insight into wisdom, on its own KPIs merely offer data. Interestingly, as we will go onto to review in its raw form data provides little or no value, it is how we then go about its interpretation. This factor is the key aspect of attaining business wisdom.

**Business Wisdom**

Qualities of Wisdom

Seeking and gaining business wisdom is understanding that your knowledge is incomplete, there is still more to learn. The point here is for every iteration of change, whether a reactive or pre-emptive you gain wisdom. Personally, I believe that wisdom is a life's journey in its own right. For me

218

it's always been about the never-ending pursuit of excellence, being unreasonably good. And I'm still a long way off.

Business wisdom forms a part of the business orientation because it's key to understanding and change. As the famous quote 'do what you've always done and you'll get what you've always got'. Essentially do nothing different, fail to change, develop and ultimately grow and you miss the opportunity to gain wisdom. What's worse you'll start down the road to failure and ultimately business death.

Indeed, in Chapter 1 I have already highlighted the fact that learning is an intrinsic element of your business growth, ultimately of the journey towards making your dreams come true. So, there is no surprise that business wisdom is a key element to who you are as the owner and remaining oriented within the business.

As the business grows so do you as the business owner, that's inevitable. As you gain the confidence and discipline to keep your head above the parapet, taking ownership, you'll find you will gain that critical experience. As you gain more and more experience it increases your knowledge. If you have been in business for some time are you the same person from when you started, or have you gained experience? If you are a new start-up business has it been an easy transition from being employed or has there been some lessons along the way?

Whatever your circumstances as you gain experience you grow in knowledge. The slight difference with being truly orientated to your business, being the business owner is through being aware of the need for agility when change is required or happens you have the ability to learn from it and learning leads to experience.

Your experience essentially embeds the knowledge, which are the facts, information and skills acquired through experience. When we are young we very early on learn that we should not touch hot things, like flames. The first time you touch it we are able to determine the fact that a flame will burn our skin, which gives us the information in relation to what flames look like, where we find them and then in turn leads to the skill to avoid touching them.

In business, we go through the same process. With each iteration, we build and reinforce our ability to make sound decisions, we gain sound judgment. We are able to use our wisdom in the decisions we make going forward. It maybe that we are entering into uncharted territory, non-the-less our knowledge affords us the insight, vision, assumptions that based on what we already know we can predominantly determine the outcome. Our judgement allows us to orient truly to the opportunities our business offers. The true course of applying our business wisdom.

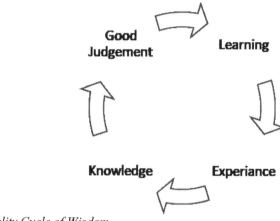

*Quality Cycle of Wisdom*

**Strategic Agility**

*The ability of a business or organisation to continually strive to maintain the competitive edge by adjusting and adapting new innovating ideas, using these ideas to create new products or services as well as the business model.*

Business life is an ever-changing environment one which can shift with little or no warning. The balance of business can be shifted from a negative to a positive situation in the blink of an eye. It could be the impact of a decision, change in the business environment, disruption from a competitor, the changing circumstances in the financial world or the shift in governmental policy. The key here is the preparedness, response and reaction you and your business have.

Interestingly the opposite is strategic paralysis. Having the inability to react in a manner other than what had been predetermined. It is this inability which will result in the demise of many businesses. Not being able to respond to the changing circumstances of business. Strategic agility will enable you the business owner to determine what the options are when things change. You are likely to remain on the same long-term journey, have the same destination in mind, it's simply the fact you have hit a roadblock and have to take a diversion.

Sadly, all too often I have seen first-hand the impact of coming up against a roadblock without having the strategic agility to seek an alternate diversion. Interestingly when you think back to Chapter 2 it is often the resistance which causes the inability to re-route. Burying your head in the sand, allowing the resistance to build will only go to cloud your judgment, stop you from being able to take the strategic view, the big or bigger picture and respond to it accordingly.

Strategic agility isn't just about being responsive it's also about being an innovator or early adopter. Don't think for a moment that the focus on agility here is being reactive, it's about being pre-emptive, proactive and forward thinking. Agility allows for you to 'think outside the box' all too often businesses are stuck in the mire of industry norms. That's not the way things are done in this industry. All too sadly there are far too many examples where big business has fallen foul of such a mindset and belief. Blockbuster, didn't think mail DVD service was sustainable, let alone online and downloading. Kodak failed to recognise the impact of the digitalisation of photography and film. And there are plenty more examples.

There is a very famous quote which in many respects sums up strategic agility from Charles Darwin:

*"It is not the strongest of the species that survives, nor the most intelligent that survives. It is the one that is the most adaptable to change."*

Understanding that change is in actual fact an element of success, to be expected and indeed embraced. Are you and your business prepared for change, how have you previously responded to change? Were you aware of it? Did you resist it? Did you embrace it and see it as an opportunity? And the cycle continues, as you will have grown so will the need for you to ensure business awareness is constantly tuned into and oriented with the business.

It's important to remind ourselves that this process is predominantly owned by you the business owner. The key part of the cycle here is how it is then linked to and empowerment for the team. You need to ensure there is a focus of aligning and empowering the team to deliver.

**Application**

In the simplest of terms, application is about utilising the wisdom being gained, applying the knowledge. We have highlighted on many occasions throughout this book the link to action and getting into action. The key here is committing to activity this is about being smart in what you do. There is a deeper understanding of what you do, credibility with what you seek to achieve and even in circumstances where you venture into the unknown, you have a greater sense of confidence owing to your understanding. Look upon it as applying the theory of your business.

You will no doubt be familiar with the term knowledge is power, is it? In my opinion, the journey to wisdom is charging the battery and application of your wisdom is about releasing the power. The reason I use the battery analogy is that the battery needs to be constantly charged as you utilise or apply the wisdom. Without that continual charge, gaining of wisdom, once the battery is discharged it is of no use. As I have already mentioned the journey to gaining wisdom is never-ending and therefore as you grow, you discover new and fresh focus. Increasing your wisdom step by step. Its application, the releasing of power is where the real power lies. Power on its own doesn't do anything. Unless the battery is powering something, it doesn't have an impact.

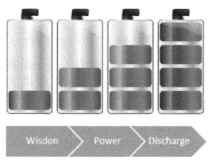

*The Wisdom Battery*

Now the other element of application is the controlled release of the power, being controlled in the application. Being controlled related to the ability to have a measured approach, not squandering the knowledge. This is about the wise application of what you aim to do. As we will go on to discuss later in this chapter having a measured approach and being tuned in to test the results. Essentially decision-making.

Decisions - Speed versus Velocity

So, what is the impact of your ability to make decisions which are informed, factual and objective? It essentially boils down to the difference between the speed of decisions being made and the velocity of the decisions.

Speed is defined as the rate at which someone or something moves or operates or is able to move or operate. Interestingly as a coach, I often come across business owners who operate at speed or are seemingly very busy. They have no issue with making decisions, the challenge here is often the decisions being made are ill-informed, hunches and at best reactive to a situation.

'I KNOW' will often play a significant part of the business owners' mindset, resulting in the swiftness when decisions need to be made. Additionally, it wouldn't be unusual to see a business with no KPIs in place, the knowledge resides with the business owner, being the 'all-knowing oracle'. The 'tell' will be a business and business owner suffering busyness! No doubt working really hard, just without focus and likely to be speeding in the wrong direction or with no focus on direction. Interestingly working at speed doesn't necessarily mean you're going to succeed, having that feeling that 'we are working really hard, so we must succeed'. Not the case.

Velocity conversely is defined as the speed of something in a given direction. There is a significant difference here in the context of speed in getting things done and then actually decisions which move you in a given direction at speed. With supporting KPIs it means the decisions you make will allow you to move in a specific direction. Having velocity in decision making keeps you focused on the key aspect which will lead to meaningful results. It will ensure your activities are always impactful in the direction of travel of the business.

*Speed v Velocity in Decision Making*

A business which is more likely to make decisions with velocity, thus creating momentum will have a clearly defined vision, mission, set SMART goals, will be focused on growth and higher levels of productivity. Planning will form an intrinsic element of their business rhythm.

## Align

Business orientation has been focused on the ensuring you, the business owner or leadership team have clarity and the ability to interpret where the business is at any point and that you are heading in the right direction. There is also a high focus on the assimilation of the available information to create velocity within the decision process, to drive the momentum of the business. Essentially to ensure it is moving in a direction towards growth and ultimately success.

Alignment requires clear and concise communication and coordination of multiple activities across the business and its fundamentals. Whether you are a sole trader or owner of a business with a team, you'll need to align others and orientate to the business, the direction it's going and its velocity towards getting there. Alignment is the glue between the people, the plan and purpose which equals higher levels of productivity in delivery.

During my military service alignment played an absolutely critical element in any operational deployment. Alignment was established with a clear and concise delivery of orders; the plan. There would be a clear and concise explanation of the environment where the operation would be taking place. The mission would take centre stage and as such would be verbally repeated twice when delivering verbal orders. The mission was the ultimate in establishing alignment with the soldiers (the purpose) and tasks and responsibilities would be assigned to ensure alignment of the people, actions and effects required on the field of operation. All this would then be discussed and explained in terms of the operation execution; we'll discuss this in more detail in the next section.

Through your focusing on the business orientation, you'll define the direction of travel for the business, where you aim to get too and when. Interestingly you'll need to make sure you and everyone with you, both your external team and internal team understand and have focused and coordinated effort. For a small business or sole trader, it will be ensuring your external team, that is your accountant, marketer, IT support, coach and other external support elements understand where you are heading and their part within the strategic picture and the tactics they need to deliver for you. We'll be talking about tactics shortly.

For businesses with employees, their own teams, you'll need to be aligning them. External or internal there are challenges with alignment. How do you ensure everyone is in tune with the strategic direction of the business, understand the part they play and most importantly are able to deliver it? It's also about the unity of effect, making sure everyone is pulling in the right direction, understand the part they play and why it's critical to the overall success.

In Chapter 1 we took a look at where you want to get too, what you want to achieve and why. Understanding your dream and gaining the clarity through your vision and the vivid vision allows you to define the strategic focus and through your goals, planning and learning you now find yourselves ready to act and engender action.

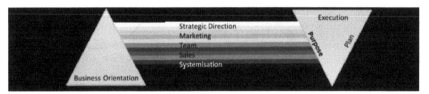

*The Alignment Prism*

Coordinating effort is absolutely key when we seek to ensure alignment, the question is how and where to align. The business alignment prisum depicts loosely, how light is expanded to show its many different wavelengths, the rainbow. As it enters the second prism it is the wavelengths that are then refocused into a laser. Whilst I have no doubt this is not scientifically robust, it offers a good depiction of the importance of alignment.

The diagram doesn't highlight the definitive list in terms of what needs to be aligned. What's key is the need to break down and expose the areas which need to be aligned, where clarity and direction need to be given and ensuring all key functions of the business align. This is where Chapter 1 will assist in the need to break down all the areas of your destination, establishing your plan of action, the business plan and the mission based on the vision.

**Execution**

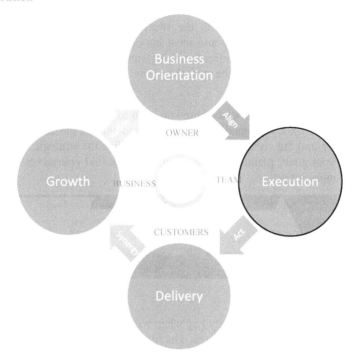

*Application of Execution – The Bus Pass- The Art of Delegation*

As a factual book, it is no different, I suspect, then any other book you have read. You will have been given insight, read accounts to reinforce new learning and offered actions to take and apply; Chapters 1 – 4. Interestingly it is the execution where, sadly, the vast majority will fall down. Let's be clear without execution you will not achieve your vision and will live merely a mediocre life.

In many respects, this book, if you have utilised its structure should by now have you in a position poised and ready to execute. After all, what's the point of having all the thoughts and ideas and then doing nothing with them. When we talk of the formula for abundance (p 190), doing is intrinsic and doing is fundamental to execution. Let's also be clear that the responsibility for execution within your business is you, the business owner. In my experience from the military, business coaching and employee engagement working with both small and large teams I have derived the following as an outline to effective execution. The initial key to execution is discipline or as I term it your 'pig-headed' discipline.

One thing execution is not, is a constant focus on merely getting stuff done. Merely a process of work. Execution should and needs to be a continual evolutionary approach to qualitative delivery of the business objectives.

**The Disciplined Application of Execution**

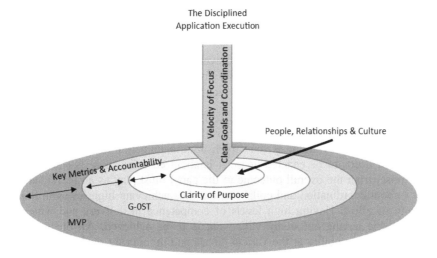

*The Disciplined Application of Execution*

Execution is about precision in application of strategy, having a clear focus on where, what and how activity and the application at the tactical or grassroots level are delivered. In the book Execution (Charan, 2002) Charan and Bossidy clearly highlight the difference between execution and doing things, they highlight that in the process of defining strategy the organisation has the ability to execute. It is here where so many business owners make the mistake of assuming the act of doing things, focusing on a series of smaller activities which should result in achieving the strategy.

Charan and Bossidy also highlight the three key points of execution; discipline, it being the key focus of the business owner and its need to be intrinsic within the business or organisational culture. Now ask yourself if you have ever defined a strategic approach to growing your business, the big picture, highlighted what needs to happen and then started to do stuff. The only problem is the fact you never achieved the desired outcome at the strategic level. The goal or goals weren't achieved, the results weren't what you expected or anticipated. Now ask yourself these 3 questions:

1.      How disciplined was I as the business owner, did I have a truly disciplined approach to success? Pig-headed discipline.

2.      How much time did I expend focusing ON the execution in comparison to the time expended on completing stuff, being the busy fool IN the business?

3.      Does there exist a culture which embraces the required focus on execution and understanding behind our actions, a drive to succeed?

Now in all likelihood 1, 2 or maybe even all 3 of these aspects were non-existent, whilst we thought we had focused on the execution towards achieving the growth and ultimately achieving the goals and objective, the reality was starkly different.

We can begin to see that execution isn't just about a continual focus on activity, rather having the systems to ensure dissemination of information to where it needs to be enacted upon. It is about ensuring there is clarity of purpose, from the overall outcome to the part I must play as an individual. It's about coordination and collaboration, thus achieving high levels in the unity of effort. Having high levels of competence in delivery and where applicable having autonomy with what is to be achieved. All the while having accountability at the various levels and monitoring the key metrics to ensure everything remains on schedule toward achieving the goals and ultimately the objective.

Having a pig-headed disciplined approach to execution has remained a critical focus in my business today and was born through my military training. In order to approach any military operation, there is a critical need to ensure the desired outcome is stacked in your favour. You set the condition for success. Instrumental in this process was alignment through the orders process. The key aspect having achieved alignment would be execution, which was referred to as the concept of operations, within the order process.

The order process was a critical aspect to each and every military operation, whether you were giving a comprehensive and full set of orders which could take over 2 hours to deliver or snap orders in 5 to 7 minutes. The point being the consistent discipline of following the process before execution was key to setting the conditions for success. Let's be clear when you're committing troops to task the outcomes have consequences. So, you absolutely want and need to ensure your execution is as focused and prepared as is possible to determine the right outcome. Just running in blind rarely ends well.

'Concept of Operations, Execution' would be delivered in three elements; the Intent, Scheme of Manoeuvre and Main Effort. In a business context, I term this the 'Velocity of Focus' and the key component for the application of execution. Interestingly this correlates with the velocity of decisions, essentially ensuring progress in a certain direction at speed, in order to gain ground or growth. In the military, the concept of operations would be produced to cover the overarching higher commander's intent, which would look at the big picture for a formation deployment, such as a 6-month deployment to Afghanistan.

From here, the process would be replicated and at each level, the commanders would extract the information which would assist them in producing their orders at each subunit level. This would then form the outline for each and every operation undertaken throughout the operational deployment. In this manner, the entire formation would at each and every turn be focused on the overall outcome at the completion of the operational deployment. When we look at this in the business context and take a view on the application of execution, the process follows the principles, I have merely devised a focus on their utilisation working back from the long-term vision, 5 to 10 years, the 12-month goals and respectively the quarterly goals and the daily routine of working IN and ON the business.

The concept of Operations (CONOPS) is almost delivered in a story like fashion, offering a direct insight into what will happen. There is a great temperature check here for a military commander offering the CofOPs as there is for a business owner offering their version of Velocity of Intent. If you are able to tell the story of what you aim to achieve, without the aid of notes, in other words, it comes from your inherent understanding, your heart, then you will have planned thoroughly with sufficient detail.

Knowing your own plan with this level of detail will give your team more confidence in you as the business leader and or business owner. The power of understanding your own plan should not be underestimated. Having received orders from commanders who have demonstrated significant confidence and depth of understanding their plan, I can say first-hand it makes a difference. The focus we have already offered on planning sets you up to deliver your Velocity of Focus (VofF) and underpin where and how to achieve a real understanding of your plan.

Within your VofF you will offer clarity of purpose (your intent) to your team, this is your purpose, you're why. How, when the plan is executed, will the goals be achieved and what is the desired impact they will have. Setting out your VofF will greatly assist in the promotion of unity within your team, the unity of effort. As mentioned, everyone singing off the same song sheet. I can't tell you how many times I have spoken with a business owner who have the plan in their heads and wonder why their team just don't get it. Well, have you got clarity yourself and have you shared that clarity with the team?

The VogF will motivate, inspire and empower the team, you will experience higher levels of productivity and performance. Having articulated the purpose you and your team will be equipped with the ability to make informed decisions merely with that understanding. As we will see this will have a major impact on the levels of autonomy, which in turn will increase productivity, performance and empowerment. The following table will offer the correlation from my learnings in the military to how I now work with the business owners I coach.

| Execution | |
|---|---|
| **Military** | **Business** |
| **Concept of Operations** | **Velocity of Focus** |
| This allows the military commander to make his intentions explicit for the subunit commanders. They will offer mission and tasks for his subunit commanders. They will describe in some detail how the commander intends to complete the mission. The CofOps as a statement should also include, quite clearly the following: | The business owner determines the objective which needs to be achieved. This will offer the team clarity in terms of the goals which will need to be achieved and insight to the coordination which will be required to ensure the focus remains in the right direction and velocity. |
| • **Intent** | • **Clarity of Purpose, the Why.** |
| The intent is a statement of what the commander wants to achieve, in the field of operation this will be expressed as an effect. i.e. support, surprises, defeat, capture etc. | When we look at purpose or asking the why question it is normally associated with a long-term vision and destination. In many businesses, this will be articulated as the vision |

| | statement. In the same context as having a long-term vision your purpose statement set out what is to be achieved, it could focus on the number of leads generated, increased profit, new venture, new product launch etc. |
|---|---|
| • **Scheme of Manoeuvre** | • **G-OST** |
| Having set the scene in terms of what is to be achieved, the intent. The Scheme of Manoeuvre sets out in more detail and expands on how the commander sees the operation unfolding. There will be an overview in regard to where, when and how, without going into the who. | The G-OST (Goals, \|Objective, Strategy, Tactics) sets out the overarching goal or goals and then the subsequent objectives which will need to be achieved in order to succeed. This will then be broken down into the strategy which needs to be adopted and the tactics of delivery. |
| • **Main Effort** | • **Most Valuable & Profitable** |
| This is a key aspect which the commander will see as the most significant outcome, which if not achieved will make the operation untenable, have to re-establish direction from the higher commander or seek out a predetermined course of action. The focus on the Main Effort helps to focus activity towards its achievement. | The focus on the Most Valuable and Profitable, in a similar vein to Main Effort, keeps the team accountable to the right activities, at the right time and right focus. Most Valuable and Profitable (MVP) activity is a way of ensuring accountability throughout the business. With each team member or employee having certain criteria to perform, they can ask themselves 'right now is the activity I am undertaking the MVP use of my time in the business?' |

*Execution - Military to Business*

**People, Relationships and Culture**

At the core of the application of execution, unsurprisingly, is people. In every organisation which has a focus on growth and profitability, people are the key element. If you remain the sole employee of your business, guess what? You own a job and will continue to do so until you start to grow a team. Additionally, there is the focus on creating a business which isn't reliant on you, as the business owner and most likely 'all-knowing oracle'. Yes, there are some .com businesses, or to be more specific individuals who have made their fortune on their own, I'm sure that if you talk to them you'll find they now have an external support team. It is safe to say that for 99% of business you're going to require to attract and draft in the efforts of others, be they external or internal team members to grow your business.

As I have already mentioned, for the vast majority of business owners they remain the busiest person in the business. Ask yourself the question right now, how busy am I? If you are working harder than your team then you need to review where you are and what causes this imbalance. The whole point of employing people, growing a team is to grow your business. To leverage their time in return for a payment. Now, this sounds simple, for most business owners this is one of the hardest elements to master.

Essentially this is about truly aligning and engaging your workforce. Sounds obvious doesn't it, that's why I pay them. The reality for the vast majority of business is starkly different and it's why at the centre of the application of execution resides people, relationships and culture. Our people need to feel a part of something meaningful, aligned with the business and fully engaged. When these elements are in place you'll find that the cohesive ability of the team, organisation and business will be tremendous.

It's a useful point to take a review of your team. How engaged are your people and I mean really engaged? There are three levels of engagement you should be able to identify within your business, the question here is what proportions do you see within your business? See the Values Performance Matrix.

> 1.      Actively Disengaged – These are your dissidents, your bad apples, they will likely be effective in their role insofar as they are able to perform their task and likely to be good and experienced at it (not in all cases). They will also have a very high opinion of their own place within the team, believing they add more value than they do, they are a key to the success and you should be thankful. Interestingly they would very unlikely (less extreme occasions) to be bold enough to tell you directly. They will seek to encourage more followers.

2.      Disengaged – Now let's be clear these aren't bad people, they are merely not engaged, aligned or enthralled to be working for you. For these it's a job, a means to an end. They will do what's asked of them and generally nothing more. It is merely a transaction between you paying them and them giving you their time.

3.      Fully Engaged – This group are aligned with the business, enjoy their work and the position they hold within the business. They will go the extra mile for their teammates and the business. They will seek to add value where there are opportunities. They will be empowered, engaged and excited about where and what the business can achieve.

In broad terms, you will be able to assess your team with these parameters. In the first instance, there is no place in any team for the dissidents (actively disengaged), we'll take a look at what to do about those shortly. Your levels of disengaged people are and should be seen as an opportunity. What and how can you improve the levels of their engagement? Vast opportunity resides here. Significantly those who are already fully engaged will probably hold for you the key to unlocking potential across the remainder of the team.

With the core ingredient being the people, attracting, retaining and indeed growing the right people is a critical function for any business. Essentially ensuring you get the right people on the bus is challenging, so it is that area I would like to focus on. What determines someone being able to get on board your bus, gaining a bus pass for your business? Let's take a look.

The Bus Pass – Getting the Team Right

Jim Collins's (Collins, 2001) use of the bus analogy is the best and simplest to understand. His focus on the journey from good to great stresses the need to have the right people on the bus and where applicable get the wrong people either in the right seat or off the bus completely, will serve you well. Let's be absolutely clear having the wrong people will not serve you or the business. There's a reason we call people who are not good team players 'bad apples'. Now reflect for a moment, as I will be sure you will have personally experienced a bad apple or maybe even have one in your business right now. What happens if you have a bad apple in your fruit bowl? It infects and rots all the fruit around it and if left, the entire bowl. Frankly, it's the same in business.

There is a simple way to review your team and take a look at who is in what seat, if they are in the right seat and who may need to give a bus pass too. If you have worked your way through this book you will have a far better idea in regard to the potential of your business, what you aim to achieve, your purpose and insight to your behaviours and values. When we look at your team and measure their place against performance and values you will be able to determine if they are in the right seat and or whether they should remain on your bus.

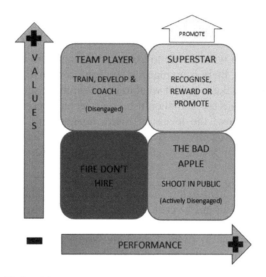

*Performance Value Matrix*

The Performances Values Matrix

This is a simple method to determine your team and their level of investment and where they fit.

Low Value and Low Performance

Let's make this really simple. There is no value for you in your team with this type of person. You will ultimately be doing all the work for them and here's the thing they won't thank you for it. In the first instance do not hire these people. If you have team members of this nature, then it's time to let them go. You are wasting your money as these will be costing you time and time, as we are well aware, is money. I'm not saying these are bad people, rather they have value to add, just not in your business. A focus here in the hiring process is to always ensure you have a sufficient probationary period. Hire slow fire fast.

Low Value and High Performance

You will know who these people are, you will have encountered them or indeed have them in your team now. Whilst they may have great skills and ability, they will not be a team player. Bad apples (actively disengaged) will seek to undermine you, the business and most worryingly seek to surround themselves with like-minded individuals. In other words, cause a rot within the business. They will have a major below the parapet attitude, feel that success is down to them, they are the glue that holds the business together. They will complain about everything and be change resistant.

Interestingly they will very rarely direct their discord directly or openly to you unless you have accepted their poor behaviours and allowed that to happen. Ultimately, they need to go or at the very least cease their disruptive and destructive behaviour. Now, I always get myself in trouble with HR experts with my next statement, bad apples need to be shot in public (metaphorically speaking). Let me explain. They gain their confidence and power from infecting others, they will undermine you and corrupt good people or worse still have good people leave your business. I am sure you know who they are in your business. They must clearly understand that you know their behaviour and that it is not acceptable within your business. If you witness their behaviour directly then they should be corrected there and then.

Under no circumstance should you allow this behaviour to be acceptable within your business? Where applicable evoke disciplinary proceedings, talk to a good HR professional and work out how to have them removed from your business. Let's be clear and I know some will at this point be in fierce disagreement with me, this is your business, your future and you are paying the bills. In all likelihood, they asked you for the job, so be clear about what seat they hold and the value you get for buying their time.

High Values and Low Performance

These are in fact great team players and an area of significant investment for you (Disengaged). They will be willing to engage with you and the other team members, they will be enthusiastic, they will have the drive to learn and add value to the team. They are an investment for you in business and the area of focus to unlock their potential and increase their levels of engagement. Yes, you may need to invest time and money in them to train, develop or indeed coach, one thing that will be clear is you will be rewarded for doing so.

They will be right for the future of the business and in many cases, will be where you will find your emergent leadership, those who will step up to positions of management and leadership as the business grows. It is in this quadrant that we find a rich source of good quality people and goes to reinforce that age-old question of attitude or skills. For me every time it has to be the attitude. As Jim Collins states (Collins, 2001) great businesses have a real focus on who first then what. Determine who deserves to be on the bus and then you can work out what seat they take.

High Values and High Performance

These are your superstars (Fully engaged), they get it, love what they do, are open to change and challenge. Now it's important with these and the team players that you recognise their efforts, results and commitment. Celebrate success, reward them make sure the team know that it means something to do good work within the business. Now as obvious as this sounds it's lacking in business today.

Ask yourself what was the last positive celebration you had as a team? Did you celebrate the sale, the new product, the team's innovation, a business or team members milestone? Sadly, not as much as you should. More likely you focused on the negative and the need to do something about that and most likely your team players and superstars just got on with it. Well if you celebrated the wins with as much vigour as the negative and challenging aspects what's the likely outcome going to be on performance and productivity?

Another area of focus here in terms of reward could be promotion, offering your superstars the step up to the next level in the business. One thing to be very mindful of when promoting someone is that you don't promote them into a position of weakness and poor performance. They will either need to know they have the confidence to step up or you're going to ensure they are trained and ready. The worst thing is to have a superstar feeling demoted because they aren't able to step up to the challenge. Conversely, I am always a keen advocate of challenging people, taking them out of their comfort zone to expand their ability and belief. The trick is to make sure they are comfortable with that.

The Bus

Let's take a look at the bus for a moment. Having an idea of the team you desire and assessing where you are now we can ask how that actually fits with your ideal bus. Well, let's look at each aspect of the bus and simply ask yourself how it fits with the state of your bus today?

- **The Driver.** As the driving force in your business, how well are you able to manoeuvre through the speed humps, traffic delays and barriers you face. Are you a good leader or is this an area where you may need to develop? Just because you own the business doesn't mean you're going to be the best driver. You need to have a clear focus on where you are going, a clear windshield. A good look at what's happened in the business, its history and the administration that results in a good view of the rear-view mirror. You also need to have a good fix on what's going on now, the technical delivery of your business. Remember the entrepreneur in you looks to the future, the manager has a fix on the past the administration and as the technician what's happening in the present.
- **The Sat Nav.** Do you have a clear road mapped out for the future where you are going? What's the dream destination, vision, the current goals and objectives? Equally, does the team have sight of the map, are the rear seat TV displays working so they can check in and see just where they are and their part.
- **The People in the Right Seats**. Are your team all sitting in the seat assigned to them? Having the right people on the bus is one thing, the critical element is they are in the right seat. Now, remember that with all likelihood there will be some who move seats along the journey and that is to be expected. Their seat isn't fixed and nor should it be, rather you have the focus to be adaptable and flexible for the needs of the business.
- **The Right Fuel.** Ever put petrol in a diesel car (or vice versa), I have and it's not good, it doesn't go very far and if you don't stop and drain the tank you'll end up with long-lasting damage. Having the right fuel to motivate and drive your team is a real key aspect. Knowing what motivates your team is vitally important. As such I want to touch on that next.

The 3 Core Needs Within a Team

As if owning a business isn't hard enough, you will by virtue develop into a business leader. You will have a number of people who you employ who will become your team and you will need to lead them. Having already looked at the requirement to focus on building the right team, having the right people on the bus, it's important we understand in the simplest terms what makes a team or more specifically the team members tick. There are 3 elements which will dramatically shift the team's ability to perform coherently dependent on their presence, level of importance and impact on the organisation's culture. Multiple and meaningful relationships, personal competence and high levels of autonomy are always present in high performing teams.

Relationships

We are a social species and to one degree or another, we all need to know we are in and have meaningful relationships. Let's be clear in our lives we will establish and continue to seek multiple meaningful relationships. Within our families with our loved ones, with those with whom we share passion and love and within the many levels of friends and acquaintances, we will encounter throughout our lifes journey. We each of us need to know we are needed, relied upon and ultimately loved. It's no different in business and the teams we work within.

I was fortunate enough to attend a seminar by Manley Hopkins (Hopkins, 2014) whilst I was serving in the Army. Manley, who at the time had completed the BT Global Challenge renowned by many as the world toughest yacht race, offered insight into leadership culture and how relationships impact any team. His seminar was based on his account of being selected as a member of the BT Global Challenge team and how the remaining crew developed a strong bond together and fought through some of the harshest conditions the world can offer to complete the challenge.

During the presentation, we undertook a very simple exercise to discover just what would be required to undertake such feet. He asked the assembled officers and soldiers to take a number of post-it notes and write down for us as individuals what it meant to be chosen for a similar challenge. Had we have been selected what emotions, values, behaviours would it evoke in us as individuals. Once we had written out our post-its we were then asked to stick them to a whiteboard under the heading me. Next, he asked us all the same question, although this time we had to answer with the focus on having been selected amidst the rest of the team. This time we had to stick our post-its to the board under the heading team. Finally, he asked to do the same with the understanding that we were going to answer with a view of what it meant to represent the organisation.

Manley took us through an exercise I have since used with numerous businesses and teams and it is an excellent way to reinforce the impact of relationships. Whilst Manley uses the example of extreme hardship and indeed much of my experience from the military has been in difficult and dangerous circumstances, the final question he asked was the one which has driven home a valuable lesson for me. Reflecting on the context of the exercise Manley simply asked:

*So, what's different right now today?*

Frankly, nothing, whether on a challenging expedition, on military operations or turning up for work tomorrow, nothing changes. Yet we struggle to evoke the behaviours and values we would suggest are critical for exciting and dangerous endeavours. Ask yourself right now where your team is? Within any organisation team relationships are key and the numerous times I have run this exercise merely goes to reinforce that notion.

Everyone needs to know they are part of something bigger, have a place in the team and feel valued. A fully functioning team needs to have a network of relationships, a collective bond, a common goal and purpose that together can be a motivating factor. And here's the important part these relationships need to be meaningful. So how can you develop these relationships? Well here's some ideas to get started:

1.      Widely publish the vision and mission. If you have a vivid vision, then send a personal copy to all the team members.
2.      Make sure that everyone knows and is bought into the common goal.
3.      Encourage the team members to talk to each other and find out something new. Ask them to share stories. Stories are the best way to break down the barriers.
4.      Have team days.
5.      Encourage healthy conflict and challenge.

The key here is to ensure that you promote and encourage relationships to be forged. I know this may sound like a utopia, it isn't. Through these relationships we will vastly increase trust and trust is the bond which keeps a team together and productive. It also means we don't always have to agree with one another, far from it, it allows healthy conflict to prevail. We don't just agree because you're the boss rather we feel there is an open passage of communication which encourages wider thought and contemplation.

Personal Competence

Whilst this may sound quite obvious, all too often it is not. To work effectively within a team, you need to know and have a level of confidence that the role, appointment or task you have been given, you are able to complete. On many occasions through my military career after promotion, I found myself having doubt and wondering how on earth did I get here. As I reflected on the qualifying courses and efforts I had made to attend promotion I was able to reinforce my confidence that I did, in fact, have the competence. This in turn naturally increased my level of engagement, I loved what I did and worked hard to do it as well as I could. I, in essence, sought to be the very best version of me at each and every rank and appointment I held in the Army. That continues today in my pursuits as a professional coach.

Your part in a team hinges on you being able to perform. Take away your confidence to perform and suddenly your confidence goes, you start to have doubt and feelings of anxiety. You will not be able to perform and ultimately will weaken the team. When you take the view on this as the business owner or leader the importance here is to ensure your team members are in the right seat and that means they have the abilities required. In turn, this will ensure they are engaged and aligned.

Now when we think for a moment and the focus on 'who first then what' we have room for manoeuvre. Essentially having the right attitude may result in someone with less ability but equal competence. In other words, they have the capability and the basics to perform the role, more importantly, they have the desire, drive and motivation to gain even greater competence. They are a team player. Whilst you may have to invest in these people the long-term outcomes out way having someone who is competent without the right attitude. These are your team players.

In a similar vein when you take your superstars, be mindful of promotion. You can very easily, for all the right reason take a superstar from their seat and with a view to offer and assign them a better seat reduce their competence. In turn, weaken the team. When seeking to promote be clear they have or will receive the necessary training and support to take the next seat with confidence. Don't risk limiting their confidence because they perceive to not have the competence in their new role.

Autonomy

I'd be pretty confident that each and every one of us likes to have the feeling of freedom, to just do what we want to do. Or in some cases not do. Autonomy and the ability to think for ourselves is a key aspect. Yet in business we seek the course of least resistance, to be less than autonomous, to just be a part of the herd. There is no surprise that the business owner will more often than not be the busiest person in the business. They allow themselves to become the default setting.

Autonomy is a key factor in any high performing team, indeed without it, productivity will be low, morale will be low and your team will not be fully engaged in what they do. As a coach from a military background, I have found this quite bizarre. Now you may think that the military merely trains and indoctrinates its people to be utterly compliant, follow orders to the letter and not be able to think for themselves. Which can be construed, especially when you use terms like 'Chain of Command'. Thankfully in today's armed service, the opposite is true, as there is a focus on creating soldiers and officers who have the ability to work through and make complex decisions without the need of orders.

One simple methodology which can be widely embraced with business is mission command. Mission command is widely described as a style of command that seeks to convey understanding to subordinates about the intentions of higher command and their place within the plan, enabling them to carry out missions with maximum freedom of action and appropriate resources'. In short, go back to Chapter 1 and look at your mission, it is clarity in this which will ultimately enable autonomy in your business.

The mission is the overarching statement of your intent, from here you then need to ensure the team have clarity and all share the common goal of the business which is relevant at that moment. Having a common goal will encourage an environment of autonomy within the team. Understanding where the business is heading and that in short as long as the decisions being made are in line with that common goal individuals are acting with utter commitment to the very best outcome.

Essentially this practice defines the 'rules of the game', ensuring where appropriate and applicable to what depth and level can decisions be made. At what point do individuals need to seek clarity or permission? Now, this does renege on the need for autonomy but rather afords a level of protection to the team, the business and you the owner. The rules of the game offer the

241

conditions for autonomy to flourish. Let's take a look at the rules of the game and the two distinct sides of the decision coin.

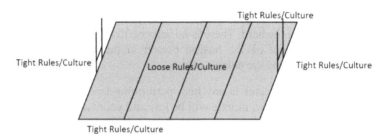

*Loose and Tight Rules/Culture*

- The loose rules/culture. To explain this, I'm going to use the analogy of a field of sports, a pitch of your choice. In most cases, there will be white lines depicting the outline of the pitch, court or field of play. It is these lines which define the loose rules. Everyone on the team understands the role they play within the team (competencies and relationships) within these lines. They will have clarity of what and how to act, respond and the level of the decision they can make. You will likely have a team captain (manager) and referee (industry, compliance, law, principles). So, we can even see there is direction available within the loose rules and culture. Freedom of movement commensurate to the position, task and responsibility everyone holds. There is even clarity in the mission, the mission is to win, the objective is to score goals, the tactics are how we then undertake that.
- The tight rules/culture. Now the white lines are there for a reason, they form a reference point where team players will need to seek clarity. Outside of these lines resides the leadership and as you will observe the coach. When the ball crosses one of these lines, generally play has to stop. At which point we need to seek clarity, which can come from the referee and the leadership or coach. Essentially team members will need to seek clarity of what is to happen next, confirm they remain on task and seek to understand if there are any constraints imposed.

Unfortunately, in many teams and this has been my experience, the loose and the tight rules are undefined and a culture of understanding doesn't exist or isn't clear. Marginally the focus is to default everything to the business owner or leader. There is an ever-decreasing limitation on the ability to assess situations on the playing field and make meaningful decisions for the benefit of the team and organisation or business. The rules of the game will in a paradoxical approach enable and empower far greater levels of autonomy.

When we take a really close look at the organisations who have developed extremely high levels of autonomy they will have in place the Loose and Tight Rules and have a strong culture. In his book Turn the Ship Around, David Marquet (Marquet, 2012) tells the story of his appointment to take command of a USS Santa Fe and the shift from being the worst in the fleet to become the first in the fleet. He introduced a focus on leadership which challenged the underlying assumptions of taking control to one where the team were empowered.

There was a major lesson reinforced from his insights and one which I could take from my military experience. It revolves around the question of leadership, what is the purpose of leadership? Now if you type that into Google you'll be offered quite a wide variety of results, at the time of writing there were 60,800,000, funnily enough, it's more than the age-old question 'what's the meaning of life, which came in at 17,400,000. The point here, is I believe there is one overarching focus and meaning for leadership and that is to grow and develop new leaders.

Now think about that for a moment. In order to grow new leaders, you will arguably need to have in place all the focus on developing leaders and leadership. To grow new leaders you need to encourage, inspire and empower the will of others towards a given outcome and or task. You need to be a decision maker and encourage others to do likewise. You need to be committed to a cause or belief and enrol others. We could keep this going for a while, I guess you get the idea.

David Marquet, had that simple focus to empower his crew to take responsibility, make decisions based on the needs of the ship and to think for themselves, have heightened autonomy. David termed this a 'Leader Leader' culture where he empowered commensurate responsibility and thinking at each and every level of command, from sailor to XO. He offered some very simple rules of the game. Over time these created long-lasting transformation throughout the crew and performance of the ship.

He eliminated the need for permission to act. He empowered the crew the ability to make and see through decisions with commitment. On the occasions where the crew would traditionally ask permission (the tight rules), they would offer an intention, make a commitment to what they intended to do not ask permission to do it. 'I intended to....' This ensured great communication, a simple unassuming method to ensure the right course of action was being undertaken without being impeded or delay. Should clarity need to be given it could be through a simple request for confirmation.

He encouraged a culture of deliberate action, ensuring the crew always remained committed to a course of action. This, in turn, created extremely high levels of engagement, alignment and autonomy. The crew owned their positions and appointments, conducted themselves in a manner which created far higher levels of productivity and ownership. In addition to this, it also encouraged a focus on excellence, seeking always to go that bit further, do that bit better, as I have highlighted to be unreasonably good.

## Act
When all is said and done the application of execution is wholeheartedly reliant on the actions and activities undertaken by the team. Having an engaged and empowered team or at the very least on the road to achieving that, now relies on the need to get stuff done. The application of execution could be very much viewed as the application and development of leadership within your business. Now developing a good team, having good people is key, I am also very clear that not everyone in your team will demonstrate leadership and high levels of autonomy. Let's not forget that many people are more than happy with being an employee, having clarity in what they are required to do.

Getting into action is where management comes into play. Management shouldn't be seen as a limitation on the 3 factors within a team, far from it in fact. Management is the means toward delivering the tactical aspects within G-OST. It is also the focus to underpin the loose and tight rules. As already mentioned the team captain would be an element of the management.

Let's be clear management isn't about micromanagement, although there may well be occasions where that may be required. It's making sure the tactics being undertaken are in tune with the strategy. Management plays a key function in achieving the business objectives and remaining on track to achieve the goals. Good management is always a significant contributing factor to creating and maintain a high performing team.

Now I have no interest in adding to that age-old question in relation to leadership and management, you didn't buy this book for that debate. Rather I seek to clarify the importance of management in action, not to mention the fact that you can be the leader and manager, you just need to be able to differentiate between them. If you want to ask yourself that question, go back and review your organisational chart. Where are you currently responsible for delivery and focus on strategy versus where are you, the default setting for the delivery of the tactics? I'm sure you'll realise this is where you act as a leader and manager.

At one end of the spectrum is the maintenance of what needs to happen and at the other end change. As a manager or in the managerial mode you are focused on systems and process, whilst as the leader, you focus on engagement and empowerment. It's very much the journey between the two sides. The shift between transactional, following a processor system and transformational in achieving growth and change. Indeed, as we have previously highlighted these will be the areas for growth within the business. You lead and develop or hire managers.

So how do we have a focus on management which is in tune with the three core principles of the team? Have a level of management which encourages, empowers and engages and doesn't have an adverse effect. Essentially, it's about delegation, and stopping being totally responsible for all the activity all of the time.

The Art of Delegation

Effective delegation has multiple benefits to any team. For you, as the business owner, it creates an opportunity to vastly increase your productivity as a leader with a greater focus on the business and less where you're in it. Before I go onto offer my insight to the 'Art of Delegation' let me first highlight the wins from delegation:

- Training and Development. Delegation is a great way to develop your team, give them additional responsibility, stretch them in their position. This can also form a part of your team's personal development in regard to specific individuals and their roles and responsibilities. Take for instance your emergent leaders, delegation can empower them, give them greater responsibility which can all be a part of their transition into a new role or promotion.
- Build Strengths and Weakness. Delegation can be seen as a focus on a team members strength, giving them the task and

245

responsibility, which suits their skill sets. Conversely, it can be a focused activity on a weakness which the individual requires development in.

- Team Ownership. In this instance delegation can focus on specific projects which encourage a team member to take full ownership, in these instances, there are significantly high levels of autonomy. They complete the project and then look to assume the responsibility for the following elements or similar projects. Essentially you can have a project run itself.
- High-Level Engagement. This in the simplest terms allows the team member to feel a significant part of the team. Their personal levels of engagement will vastly increase along with a sense of empowerment.
- You will gain far more personal and business time. It will assist your shift from a reliance of being in the business towards having far more quality time. Essentially this will give you the opportunity to do more and therefore to achieve more.
- Delegation builds autonomy and a direct output is a speed at which the business will grow. The productivity and efficiency will significantly increase, in both yourself and of your key people.
- Responsibility. Probably one of the most significant aspects and benefits and links back to the principle of Leader Leader, your team accept more responsibility and become more valuable to you. Solidifying the right people on the bus.

A major reason why there is often low levels of autonomy and by virtue low levels of delegation is the associated risk that accompanies the task being completed, achieved or effectively completed to your standards. Often this will be directly associated with a financial outcome. The root cause, without doubt, trust. Trust is the glue which bonds a team together, it affords strength in relationships, confidence in position and the leadership.

When we reflect on the 3 principles which contribute to a winning team you will see trust is an intrinsic ingredient. Think if there is limited trust just how authentic will the relationships be? Just how empowered and likely will the levels of autonomy be? And what of competence without trust, we will cease to get anything done efficiently. Take for a moment the emphasis Steve Covey (Covey S. , 2006) placed on trust. In his book on The Speed of Trust, he states trust as tangible and when developed and leveraged has the potential for unparalleled success. It is the one thing that changes everything. Interestingly he has highlighted 13 behaviours he associates with trust, which link very closely with the with our 3 principles; talk straight, respect, transparency, right wrongs, loyalty, deliver results, get better, confront reality, clarify expectations, listen, keep commitments and extend trust.

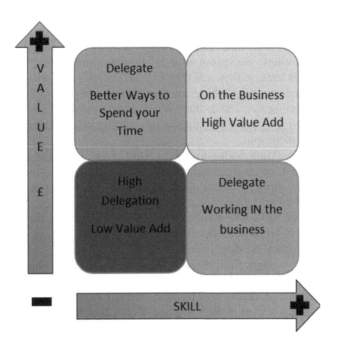

*Values Skills Quadrant*

In the book the 5 Dysfunctions of a Team, Patrick Lencioni (Lencioni, 2012) states the foundation for team effectiveness is the absence of trust. When we look at delegation it's clear there needs to be a level of trust, indeed the higher the better. Here's a great rule of thumb, when you are seeking to delegate or start delegating ask yourself this simple yet challenging question. What's the worst that can happen? Now as we have looked at and you may have started to or have in place the rules of the game could you now start to delegate more effectively?

If you are still a little reticent in regard to delegation, then you will also need to ask yourself what the cost is in your inability to delegate. In terms of costs, what is the monetary value? In terms of the value, you add on an hourly basis to your business in comparison to your team member or indeed outsourcing. This really doesn't take a great deal of thought that if your value is in the £100 and the job generates in the £10 then what may you need to do? One way to look at where you may need to start delegating is in the values skills quadrant. In this quadrant, you will be able to determine where and what you should start to focus on in terms of delegation.

- **Low Skill and Low Value**. In this quadrant, you will be wasting your time and ultimately costing the business money. Interestingly the reason so many business owners find themselves here is because they feel they will save money or it will be quicker to do it myself. Nothing could be further from the truth. This will be costing you and is the place to start to look at delegation and indeed it may even be the area to start to look for recruiting new team members.
- **High Value and Low Skill**. Here the business owner is deluded, conducting tasks which offer high value to the business, yet the business owner does not have the skills to do it effectively or efficiently. Once again costing the business money. Now, these may be tasks where trust is a significant issue and the money an issue in terms of the level of financial decision making which may accompany the delegation.
- **High Skill Low Value**. In most cases, these will be technical tasks the business owner is more than competent to complete. Often relates to the business function and what got the business started in the first place. Going back to the tools may well be bringing value into the business, however, as the business owner, it is often not the value which they now add ON the business.
- **High Value and High Skill**. This is where you as a business owner add the value, you may be applying your technical ability, your entrepreneurial focus and your managerial focus ON the business, all of which are revenue adding.

As a rule of thumb going through this quadrant is a simple and effective method to assess where, commensurate to your business, you need to start delegating or in some cases recruiting. Let's be clear recruiting is the ultimate in delegation, you leverage other skills through paying them to increase your business outputs.

Now I want to be really clear that delegation isn't abdication, you are not merely relinquishing the responsibility you have to the business. Whilst it is the end game to create the business which works without you, it doesn't happen overnight. So, here's a focus on what you will need to do to make sure you have a structured approach to delegation:

- Have a clearly defined set of policies in place (rules of the game) that the staff member can refer to for guidance and be prepared to stand behind the staff member's decisions based on those policies.
- Give them the skills and training needed to do the task.
- Give them the responsibility (autonomy) to take the action required.
- Give them the authority (autonomy) to be able to take the action required.
- Give them a time frame to complete the task.
- Give them a clear picture of what outcome you want.
- Give them feedback so they know if they are producing what you want.

Now everything we have discussed so far is to ensure velocity focus of execution. Ensuring our people have clarity in the part they play and being an intrinsic part of the business. Set out our G-OST and have the MVP at the top of the agenda to ensure the activity and actions deliver our service or product to our customers. Now seems like we have covered significant ground, here's the really important part in all this and the key to our success, profitability, growth and ultimately survival is the ability to then get into action, to act.

**Delivery**

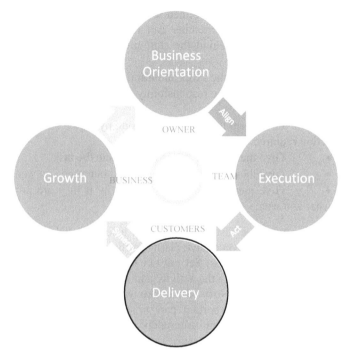

*Predictability – Consistency; Test & Measuring*

Delivery focuses on two aspects which are key for the business to survive and thrive and they are consistency and predictability. The business needs to consistently deliver on its promise and more often than not over deliver on expectation. In order to maintain the business rhythm, it also needs to be able to predict with an air of certainty what's coming. So how do we do ensure consistency and predictability?

**Predictability**

Interestingly I have found many businesses who will happily give me their predictions for the business to slump, as I term it the seasonal drift and variations throughout the year. Yet very few who will with confidence offer predictability for business all year round. It almost seems there have to be the highs and lows, which frankly it's ludicrous. I concede there will be those of you now telling me I can only reap my crop at certain times of the year and I agree. Although interestingly today there are ways to harvest and store crops to enable an all-year-round availability. There will be those of you who will be adamant that the holiday let can only be let in the summer yet have never established a market segment who seek those winter breaks.

So, what is predictability?

Predictability is essentially your ability to have a level of expectedness. To be able to pre-empt opportunity or issues as a result of having the significant insight into what's happened, happening and as a result what is most and least likely to happen. In this fashion, you will find you have the ability to act with a greater air of certainty, although it's not an exact science.

Today with the current technical advance in our ability to gather and analyse data there is a positive impact to be gained in predicting the future. Whilst we still remain a long way off from time travel, we can currently start to predict behaviours. What's interesting is the fact that the notion of 'Big Data' is no longer a corporate organisations advantage. Today any business can now gain access to their clients, suspects and prospects habits.

From traditional surveys to the interrogation of digital data from a website activity, social media, to the fine detail relating to the length of time spent on a website. Compound this with time and you can even determine the variations month to month and year to year. You can, in fact, begin to predict your delivery, when and what increases of stock may be required. At what point we need to increase manufacturing production in relation to specific clients or customer need. Even predict with some level of certainty what your stock holding will likely need to be and by virtue run a lean business.

Predictability is a key aspect of your marketing and the sales pipeline. Having the insight into what works and doesn't in marketing which will allow you to make informed decisions as to your marketing strategy.

It also offers focus in terms of the predictability of your customers and their interaction with your business. Predictability can also increases the perceived value you offer, or they gain from doing business with you. Being creatures of habit, knowing what we can expect is a comforting experience and one which will aim to have repeated. In other words, if we know we are likely to have returning customers we can assume and indeed predict growth as new customers are attracted and current customers return.

A clear knowledge and understanding of what you offer and how will also vastly increase predictability. Have you ever been sold a service or product with an understanding to expect certain criteria and then it didn't match expectation? Take as an example a builder, who state they will arrive at a certain time and have the work completed for a certain price on budget. They arrive late; the works doesn't go to plan and it's over budget. Or you buy a product that claims to do X, Y and Z. When you buy it doesn't match its description and is not what you expected. A final example and one which is probably the most obvious, when you buy take away food and it bears no resemblance to the image portrayed on the menu.

In each of these instances and examples of a focus on predictability, you can identify growth and growth opportunities, predict what's going to happen. Which ultimately means a clear understanding of what works and doesn't; test and measuring every aspect. We'll talk about this in a moment.

With our focus on predictability, there is one key to applying it successfully and that is consistency. We can gain significant benefits as mentioned from predictability if we also act in a consistent fashion. As we will go onto see consistency is the other side of the delivery coin.

**Consistency.**

Consistency is defined as:

*'The quality of achieving a level of performance which does not vary greatly in quality over time'.*

When we start to take a view on consistency within the business context it impacts on everything you, the team and the business do. It's a focus on the delivery through systems, it's a focus on routine, expectation and a high level of compliance. Now it should be said that with each of these they can be consistently poor, this is where pursuit of excellence, as one of my former Commanding Officers positioned our consistency, to always seek to be unreasonably good.

In order to understand the context of consistency, it is important to grasp the benefits of application. Where, how and what impact does consistency bring to the Business Rhythm. Consistency as a concept should run through the DNA of the business. A constant focus on delivery at the highest level. It should be a constant drive to wow the customers, building upon your consistent approach. As you develop Business Rhythm and build high levels of expectation through predictability and consistency the rhythm gains intensity. You will ultimately wow your customers with what you actually do.

A cautionary note, getting the customer's expectation right is merely the ticket into the sandbox, what you offer is as a minimum of what your customers seek. Seeking to offer the wow effect, stun your clients with the level of service they get is the real goal. What is the height of value received from doing business and investing with your business? You need to have a focus here in order to ensure consistency and predictability underpins your business rhythm. One killer for any business and impact on lead generation, retention and customer loyalty is that of 'perceived indifference'.

Let me explain what perceived indifference means? 'Perceived indifference' is when customers feel that you don't care about them; that they don't matter to your business and that you couldn't really care less whether they purchase from you or not. Interestingly it doesn't matter if this isn't the reality, remember it's called "perceived" indifference.

Prof John Gattorna a visiting professor at Macquarie University conducted a study in 2008 into the reasons we lose customers. His study concluded that 68% of your customers will leave you because they don't know that you actually do value them! Additionally, he determined:

- 4% due to natural attrition (moved away – passed on, etc)
- 5% are referred to a competitor by their friend
  - o 9% for competitive reasons (price point, product features, etc.)
- 14% because of product/service dissatisfaction

Essentially perceived indifference is the single most common reason you may lose your customers to your competitors. Interestingly with consistency. Perceived indifference sends customers away nearly 5 times more often than dissatisfaction with a product or service and over 7 times more often than for competitive reasons. Clearly, we need to pay far more attention to our attitude towards our customers.

We often assume that our customers' key concern is price, little do we realise that we can differentiate ourselves and win over our customers time and time again by simply demonstrating that we value them. There is the opportunity for repeat custom and consistency and the ability to build a solid referral system based on satisfied customers. Thus impacting on both predictability and consistency.

A key to success here also goes back to the emphasis we have on the team. One key aspect of having the right people on the bus is the impact they will have on your customers. Imagine if you never had to worry about your customers ever again. Well, you can. As a business owner, you need to value your team more than you do your customer. Treat your team as if they were your customers and you'll never have to worry about your actual customers again. In other words, really value your team.

Reputation is a natural consequence of consistency. Take what we have discussed so far, through a continued focus on your level of service and a continuing aim to go that bit further you will establish a solid reputation. Now, this is where the continued focus on consistency is critical. As you will be aware of building a reputation takes time. Losing your reputation takes moments. More often than not loss of reputation results from poor judgement, bad decisions or not sticking to the system. All of which are a result of poor consistency.

Consistency also vastly increases a sense of being and remaining above the parapet. Indeed, the very notion of remaining above the parapet requires the highest focus on and aspiration to live, work and interact at a higher level. It maintains the focus and momentum towards the destination and vision, essentially focusing on the opportunities of the future.

Another clear outcome from consistency is the ability to monitor and measure, to have a focus on Test and Measuring. Consistency ensures any undertakings have an opportunity to have an impact. In other words, you allow them time to work, which means you are able to gain sufficient data to establish, with fact, if a strategy, tactic or plan has the desired outcome. Having consistency to making a change in a way which you can measure and test the assumptions and results.

**Test and Measuring**

No matter what the strategy, tactics, systems you utilise for delivery in your service or product you need to have an analytical focus towards ensuring it works. Having a truly commercial focus within the business will sometimes mean that even your best ideas will not work. We so often act on feelings, gut instinct, just knowing it will work, only to then establish that it hasn't! Guess what, that will cost you and the business money. Now there is no sure way to stop wasting money entirely, there is a way in which we can massively limit the risk and by virtue waste less.

It is here that test and measuring comes into play in a very significant way. Now interestingly test and measuring is nothing new, it's just very rarely committed too, and funnily enough, without any consistency. Yet one thing you will all be aware of, have experienced and maybe even struggled with is the ever-changing environment within the business. The changing environment is consistent. So, having a focus on the need to measure and then test everything in your business is one sure way to remain committed to success and limit the impact of failure.

Now more often than not for those businesses who actually do focus on test and measuring the focus is almost entirely on the marketing activities and that is a great place to start. All I would suggest is having read the insight to KPIs in the next few pages, you'll suddenly realise there are numerous areas to focus and set up the process to test and measure.

To get started to ask yourself if you have insight as to where your customers come from? How did they find me? What do they buy? What don't they buy? How much profit does each customer offer? As you can imagine the list can go on. It is therefore vital you start to set in play what needs to be measured and then tested. It's not good enough to simply be guessing, you'll get it wrong and that will be costly.

Having the key metrics in place will allow you to make powerful decisions and maintain the focus on effective delivery. Understanding what works and what doesn't in marketing, throughout your sales pipeline, enables you to make key decisions. It will also vastly improve predictability and consistency.

When it comes to testing, it amazes me just how many businesses do very little if any testing of their marketplace, marketing tactics or sales process. Rather they will have a wonderful idea and just go for it without any concern as to how much it may cost. Sadly, all too often going in blind results in costly mistakes. In other instances, you throw lots at the wall and aim to see what sticks, lots of little activities with little or no thought about the application. All too often business owners are looking for the golden egg, the nugget that's going to give them the edge, to make everything ok. Well here's the thing it's there you just need to test, test, test and test again, all the while measuring the response.

With a dual focus on testing and measuring you'll be in control. From having numbers to support specific activities before you make a commitment, to testing new ideas in a measured way, without over-committing. Interesting testing and measuring is an intrinsic element of maintaining your Key Performance Indicators. As you will have discovered business rhythm is a cycle and as such, you set out and determine what your KPI's are to be in business orientation, it is here in delivery that we collate the numbers and where you assimilate the data.

## Synergy

When we talk of synergy we are essentially focused on the sum of two halves coming together and being greater than the individual parts. 1 + 1 = 4. It's about having a well-oiled machine, process and procedures, a system that works. In that manner, we end up with results greater than the sum of the parts. Synergy means the organisation, business or company is now running smoothly to keep it that way it is imperative to keep a finger on the pulse. Having a clear focus on synergy will lead to the business multiplier. Meaning your business could be worth significant multiples of its revenue. More on that shortly.

Synergy focuses on multiple levels, there is the focus of synergy between the business owner and the team, between the team and the process of delivery, the marketing, sale and customer interaction. There has to be a continued assessment of each and every aspect within the business. In many facts, there is a paradoxical synergy in the continued and disciplined review of measuring, KPI's, testing and continual feedforward.

The most important aspects of synergy are financial. When all is said and done it boils down to the business's ability to turn a profit and so for every pound invested into and within the business growth can only be achieved through making more pounds in return. The easiest way to articulate is to review the profit and loss sheet. Taking a close look at the two aspects of the P&L there are essentially; profit or the sources of business revenue; loss or the costs and expenses to the business.

Now here's the key to synergy, you can't manage what is not measured. If you don't currently have KPI's in place, a clear understanding and focus on test and measure activity within the business or a team dynamic which encourages feedforward you will never achieve synergy. Review business orientation where we seek to establish business wisdom and you can then see the importance of its ability to achieve synergy.

The review of your business and the determined areas where you could or need to focus in order to achieve and maintain a focus on the overall results and destination. Remembering within the business rhythm having synergy is the link to growth. The following areas are where synergy needs to exist.

Let's be clear this will lead to the synergistic, smooth running of your business through a consistent drive to implement and achieve synergy.

Planning Synergy.

Regular reporting ensures the business direction remains true to the vision, mission and delivery of the plan. It also creates checkpoints or decision points along the way. Regular reporting starts with a quarterly review. It is at this point we are able to examine and determine the progression and currency of the plan. Having maintained the KPI's day to day and week to week, as we discussed throughout the delivery, it is at this point patterns will emerge. As a snapshot of activity day to day, we can build the bigger picture of what is happening each quarter.

A quarterly business review starts with a review of the business goals, are they being accomplished and on course? What impact with the financial growth in the business? Here we can take a look at the ratios, what's the working factors per £100 within the business? There is also the accountability issue, how are the team performing?

Other areas which will almost certainly need to be covered include:

- Operations (production, waste, innovation, new development).
- Team engagement levels.
- Customer input, sales trends, new product development, component technology trends, outsourcing strategy and objectives.
- Sales history of customers.
- Quality performance, product returns, corrective actions.
- Delivery performance and any issues affecting deliveries.
- Programme performance and efficiencies.
- Quotations, information required/desired, quote turnaround time, new product quote, quote of existing product(s), quote clarity/format.
- Cost reduction initiative and cost savings, other issues (invoicing, terms, etc.)
- Inventory levels.
- New program introductions.
- Goals and objectives.

With a quarterly review completed the business owner should have enough information to make a clear evaluation of where the business is right now.

There should be a solid understanding of the current position in order to then determine what needs to be achieved in the next quarter. This in turn then enables the business owner to plan in detail what will be the goals, objectives, strategies and tactics (G-OST).

This quarterly process allows the business to review the overall strategic plan making sure the business is on the right track. If it is not, there is ample opportunity to make the corrections and alterations required rather than waiting for the end of the year and asking, "What happened?".

Team Synergy

There will be no surprise that there is a significant requirement to ensure the team operates in synergy. Interestingly this is an area where many businesses may never truly achieve synergy. A simple test is to determine how busy you are in comparison to your team. If you are the busiest person in your business, then synergy does not exist in the fullest context and likely not at all. Remember you are paying for other people's time. The synergy here will result in you gaining more from their time and talent than the investment.

Team synergy, in essence, is all about the ability of the team to perform their task efficiently, productively within an empowering and fun culture. Just think for a moment when you enjoy what you do, it first doesn't feel like work and you get so much more done. So, engagement and empowerment are key to the synergy of the team.

Additionally, is the matching of talents to outputs in your business. Having the right people in the business doing the right job/task will be key. Remember synergy is about the sum of two parts. In this case talent and process or talent and technology. Take for a moment if your business makes a widget, having the right operators will result in the very best outcomes from the machine. Maybe you're a service-based business in which case the very best at a particular discipline, ensure your service is delivered consistently at a higher standard. Take for instance coaching. I will gain synergy in my business when I employee a better coach than me, they will get better results sooner, great synergy.

Financial Synergy

Financial synergy relates to the balance of what's coming versus what's going or being spent by the business. Now as we've already mentioned the need for KPI's here there is a focus on what to measure. Essentially within any business, there needs to be a clear focus on costs and cost reduction. In actual fact, the constant focus on cost reduction is a major key to synergy. There are predominantly two specific financial focuses:

1.      Cost synergy: where cost savings are achieved as a result of external growth.
2.      Revenue synergy: where additional revenues are achieved as a result of external growth.

Cost Synergies

Here when we seek to increase the sum of the individual parts it will be as a result of:

- Eliminating duplicate functions & services. Such as double tapping, doing the same thing twice, reparative operations, combining departments.
- Getting better deals from suppliers.
- Higher productivity & efficiency from assets, which may include closing redundant processes.

Revenue Synergies

Potential revenue synergies include:

- Marketing and selling complementary products.
- Cross-selling into a new customer base.
- Sharing distribution channels.
- Access to new markets.

The focus on all aspects of synergy aims to shift from a percentage growth each year to determine the true value of your business using your business as a multiplier. As the focus and results on synergy start to take hold, your business becomes a truly valuable asset. There are many variables when it comes to determining the value of your business; industry, owner led or not, reliance on the owner, retained customers, lead generation, identified niche etc.

In general terms, a business will have a value of between 1x and 10 x its annual net profit. There is a general consensus that owner-run businesses will struggle to achieve a value higher than 2.5x. For those businesses with an annual net profit under £500k, they will attract 2x to 5x. Those businesses over £500k can achieve between 3x and 10x.

Throughout this book, we have had a focus on defining the outcome of a successful business as 'A commercial and profitable enterprise which works without the business owner' we can begin to place a value in that achievement. At that level, there are some key aspects of stepping up the synergy to the next level. They will also form a focus on the growth aspect of Business Rhythm.

**Growth**

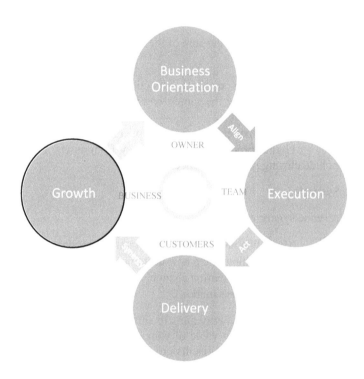

Although growth creates the closing element of the Business Rhythm cycle it's the most critical area to have a consistent focus. Jim Collins in his book 'Good to Great' relates to this in the context of the flywheel effect (Collins, 2001). Getting the flywheel underway, gaining momentum is extremely hard in the beginning. Sound familiar when you look back to getting your business underway? Yes, probably. The point here is to maintain momentum or as I have positioned it maintaining your rhythm.

For so many businesses the challenge here is the necessity to maintain that momentum. Slow down or stop, change a direction in the business, keep stop starting strategies in a frenzied bid to get results and it's tough to maintain momentum, rhythm. Remember the focus is to keep spinning with a drive to ever increase the speed. Maintain the rhythm. The rhythm will steadily increase as with each cycle, day, week, month, quarter, year. At each stage, we have now a focus on setting the goals to achieve, the vision we have in mind as the driver and the guiding principle of our mission.

The funny thing is with growth comes interFEARence, as we start to expand, offer new products or services, recruit new team members, expanding premises etc... All the while the burden can weigh heavy on your shoulders, or it can feel that way. Having a clear focus on where and what needs to grow within your business will drive your focus and commitment and keep you on track. Go back to Chapter 1, where we focused on getting out of your own way. Growth will be wholly dependent on what you aim to achieve, your vision and a continued focus to learn.

Now it may seem that growth comes last in the business rhythm, that's not the case, it is neither first or last, rather part of a self-perpetuating cycle. Now to be clear we need first to determine what growth. Its simple definition is the process of increasing in size. Taking the literal meaning of growth is the increase in the size, in this case of your business, what it does that look like?

Growth as a process is the focus of divide and multiply, in many respects what we have already determined as synergy. In nature, cells divide and with each division there is growth. It's the same in business, it likely starts with you, you then employ someone, thus dividing the workload and getting more done. Having a direct increase on business productivity. Business growth.

Interestingly the process for growth in your business starts with you the business owner. There is no surprise that you are the sole key to the growth of your business. In fact, I have placed such significance on it that the bulk of this book is aimed at shifting you towards being the ideal version as a business owner. So, I hope the penny has dropped. At this stage the saying the more you learn the more you earn really does have its place cemented in your success and that means growth.

The Growth Quadrant

The growth quadrant offers a basis in relation to the process of growth within the business and unsurprisingly it will start with you. As the title suggests there are 4 areas we will look at, intellectual growth, physical growth, intellectual opportunity and physical opportunity. No matter what type of business your growth will be nurtured and evident through the understanding of these 4 areas. Being able to shift from the non-tangible understanding to tangible results, putting your learning experiences into action.

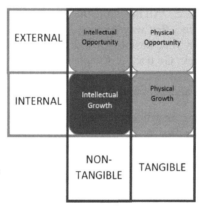

*The Growth Quadrant*

Intellectual Growth

In the very simplest terms, this is about what you are learning right now for your business. As the business owner, your knowledge will be key in terms of what you do, how you do it and where you aim to get to. Understanding business is complex and multifaceted. Essentially there is loads to learn and in many respects, you never stop learning, ever!

The catalyst for growth is knowledge and as the primary focus your knowledge as the business owner. Let's make an assumption that you decide not to invest in your learning where do you think you'll end up? Quite frankly knowledge is power, in this context, it is the raw energy which ignites life in your business. The more you learn the more you'll earn and it is that simple. You will need to establish the learning agenda for your business. Where do you start? As your business rhythm intensifies your learning agenda will too. It has to or you'll find your business gets to a point where you have no idea what to do, guess what happens then? We have already explored and placed an emphasis on learning, now we can see how it stitches together within your business rhythm.

- Chapter 1
  - Dreams x Vision x Goals x Learn x Plan x Act.
  - Learning.
    - Your Upgrade.
    - The journey from incompetence to competence.
    - Wisdom.
- Chapter 2
  - Limiting Beliefs
- Chapter 3
  - Habit 5 the I Am statements.
  - Habit 9 Prepare to Learn.
- Chapter 4
  - Judging versus Learning questions.
  - The formula for life's abundance, Be x Do x Have.

Initially, the concept of learning is non-tangible as first the seed needs to be planted to evoke learning, an internal understanding and comprehension firstly for you and the business. In regard to what needs to be learnt, you will be bombarded with decisions, challenges and opportunities daily which you will need to address. As the business owner, your learning will first require a foundation knowledge for the routine commercial running of the business.

As your business rhythm gets underway what do you need to learn? What will underpin the success of your business? In many respects, this goes back to Gerber's 'E Myth' (Gerber, 1995) and the technician, manager and entrepreneur. Likely as the technician you will have sufficient understanding, even expertise. The question is rather one of the business owner and your technical business. So what will you need to learn? As Gerber highlights being a great baker is one thing, being an owner of a bakery business is another. You will likely need to learn as a minimum:

- How to market your baking business.
- How to sell your baking produce.
- How to source your baking ingredients.
- How to create efficiently and maybe mass production of your baked product.

263

- How to administrate the business.
- How to understand and manage business finances.
- How to plan for the future of your baking business.
- How to build a team and then manage and lead them.

The list goes on. Through business orientation, execution and delivery change will occur and your learning will reflect and likely be the source and cause of that change. This will naturally happen as you set the business rhythm in motion. It will be key to then ensure you keep up with it. The risk here is the inability to grow and adapt with the potential of your business. At the point, you knowingly or unknowingly stop you will find business becomes very tough.

The inability to apply your learning or indeed to remain at the forefront of learning will be the root cause of the demise of the business. Essentially every business challenge offers an opportunity and it is that opportunity which maintains the business rhythm and increases its intensity.

Having already mentioned the impact of an above the parapet mindset and focus, one key aspect unsurprisingly was the habit of asking 'learning questions'. This in a sense can be the foundation of continued growth. Always being focused and tuned in to the learning opportunity as they are defined and show themselves. With growth being a key aspect of business rhythm having a constant focus or habit of learning will ensure the benefits from the learning opportunities.

Intellectual Opportunity

In terms of intellectual opportunity, there are two factors at play here and are essentially external to you when we look at the manner of implementation. It's about the depth of your knowledge with time and how you utilise it. Becoming the trainer and secondly strategic wargaming?

As your business knowledge develops the knowledge you gain, your learning process shifts from a student of business to the principal teacher in your business. You essentially become the trainer and in time and with growth the trainers' trainer. Although we start with your learning as the business grows as that business rhythm intensifies the learning will spread to the team, internally and externally.

The application of your knowledge will essentially create your business manual, the step by step focus of what, where and how you do business. With the growth and expansion and the team you will add to your knowledge. In the course of time, you will create a fully systemised adaptable business manual. In tune with the business rhythm, it will also be an organic growing document, that will continue to develop, adapt, improve the delivery within the business, hence a key to growth.

Whilst knowledge is one thing the real impact comes from the application of learning. How do we start to utilise that which we have learned? Often when we start to look at the way we can begin to apply theory to a situation, project or system. Now it may be the case that the mere application, untested, unmeasured is a risk, and you'd be right. Which may result in having the knowledge and never utilising it, never putting in into action. That in itself is catastrophic. Ever found yourself in the circumstances as to not having committed to doing something even though you had the knowledge?

When we take a look at the intellectual opportunity, having great ideas, or at least what we think are great ideas it raises the question as to use them. If I may I'd like to share a procedure I used on countless occasions during military operations. Now I think you'll agree there is a significant impact of getting things wildly wrong in the military. So, we had a drive to ensure the very best circumstance and conditions were set, in place to help predict and where possible assure success. War-gaming is the ability to actually play out the scenario before committing any people or resources to the operation.

Within the military context there will be plans formulated for each phase of an operation; the preliminaries, what needs to happen before, the operation and the extraction. Very simplified. During this process of planning at each stage there will be 3 assumptions made in regard to any course of action being derived:

- The worst course of action.
- The best course of action.
- The most probable course of action.

From this, a series of deductions will be formed in order to assist in making any decision towards the plan of action. Once the outline of a plan has been created a war game will be undertaken. There will be dedicated personnel who take on the role of enemy forces. They will then respond to each and every action and phase of the plan in a manner which will be assessed in line with the current 'modus operandi' of the enemy forces. In this manner, the validity of any plan can be tested and measured before any resources are assigned and soldiers committed to the operation.

Today in corporations there is a significant focus on strategic war-gaming. Here I'm going to cut away all the jargon and demonstrate the concept within the daily application in your business, taking that intellectual opportunity and putting it into action.

Your learning and experience offer your business growth. Through delivery and the focus on testing and measuring and maintaining analysis of your KPI's, you have the chance to apply your learnings. In this fashion, you can apply the context of war-gaming. In simple terms, you can make an assessment of the probability of what will work and what won't.

If you are going to focus your efforts on a new marketing strategy or introduction of a new product or service, you can start to make assumptions. What will the market's response be if? What will the product or service have as an impact? What would be the worst case if? What is the best case if? What is the most likely case? The mere act of asking these questions is a version of war-gaming.

Going through a focus of determining the impact of a plan of action you seek to initiate, you can start to ask the necessary questions and make some calculated assumptions in direct regards to the potential outcomes. In this manner, you will be able to set the conditions towards having a successful outcome.

Now it's important to understand that this isn't an exact science. Remember we can't as yet predict the future, we can make some calculated assumptions and determine what may or may not happen. Now one key output from this process is the ability to set a contingency plan or a focus on 'if this then that'. Essentially being able to set predetermined decision points, that is if a certain set of circumstances result in a pre-determined outcome it will, in turn, define the next action. Again, this is a critical area of war-gaming in the business context.

War-gaming within your business doesn't need to be complex, complicated or overly difficult. Rather ensure a level of intimacy with where, what and how you aim to achieve your plan of action. By virtue of looking in depth at your planning, you will create a greater level of intimacy with your business direction and delivery. This level of focus leads the physical outcomes within the business.

Physical Growth

Taking intangible personal development and growth then leads to your physical growth. Essentially as you start applying your knowledge you personally develop. Let's take the age-old argument of being a leader. As you get your business underway on your own, arguably there is a limited association with leadership. As you begin to build your team there is a need to understand how to manage and lead them. This is often an area of concern, having never been or seen yourself as a leader.

From here you begin to learn about leadership, what it means, how it's developed and delivered. Maybe you seek to determine the type of leader you are or will likely become. Your awareness is raised as to the deficits, what you currently don't know. Remembering the level of competency, you currently have or indeed are lacking.

Slowly you begin to develop your leadership skills and before long have the ability to lead your team effectively. Physical growth can be likened to following structured promotion, at the beginning you have only the skills you had to start at the bottom of the promotional ladder. As you develop, grow and gain greater understanding you are able to grow rung by rung. It may be you are always looking towards that top run, reflecting that you'll never have the ability to get there, until one day you do.

Think for a moment the journey towards starting your own business. More likely you took your skill set and set out to do it on your own. Suddenly there are multiple factors you didn't know about in relation to being a business owner. Hence this book by the way. Then you start to set about your learning and before long you are not only the expert in your skill, you are also a skilled business owner.

Well, there you have the impact within your business rhythm, the learning cycle you'll have to work through. Your intellectual growth will lead to a physical manifestation in its delivery and direct growth of your business.

Physical Opportunity

Now with physical growth internally you will suddenly become aware of the additional opportunities externally. As you and indeed the team increase the level of knowledge and understanding greater opportunities start to come into focus.

Think for a moment in regard to the fundamentals of business:

- Marketing – as you understand more about marketing within the business you'll gain better results, more efficiency in communicating with your marketplace. Increased market results and by virtue a better ROI on marketing activity.

- Sales – through understanding your ability to convert through the sales pipeline improves. You and the team are far more effective at dealing with objections, positioning and understanding the customer's needs.
- Financial – Through learning, you gain a far better handle on how to interpret your numbers, become far more efficient and profitable.

As you can imagine the opportunity when it comes to learning is significant, and really there are literally no limits. The manner in which you are able to apply your learning is limitless. The growth quadrant is a self-perpetuating cycle with each iteration the intensity of the business rhythm stimulates growth firstly in yourself, then the team and ultimately the business. Internally initially and then external expansion.

Feedforward

In Chapter 1 we discussed feedforward. Feedforward is an intrinsic element of Business Rhythm and as we are focused on growth, there is no surprise we highlight the clear benefits of the feedforward mindset. In the delivery of our service or product feedforward has its place firmly set. Feedforward is key within the growth quadrant. Indeed within each quadrant, feedforward can almost be seen as the link. The ability to assimilate learning and clearly determine where in the future it will take effect.

When we take a feedforward stance we start to shift from an anchored focus on the past towards the opportunity in front of us. Feedforward is goal orientated, seeking to set the agenda for the future with a view on what can be achieved. It's all about the 'art of the possible' and by virtue engaging and motivational. It has a focus on positive change and the behaviours which support positive change.

Feedforward has a focus on the direction going forward, it's all about how to make progress. It has a higher focus on guidance and leadership. It is collaborative in its context, sharing the learning experience along the way. The focus on the leadership is one of transformation and not simply the transaction of I say you do.

It has a clarity of purpose when it comes to the analysis of the KPI's, a real sense of what we can learn and determine from the metric we have in place.

They don't become a stick to beat people with rather an insight to what can be achieved.

Feedforward creates consistency in delivery and one area which is key is communication and accountability. A real expert in effective and innovative communication is Andy Bounds. In his book The Snow Ball Effect (Bounds, 2013) he introduces a format for meetings, which will have a dramatic effect on delivery. The LION meeting is simple in its context and sets in play a process to assure a higher level of delivery from within the team. LION stands for Last week, Improvements, Obstacles and Next week. Once established as a regular meeting it will significantly increase positive feedforward and by virtue accountability across the team.

The joy of the LION meeting is the simplicity, here's how it works. It's important that you gain a contribution from each of the team member's individually. It's not necessarily a forum for open discussion in detail but you can make arrangements to pick up discussion away from the meeting. The meeting will engender a significant level of accountability. In outline, you run the meetings as follows:

Everyone contributes and everyone must listen. Go through each section listening to the team first, you offer your input at the end of each section. Open the meeting introducing the concept of a LION meeting and ensuring everyone understands the rules.

- **Last Week…."Last week I said I'd……., what happened was"**
  o       Ask the question openly for each person to reflect on 'how have we/you progressed with the activity you told me you would complete/work on/do since last week?' Everyone is then to offer their personal response. If responses are somewhat vague, you should seek clarity.
- **Improvements…. "This week…….went well"**
  o       Something that went well last week, what was it and why. Are there lessons to be learned from it that the team can embrace.
- **Obstacles….. "I could use some help or advice with….."**
  o       A current challenge they need help with. The help could come from you or from within the team. It's important here to make sure that the team understand the importance of sharing these issues. At this point it's likely they would be termed 'important' to deal with, if left they will almost certainly become 'urgent'.
- **Next Week….. "The main thing I am going to do next week is"**

o        Everyone then gives their key deliverables for the coming week. This is their commitment to action, what they aim to achieve in the next week.

## Refine

The final link in the Business Rhythm cycle is to refine. In the simplest terms, it is to ensure the growth we experience, the learning we are establishing and putting into place are in fact true to the chosen direction and destination of the business. Now that's not to say things may change and the direction and destination shift. In those cases, we need to refine the direction and destination.

Ensuring we have a focus on refining as the business rhythm intensifies ensure we remain in control, we maintain clarity. It's about making sure what we have and maintain confidence in where we are going and what we aim to achieve. Let's be really clear having a regular focus to refine what's happening in the business will increase your confidence and that of the team. It's a chance to temperature check what's going on across the entire business. That things aren't getting out of control or unwieldy.

It's safe to say that things change and the challenge with change is the impact it can have on us, what's worse is when that impact is unknown, we didn't see it coming, had no idea etc… Things can get out of control very quickly and that can have a significant impact and be disastrous for you and the business.

When we refine throughout the business rhythm there are a series of questions I find extremely helpful:

1.     Has the situation changed?
2.     If so does the situation remain within my control?
3.     If the situation is outside my control does the business plan remain current?
4.     If not what and when does change need to take place?

From here you could conduct a business estimate as highlighted on page 60 and realign the business. If it's a significant change and impact, then it maybe you'll need to go back to the business plan and reassess. Now it's not as bad as it sounds when you take into account that you have initiated the need to define what the business needs are. The challenge comes when it's forced upon you and the business because you failed to see change coming or being forced on you.

As the final link in the maintenance of the business rhythm, you should now see how a focus on the four main areas and the link between them are the keys to maintaining your momentum. With each iteration of your business cycle the rhythm increases, with the increase, the business grows and flourishes. You set in motion the cycle to move towards a commercially profitable enterprise that eventually will work without you.

Now that's when life gets really exciting because you are able to make choices, determine what's next.

## BLUF – Bottom Line Up Front
We are surrounded by rhythm in life, in fact, we exist owing to a perpetual rhythm, so there is no surprise that we can attribute success in our businesses to having a rhythm. A steady focus on intensifying our business rhythm nourishes us, our teams and the business in such a way as to promote growth. A focus on simplicity, as we have mentioned the art of complexity is simplicity and if nothing else a focus on the 4 areas of rhythm will get you underway.

Business Orientation has a focus to align to the execution, in turn, encourages and promotes the right actions. This encourages high levels of delivery whilst creating higher levels of synergy which encourages growth. Where growth opportunity occurs, we are then able to refine the orientation of the business, moving in the desired direction.

Focusing on the business rhythm underpins the definition of becoming a successful business. 'A commercially profitable enterprise which works without you. So, Rhythm initially focuses on you the business owner, engaging the team and empowering them to serve the customers in order to grow the business.

The important aspect is to get a focus on your rhythm now, get the structure in place and underway and you'll have started to proactively grow and develop your business. Make sure you understand that it's a rhythm and by virtue needs to repeatable and grow in intensity as it's the route to your success.

| My Action | The Impact | Achieved by |
| --- | --- | --- |
| | | |
| | | |

# To Your Success

I don't know about you, when I finish a book I often find myself on a high, loaded with new found excitement on what maybe. How I'm going to make a difference, put my new learnings and insight into action. Now in the manner, I have written this book I truly hope I have offered you the ability to not only reflect on what you have learned, rather have got you underway. Established the 'Bottom Line Up Front' and also encouraged you to have taken the 21-day challenge. In which case you will have already made a commitment to move towards the life you truly desire. Maybe even had a personal shift in yourself already.

If on the other hand, you completed the book cover to cover, then reflect on where you found the value and now act upon it. Don't put the book down without making a commitment. Let's be clear you bought the book in the first instance for a reason known only to you. Looking for something, inspiration, guidance, insight or something fresh to motivate yourself. I truly hope you found it.

Here's the thing, no matter what encouraged the of reading this book, there is one thing I am certain of in your ability to go on to achieve success. You need to get out of your own way. The only reason you are not where you want to be is that you are getting in your own way. Beit in your life or business you are the reason you will or will not succeed. There are no other reasons, no blame you can assign to others, no excuses for your shortfalls and certainly only your denial that you are worth the effort.

I truly want to wish you every success on the journey towards the life you truly want to live. Don't hold back, never give up, where you have to, fail forward. You set the agenda in your life. Now you just have to step forward in the true manner you wish. Remember from this point forward you have the ability to shape the infinite opportunities of tomorrow. Just remember with each wasted day that passes you limit the tomorrows you have, so don't waste a moment. Get on with your life.

Go forward and be the very best version of you.

To your eternal success.

Steve.

# Bibliography

Bounds, A. (2013). *The Snowball Effect, Communication Techniques to Make You Unstoppable.* Chichester: Andy Bounds Ltd.

Cardone, G. (2011). *The 10X Rule.* Hoboken: John Wiley & Sons, Inc.

Charan, L. B. (2002). *Execution The Discipline of Getting Things Done.* London: Random House Business Books.

Collins, J. (2001). *Good to Great.* USA: William Collins.

Covey, S. (1989). *The 7 Habits of Highly Effective people.* London: Simon & Schuster.

Covey, S. (2006). *The Speed of Trust.* New York: Simon and Schuster.

Cunningham, K. J. (2018). *The Road Less Stupid, Advice from the Chairman of the Board.* . USA: Keith J Cunningham.

Eker, T. H. (2005). *Secrets of the Millionaire Mind, Think Rich to Get Rich.* Piatkus bBooks.

Elrod, H. (2016). *The Miracle Morning.* Great Britin: Hodder and Stoughton.

Frankl, V. E. (1959). *Mans Search for mean.* Reading: Ebury Publishing.

Gerber, M. (1995). *The E-Myth Revisited: Why Most Small Businesses Don't Work and What to Do About It.* New York: Hasrper Collins.

Goldsmith, M. (2015). *Triggers.* New York: Random House Inc.

Goleman, D. (1995). *Emotional Intellengence.* London: Bloomsbury Publishing Plc.

Harnish, V. (2006). *Mastering the Rockafella habits.* New York: Select Books Inc.

Herold, C. (2011). *Double Double.* Austin, Texas: Greenleaf Book Group Press.

Hill, N. (1937). *Think and Grow Rich.* TarcherPerigee.

Hopkins, M. (2014). *Compassionate Leadership.* St Ives: Piatkus.

Lencioni, P. (2012). *The 5 Dysfunctions of a Team.* San Fransico: Pfeiffier.

Lewis, D. J., & Adrian Webster. (2014). *Sort your brain out.* Chichester: John Wiley and Sons Ltd.

Loiser, M. J. (2003). *Law of Attraction.* New York: Hachette Book Group USA, Inc.

Manson, M. (2016). *The Subtle Art of not Giving a Fuck.* New York: Harper Collins.

Marquet, D. (2012). *Turn the Ship Around.* London: Penguin Books Ltd.

Maxwell Maltz, M. F. (2015). *Psycho Cybernetics.* New York: Penguin Random House LLC.

Pease, A. (1998). *The Answer, Who to take Charge of your life & become the person you want to be. .* London: Orien Publishing Group Ltd.

Pease, A. (n.d.). *Questions are the Answer.*

Peters, P. S. (2011). *The Chimp Paradox, the Mind Management Programme for Confidence, Success and Happiness.* Ebury Publishing.

Peters, P. S. (2012). *The Chimp Paradox.* Vermillion.

Robbins, T. (2014). *Money Master the Game, 7 Simple Steps to Finacial Freedom.* London: Simon & Schuster UK Ltd.

Senik, S. (2014). *Leaders eat Last.* St Ives: portfolio Penguin.

Stanier, M. B. (2016). *The Coaching Habits.* Toronto: Box of Crayons Pree.

Stockdale, J. B. (1993). *Courage Under Fire.* Stanford: Stanford University.

Syed, M. (2010). *Bounce.* New York: Harper Collins.

Tedlow, R. S. (2010). *Deniel: Why Business Leaders Fail to Look Facts in the Face and What to Do Abbout It.* New York: Penguin Group.

Tracy, B. (2001). *Eat that Frog, Get More Important Things Done Today.*. San Francisco: Berrett Koehler Publishers Ltd.

Whitmore, S. J. (1992). *Coaching for Performance.* London: Nicholas Brealey Publishing.

L - #0110 - 080719 - C0 - 210/148/15 - PB - DID2559996